I0569930

BEYOND HELL'S FLAMES

by

CHRISTOPHER AND **JAMIE HARPER**

Destin Publishing

Published by Destin Publishing

eBook: 979-8-9910068-0-4
Paperback: 979-8-9910068-1-1
Audiobook: 979-8-9910068-2-8

DEDICATION

To my beloved wife, whose initiative and obedience to the Lord sparked this journey. Without you, this book would have never come to life. You nurtured a passion for writing within me that I never knew I could have.

To my wonderful children, who have endured so much during the writing of this book. Your support and patience have not gone unnoticed, and I am deeply grateful for your presence through it all.

And to my parents, who have never stopped believing in me, praying for me, or supporting me, no matter the season. Your unwavering faith and encouragement have been my steadfast foundation.

TABLE OF CONTENTS

Dedication iii

The Introduction vii

Chapter 1: The Party 1

Chapter 2: The Fall 15

Chapter 3: The Dream 27

Chapter 4: The Remembrance 39

Chapter 5: The Awakening 49

Chapter 6: The Demon 61

Chapter 7: The Madness 75

Chapter 8: The Outworld 95

Chapter 9: The Stranger 117

Chapter 10: The Transfiguration 131

Chapter 11: The Ancient Ones 145

Chapter 12: The Prophecy 163

Chapter 13: The Chosen 179

Chapter 14: The Repercussion 195

Chapter 15: The Morning Star 205

Chapter 16: The Creation 229

Chapter 17: The Consummation 241

Chapter 18: The Deception 265

Chapter 19: The Covenant 281

Chapter 20: The Vision 299

Chapter 21: The Dragon 313

Chapter 22: The Breach 329

Chapter 23: The True Morning Star 353

Epilogue 369

About the Authors 385

THE INTRODUCTION

I feel doomed in a world I know nothing of, forgotten by the world I was once a part of. Seated upon the scorching earth amid the intense blaze, surrounded by the confines of my own infernal prison, I contemplate, *Am I truly the fortunate one to be ensnared within this relentless flame?*

The unimaginable distortion and dementia that characterizes the reality of Hell renders one unrecognizable, stripping away the very essence of humanity that uniquely defines us all. As I gaze at my surroundings, the true horror of Hell unfolds before me—not the flames licking at my skin or the screams echoing through the darkness, but the chilling truth that something has been severed from me, as if a vital lifeline had been cruelly cut, leaving me stranded in a bewildering abyss of doubt and longing.

This realm, it seems, has perfected the craft of unraveling the very purpose for which we were meticulously shaped. It excels in dismantling the divine image and intricate imprints that once delineated my existence.

Reflecting back, it is perplexing how everything hinged on a seemingly simple choice when I was alive. Rejecting God equated to rejecting life itself and discarding the inherent characteristics within God that granted me my humanity. The consequence: stripped of all His fruits and the personal qualities He represents, what remains is Hell—a desolate void where the vibrant tapestry of life unravels into nothingness.

However, even if someone recalls my existence, *Who would be able to help me in this place?* I think to myself.

"Who could get me out of this nightmare?" I whisper as I begin to cry.

Closing my eyes, seeking the solace of rest, a routine etched in me from my days alive, Hell swiftly reaffirms that repose is an alien concept in this realm.

THERE IS NO REST FOR THE DAMNED!

Fear immediately overtakes my mind as though under someone else's control. My thoughts race with every nightmare and horror I could or would ever imagine. And, as if to play some sick joke on me, the flames in front of me project my fears in full form, as though I was creating into existence my own horrors and nightmares.

There truly is no rest here. There truly is no peace, I internalize.

"How did I get here?" I ask myself. "What paths did I take that led me to this point?"

As I search my inner thoughts for answers, I stumble upon a distant memory, a time that lingered on the precipice of my own demise. It was where the journey's threads began to unravel, the prologue to an impending conclusion.

This was the beginning of the end.

CHAPTER 1

The Party

Ecclesiastes 9:12

A person can't possibly know when his time will come. Like a fish caught in a cruel net or birds trapped in a snare, without warning the unexpected happens, and people are caught up in an evil time.

Romans 1:25, 28, 32

They exchanged the truth about God for a lie, and worshiped and served created things rather than the Creator—who is forever praised. Amen.

Furthermore, just as they did not think it worthwhile to retain the knowledge of God, so God gave them over to a depraved mind, so that they do what ought not to be done.

Although they know God's righteous decree that those who do such things deserve death, they not only continue to do these very things but also approve of those who practice them.

Psalms 49:14

The fate of fools is the grave, and just like sheep, death will feast on them.

1

"**Y**ou just killed yourself," I whisper, the chilling words escaping my own lips as I stare at my reflection in the mirror. The face that looks back at me seems like that of a stranger, not at all like the bright, blue-eyed, happy person I used to be, but rather like someone who has just committed an unforgivable act. The coldness in my voice matches the icy grip of fear taking hold of my heart.

Before I can fully comprehend the gravity of what I have done, the shadows in the room begin to converge, swallowing me whole. Enveloped by darkness, I feel as though I am being swallowed by an abyss, a vast expanse of nothingness that stretches endlessly before me, devoid of any light or hope.

As consciousness slowly returns, my senses sharpen, and I become acutely aware of the shooting pain and stiffness that grips my entire body. The physical torment mirrors the emotional anguish that drove me to utter those haunting words at my own reflection.

In that moment of despair and self-realization, it becomes abundantly clear that I have ventured into a realm from which there might be no return. The darkness surrounding me is not just the absence of light; it is a manifestation of the darkness within my own soul, a darkness that pushes me to the brink of self-destruction.

What was in that last line? I ponder, my thoughts gravitating towards the substances I just consumed. Fear seems a distant memory as I impulsively reach for yet another line, driven by the desperate hope that each inhale of the snow-white powder will either silence my relentless agony or propel me deeper into the unknown, even if it means risking everything.

My eyelids flutter open, yet all I behold is an impenetrable void. Panic surges as I lean against the cold, unforgiving bathroom sink, cold sweat beading on my skin, my trembling hands gripping the edges, and my heart racing wildly. An oppressive darkness seems to smother my very essence, and my vision blurs slightly, amplifying my disorientation. Suddenly, the bathroom walls appear to close in around me.

I shut my eyes once more, summoning a veneer of composure, clinging to the belief that I retain control over my own reality.

"Snap out of it!" I declare firmly, a self-imposed verdict on the surreal state I find myself in.

"Everyone will be here soon," I mutter aloud, the relentless pounding on the door reverberating in my head.

Knock, knock, knock

"Hey, man, are you okay?" a voice from the other side inquires. "You've been in there a while. Everyone's asking about you."

Confusion gnaws at me as I reply, "Everyone is asking about me?"

Bewilderment clouds my thoughts.

"No one should be here yet," I whisper to myself, splashing cold water on my face in a desperate attempt to anchor myself to reality. Gripping the edges of the bathroom sink once more, I remind myself, "You're in the bathroom, in your friend's house, just waiting for the party to start."

"Pull yourself together!" I mumble, a stark reminder of the need for introspection.

What was all that nonsense about killing myself? I wonder inwardly, banishing the unsettling thought from my mind as I seek to grasp the elusive concept of time that slipped through my fingers.

"Yeah," I say out loud to the voice on the other side of the door. "I'm fine. Just give me a minute."

As I stand there, trying to regain my composure and make sense of the events that transpired, a lingering disorientation clings to me. The passage of time remains elusive, leaving me perplexed by my friend's question.

When I open the bathroom door, hoping to escape the bewildering thoughts that besiege me, I am immediately bombarded by the sight of people, music, and debauchery. It is only then that I realize I must have passed out from the drugs I took earlier in the evening. The party is in full swing, and despite my previous belief that everyone would arrive soon, I find myself fashionably late to an event that had been ongoing for some time.

"About time you decided to show back up!" my friend says to me, wondering where I went.

I observe my friends, catching glimpses of their joyous, somewhat inebriated smiles. My buddy, with a half-drunken grin, gives me a thumbs-up as he swings open the front door, ushering in a crowd carrying boxes of familiar beers and various brands of alcohol. Typically, this is my scene—I am the one orchestrating these gatherings, setting up the parties, and ensuring everything runs smoothly. However, tonight is different. Something feels off, and I can't quite put my finger on it. There is an unfamiliar weight, a profound heaviness settling over me, infiltrating the hollow spaces within that I hadn't realized were so vacant.

From this emptiness emerges a peculiar sensation, one that lingered throughout the day and now solidifies into repeating words. Whatever this feeling is, it has taken shape, echoing within me a persistence I can't seem to shake.

You're going to die! The words echo in my ears, as if spoken from an external source that I can't quite pinpoint.

"I'm going to die?" I say aloud to myself.

Are these thoughts somehow tied to my earlier inclinations that I killed myself after hitting too much blow?

"Nah . . . I'm fine," I say in reassurance.

"This wasn't the first time I hit angel dust, and it won't be the last," I declare aloud, casually inspecting myself before heading to the kitchen.

Pouring myself a drink from the first bottle of hard alcohol I see in front of me, I throw them back one after another. One shot, then another, and another. I hold nothing back as I raise the bottle high in the air for everyone present to see, kickstarting another great night.

As the evening unfolds, a palpable buzz fills the air, and my surroundings gradually blur into a hazy backdrop. The remnants of the drug I took still numb my senses, and each sip of alcohol deepens the fog in my mind. It becomes increasingly difficult to comprehend the amount I ingested and the potential consequences that might follow. The combination of substances casts a shadow over my ability to make rational decisions, leaving me caught in a swirling whirlwind of uncertainty.

But, a sense of calm immediately washes over me, and a gentle smile graces my lips as the effect kicks in. The alcohol's soothing influence begins to envelop me, wrapping me in its warm and intoxicating embrace.

"Did you drink most of that bottle by yourself?" I hear someone ask.

Holding the bottle back to get a better look at just how much I consumed, I noticed I must have drank a lot more than I thought I had but not feeling like I drank as much as the bottle reveals.

I nod my head with pride, declaring, "Hell yeah, I did."

"Oh my gosh," he says. "You're a beast!" he declares, his recognition of my "achievement" is broadcast for all to hear.

"Down it, down it, down it," he voices, as many others in the room join in, daring me to finish the last of the bottle.

I gaze at the foolish grin plastered on their faces, seemingly treating this as some kind of accomplishment—a sentiment that resonates with others in the nearby room as well. Without hesitation, I reclaim the bottle, proceeding to down the remaining contents within. His encouraging remarks, along with the cheers from the others, push me to finish the challenge. I triumphantly slam the bottle onto the table, asserting my "victory" over this imprudent feat. The room erupts in cheers, pats on the back, high-fives, and various expressions from the other partygoers who witnessed my conquest.

"My victory!" I think to myself in reflection. It is amazing how something so primitive and insurmountable as drinking a bottle of alcohol is considered an accomplishment.

After the praise settles, I glance at the commotion coming from the front door, only noticing more and more people still arriving. I hear the laughter and the shouts of greetings from newly arrived friends with excitement from those at the party noticing each other. The constant sounds of beer bottles hitting the floor and the ever-growing praises from the people in their drunken stupor make my ears ring with annoyance. However, even in the midst of this uproar, four familiar words cut through the noise and reached my ears in a certain clarity that made my hair stand on total and complete edge.

"You're going to die!"

I gulp, a distinct burn lingering from the alcohol. My throat tightens as I survey the room, scrutinizing each face with heightened awareness of my surroundings. The once cheerful faces surrounding me undergo a stark transformation, shifting from joyous to ominous, with sinister glares now upon me.

"Who said that?" I shout, loud enough for all to hear.

Met with only a few awkward glances, their faces quickly revert to normal. "Wait a second," I say, "these words aren't coming from anyone nearby. They're coming from somewhere else, but where? Where have I heard that voice before?" The voice sounds distorted, as if manipulated by some device into a demonic and stretched tone. Despite its eerie quality, I can't shake the feeling that I've heard it before.

But where? I wonder. Where had I heard that voice? Why was my heart racing with an overwhelming sense of fear as if some familiar entity is behind this?

I notice that not one person looks in my direction when I turn to confront the ominous presence. Everyone is so consumed in their own debauchery that no one seems at all responsible for such a menacing prank on me.

Unwilling to wait for answers and clearly not getting any acknowledgment from others around me, I decide to leave the room. However, as I turn to leave, the room spins uncontrollably. The intoxication seems to be taking its full effect on me.

I know I drank too much but had not considered the weight of my actions at that moment. It's a reckless decision made to impress a few people I call "friends," even though I have only met most of them in the past few weeks. Not to mention the substances I took leading up to the party and what effects those were having on me as well. Suddenly, my stomach twists into knots, and the stark awareness sets in about the substantial amount I've consumed. The effects swiftly take hold, causing my mental fortitude to deteriorate.

"I must do something," I say in desperation. "Perhaps if I could just throw it all up, that will ease its hold over me," I mutter under my breath.

I am all too familiar with having to go to the bathroom to purge the mistakes made earlier. This is no different and clearly a way to get it over with and sleep this one off.

"That is what I will do," I think to myself. "All I need to do is throw up, and everything will be fine."

Advancing another step toward the bathroom, I hear it once more. This time, a whispered, elongated hiss echoes in my ear. The words, **"You're going to die!"**

It is an ominous, slithering voice so close behind me that I am afraid to even look. But this time, I swear I can feel the hot breath of its words on the back of my neck. Consciously turning around, my defenses on high alert, I find that the only thing between me and the bedroom wall is just a couple of short feet of empty space.

No one is there.

My stomach churns, and a wave of paleness washes over me. Despite my efforts, my breaths become shorter, and I am unable to drown out the persistent hissing thoughts of death echoing in my ear. The reminder that this is not a product of my imagination my imagination makes my blood run cold. In haste, I navigate through the groups blocking the hallways, making my way towards the bathroom. The hope of finding solace in the quiet enclosure where my evening began drives each desperate step.

Yet, as everything begins to spiral out of control, the music slows to an almost eerie pace, the rhythms in the air transform into a distorted remix of their original intent. I rub my eyes and blink, attempting to regain focus, but the world around me refuses to cooperate.

"I gotta get out of here!" I say under my breath. A sudden sense of urgency overtaking me in the need to distance myself from these people—the clamor, the pervasive scent of alcohol, and the underlying fear lurking in the recesses of my mind that something was pursuing me.

It feels as though something relentlessly pursues me, clinging to my every movement—an inescapable presence. It's as if I unwittingly beckoned forth a malevolent and all-too-familiar darkness, and now, I can't escape the ominous feeling that I foolishly invited it into my world. The air grows heavy with foreboding, and I can't shake the chilling thought that something sinister lurks just beyond that open door.

My mom always tried to convince me that "it" was only my imagination. Dad tried to make light of "it" by telling me that "they" were just little blue fuzzy creatures called "sock monsters" that lived under my bed and waited for a stray pair of socks to be kicked their way for them to snack on in the middle of the night. Jokingly, he said that if I saw one, I'd better hold on tight to my socks or I just might wake up with cold feet. It was silly, really, because I never slept with socks on my feet to begin with. We lived in Texas, for crying out loud. If I ever had socks on, it was only to wear them with my sneakers. But I think it was his attempt to make me feel better about sleeping in my own bed, as opposed to sleeping in a room shared with my brothers, as I had only previously known.

At only eight years old, I believed him the first time I saw them, and maybe even the second time. But after that, the sock monster showed itself more and more. And it was not so small, or blue, and definitely not so fuzzy.

I recollect a night when an incongruous shadow emerged in the corner of my room. It began as a small anomaly, gradually expanding until my entire haven was shrouded in a black mist, darker than the deepest of nights. The obscurity drew every element of my room toward that single corner, forming what appeared to be an immense, vacant void. I found myself yearning for this entity to possess a more benign appearance—perhaps blue or fuzzy, with the hint of the humor my dad had suggested. Anything to unveil its features without instilling fear. However, this monstrous presence had no eyes, no discernible face, no limbs—at least not initially. It was just an enveloping darkness, steadily reaching the height of my ceiling, threatening to engulf me entirely.

On another night, I recall waking up to my entire bed trembling as if an unseen force had seized hold of it, attempting to shake me free. In a panic, I clutched the covers tightly around me, screaming for the unsettling sensation to cease. Uncertain whether it was a nightmarish dream I couldn't escape or a tangible reality, I hesitated to leap out of bed and seek refuge with my parents down the hall. The fear of plunging into the surrounding black emptiness immobilized me, leaving me in the grip of uncertainty about what would transpire if I took that bold step. It wasn't until my parents hurried into my room in response to my screams that the shaking finally ceased. Throughout the remainder of the night, they reassured me that it was merely a dream.

But was it a dream that gave me bruises in my sleep? I contemplate as I reflect back.

Could a dream have the ability to move objects off my shelves right in front of me? I think not! I argue.

Finally, after repeated nights like this, my parents no longer called it my imagination, nor did they make up stories of little sock thieves that lived under my bed in an attempt to make me feel better so I would sleep in my own room. They called them "night terrors," and every night, my parents would pray for those terrors to go away. I even prayed with them in hopes they would finally cease. But these terrors felt more than just my imagination, or whatever it was they wanted me to believe. They felt real, as if they were alive. And I couldn't shake the feeling that they wanted me.

Growing up in a Southern Baptist family, we didn't believe in such beings . . . at least, not yet. I can vividly recall the night everything changed. It was an ordinary night for the rest of my family and anything but ordinary for me. The events that would soon unfold would forever change my family's lives and alter the course of us all.

That night, my dad was roused from his sleep by the unmistakable sound of footsteps rushing upstairs in our newly built home. Considering the late hour, he found it odd that any one of his three boys would be awake. Stealthily slipping out of bed, poised to reprimand one of us for such untimely activities, he ascended the staircase, making his way to the game room directly above their bedroom, where the commotion had originated. To his surprise, the room was now empty and eerily quiet.

Confused and chalking it all up to his imagination, he began making his way back downstairs when, out of nowhere, another sound pierced the air. This wasn't the soft patter of a child or the familiar steps of any of his three sons; instead, it was a resounding bang followed by scratching noises and whispers echoing as if traversing through the walls. A cold air brushed across the back of his neck, causing the hair on his arms to stand on end and compelling a swift return up the stairs. The eerie echoes now undeniably emanating from my bedroom fueled an unsettling urgency within him.

Without hesitation, he swung open the door and in absolute disbelief and horror looked directly upon the very being I had mentioned several hundred times prior to this. As if startled, the demon collected itself and faced my dad, standing tall in the room, nearly touching the ceiling. With an authority unknown to my father, he cried out the name of Jesus, and the demonic spirit fled to the dark corner of my room from which it came.

Shaken, I remember my dad putting his arms around me and consoling me for not fully believing me; the realization of what I had been enduring for months on end hitting him in disbelief. It was unfathomable for him to comprehend how many nights leading up to this I had spent with this demonic spirit, and no one came to my aid or rescue.

It was this moment that led my parents to search for answers. They settled upon non-denominational church groups that believed in the power of the Holy Spirit and the spiritual gifts given to believers to combat them. My parents built a ministry around helping others fight against these demonic beings. Through this, many people afflicted by these demonic spirits were at last confronted by those within this group that had an understanding of the authority within Christ Jesus and were even completely set free.

For years, I had known peace and freedom from the night terrors. However, there were still very harrowing moments when I was abruptly awakened, finding myself face-to-face with individual demonic entities.

During my preteen years in Canada, I vividly recall a haunting by one such malevolent force—a demonic entity that, on one particular night, was adamantly trying to kill me. Awakened by the sounds of thrashing claws at my door, my screams fell upon deaf ears, my covers tightly held over my head as the pounds reverberated in the room. As the cacophony of its assault faded, I seized the opportunity to flee to my parents' bedroom.

Making my way to their hallway and turning the corner, I glanced back and witnessed the malevolent force—a four-legged demonic spirit with limbs grotesquely twisted backward. Its unnatural posture makes my skin crawl as its arms extended outward, like desperate claws reaching for me. The creature's elongated head hung low, nearly touching the floor, its wide-open mouth hovering ominously above the ground. A grotesque tableau of horror, this monstrous entity embodied the twisted depths of my deepest fears, etching an indelible image of terror in the corridors of my subconscious. A profound fear gripped me, preventing any inclination to return to my bedroom. I sought refuge in my family member's bedrooms for weeks, haunted by the chilling presence that was unwilling to let go of its pursuit.

Unsure of why these events persisted, my parents continued to learn and experiment with their words and the use of scripture to combat these demonic forces. But for me, it wasn't going away. There was an ever-present darkness that I felt with me each night and as I aged, it became clear that I had to learn to accept it or find alternative ways to drown them out.

So, I found my own ways to deal with these shadows. The perception of being tough on the outside could never hide the fear that lay in the back of my mind from the unknowns that haunted me most nights. This led me down a path of anger, violence, and a lack of self-control. I was introduced to a world of theft, drugs, fighting, sex, and alcohol. A resentment developed within me towards the God my parents served so wholeheartedly, as they seemingly forgot about me in pursuit of their own ministry, while I learned to cope with my "night terrors" alone.

As long as I was immersed in the numbing elixir of alcohol and the revelry that accompanied it, the malevolent spirits relented. It seemed that the chalice of my drinking held the power to ward off their haunting presence, granting a momentary reprieve from their spectral grasp.

As I continued to drift further from my faith, the oppressive presence of my inner "demons" appeared to recede in tandem. It was as though they had found comfort in the path I had chosen, one that diverged from the teachings of God.

"No wonder the lost are so easily swayed," I mutter to myself, reflecting on the shift in my life's trajectory. The realization hits me that when we willingly stray from the path of righteousness, the forces of darkness need not reveal themselves. We become ensnared in our own temporal existence, blissfully unaware of the impending damnation that lurks in the shadows.

"What if I did kill myself?" I mumble, the weight of the day's events and my reckless consumption sinking in. The gravity of my actions weigh heavily on me, the consequences of my choices looming ominously in the air.

Despite my efforts to divert my thoughts from the grim reality of my situation, using these musings as a temporary escape from the unsettling truth of what lay before me, I can't shake the nagging feeling that this respite was only temporary.

The malevolent forces lurking in the shadows remain patient, biding their time. It is as though they know my internal descent into this darker realm is far from over, and they await the perfect moment to return with even greater intensity, ready to claim their hold over me.

CHAPTER 2

The Fall

Isaiah 5:20-24

Woe to those who call evil good and good evil, who put darkness for light and light for darkness, who put bitter for sweet and sweet for bitter. Woe to those who are wise in their own eyes and clever in their own sight. Woe to those who are heroes at drinking wine and champions at mixing drinks, who acquit the guilty for a bribe, but deny justice to the innocent. Therefore, as tongues of fire lick up straw and as dry grass sinks down in the flames, so their roots will decay and their flowers blow away like dust;

Proverbs 28:18

The one whose walk is blameless is kept safe, but the one whose ways are perverse will fall into the pit.

Ephesians 2:1-3

As for you, you were dead in your transgressions and sins, in which you used to live when you followed the ways of this world and of the ruler of the kingdom of the air, the spirit who is now at work in those who are disobedient.
All of us also lived among them at one time, gratifying the cravings of our flesh and following its desires and thoughts. Like the rest, we were by nature deserving of wrath.

Jeremiah 17:12-13

All who leave you end up as fools, deserters with nothing to show for their lives, who walk off from God, a fountain of living waters - and wind up dead.

"**M**y head is killing me!" I say out loud in frustration and agony. The flashbacks of my past and the sensation of being utterly disconnected from reality persist, haunting me amid the lively atmosphere of the party, all the while an ever-present thought looms in the back of my mind.

You're going to die, keeps echoing through my head. Whatever is whispering these thoughts of despair seems to reveal itself in the dark corners of the room, amidst the unaware partiers who continue on. The familiarity in the inky blackness reminds me of my night terrors as a kid, and I wonder, *Could it be back?*

I blink, hoping to clear my vision, while the shadows in the room seem to twist and stretch, elongating into eerie shapes that reach out toward me with long, spindly fingers.

The room feels different now, and a sense of unease settles in the pit of my stomach. The dim light casts eerie shapes across the walls, and the corners seem to harbor secrets within their depths. As I focus on the elongated shadows, a feeling of being watched creeps over me. The air is heavy with unspoken tension, and the once-familiar room now feels like an unfamiliar maze. I can't shake the idea that something unseen is observing my every move.

After minutes of struggling to move through the crowds, reaching the bathroom confirms that leaving the party and attempting to make it back home is a daunting task. Contemplating what awaits me in the next room fills me with anxiety and fear. A sickness wells up inside me, and I embrace it. As I wrap my arms around the toilet and vomit, a disturbing vision flashes in my mind, revealing a scenario in which I don't leave this bathroom alive. The mere thought of it triggers a jolt of fear within me.

"You've been here before," I reassure myself. "Just get it out of your system, then sleep it off."

Closing my eyes tightly, the words heard all night begin to take hold, planting seeds of fear and doubt. Fighting the urge to believe them, a refusal to entertain the thought of dying, I heave again over the toilet.

"God, make this pain stop!" I cry out loud, clutching my stomach, trying to make sense of the stabbing pains spreading throughout my body.

After many seemingly endless moments pass, I summon the strength to pull myself up from the floor and gaze at my reflection in the small mirror hanging above the vanity. Striving to regain my composure in a last-ditch effort to evade the internal devastation, I'm pleasantly interrupted by knocks on the door and a muffled voice yelling above the music, asking if I am okay. I mumble something back, and unsure of what I said, I look deeper at myself in the mirror.

"Look at you," I hear the voice say from close behind me, as though the words are passing by from left to right. Maybe it's the drugs having an unusual effect—who can tell the difference now?

"Look at what you've become," the voice whispers again, this time with a more ominous tone.

What have I become? I think to myself, playing into its questioning as if it were some game.

I close my eyes and let my head hang low. I used to know who I was, or at least I thought I did. Lately, it seems I have been on a journey to discover my true self and my beliefs. Over the past several years, driven by resentment toward God, I decided to explore other religions, deities, and belief systems, hoping to find answers to my questions. Yet, I found no clearer answers than when I began.

I had mistakenly concluded that there must be a universal god and a universal deity that all people, regardless of their religious affiliation, would eventually connect with if their hearts were pure and their actions righteous. This deity would assume different names and forms primarily due to the diverse cultural aspects present across the world. This variation in culture is what led the deity to be represented in various ways to better resonate with and relate to the beliefs, values, and practices of different societies. As a result, the deity would take on multiple identities and manifestations to adapt to the unique spiritual and cultural contexts it encountered throughout its presence in different regions and civilizations.

I had also believed in the reincarnation of one's soul. Life was always just an opportunity for any one being to elevate themselves to a greater awareness of their own divinity as they transitioned closer to the intellectual beings painting the grand masterpiece of our journeys. Hell, in my view, was merely a metaphor for a self-imposed purgatory for those who were not deemed virtuous or deserving of the life-giving qualities that make someone "good" or "righteous." This meant they would be denied access to eternal life or "Heaven" if they were found unworthy and thereby given another chance through another life.

I refused to believe in the God of my parents, not allowing myself to trust their words for the sake of my eternal future without further evidence or consideration of other religions, gods, and intellectual viewpoints.

"Besides," I utter aloud, annoyed that these thoughts even matter at this moment when my insides feel like they are being ripped out of me, "if the God of my fathers was so great, then how could He allow all the pain and suffering in the world? Why don't I see miracles today like the ones they shared with me as a child, professed in their precious Bible? And why, when I used to cry out to Him in desperation, did He choose to remain so silent? For Heaven's sake, why were the demonic spirits that haunted my childhood nights more prevalent than this 'God' my parents believed in?" I say out loud in frustration.

I never witnessed God, an angel, or anything of a "heavenly" nature, but the presence of the demonic was all too familiar to me. I could discern their various forms, sizes, strengths, and the fears or deceptions they used against me. Their aura haunted my room, lingered in the mall, and even infiltrated my friends' homes. I knew them by name; the eyes of the oblivious could never hide their presence from me.

Why have I encountered years of the demonic and NEVER SEEN EVEN A GLIMPSE OF GOD? I continue to debate within myself.

It was because of these profound questions that I believed He—Yahweh, "Jesus," or whatever His name is—had left me with no alternative but to forge my own path, seek my own way, and formulate my own beliefs. Despite my rejection, a small part of me yearned for the comfort and peace I once felt when my parents used to describe Him to me. Curiously, in this dim moment, a memory of a bright, sunny day begins to dance in my mind, and I find myself becoming immersed in its warmth, as if a higher being is trying to remind me of better times.

The memory of my baptism invades my consciousness. I am only twelve, but I feel like a man when I look into my dad's eyes, brimming with pride. We are in our backyard pool in Lake Jackson, Texas, my hometown. It is a place where everyone knows most everyone else, and the neighboring kids are more like extended family. My friends and I are very close, bound together by church and our Christian school. The church we attended made you excited to grow your faith in God. That day, with my parents by my side, I want to make a declaration to myself and to God, to grow closer to Him through baptism.

I can still remember how sweet the air smelled from the freshly cut grass. The warm Texas summer breeze plays with our hair, drying the sweat that formed along our brows. The shades of blue surrounding us, the small, white, puffy clouds contrasting against the sky, make it look more azure than usual. The sky's reflection in the pool's water sparkle in perfection.

I remember picking out my favorite blue shirt to wear for the occasion. Looking down at my own reflection in the water, I notice my eyes match the same blue hues around us. I am the only one out of my brothers who has blue eyes, and today, it seems like nature's natural color of blue is trying to match the clarity of my own blue eyes. Blue—a color of refreshment, renewal, and endless possibility.

As my dad gently immerses me under water, I come up feeling an overwhelming joy throughout my whole body. I feel the pride not only from my dad, but from my Heavenly Father, and I think, *I will always be a man of God.*

"A man of God," I say out loud, spewing vitriol. "Where was that man now? Where was God?" I question, contemplating my current situation.

I find myself immersed in a shroud of darkness as the memory I hold onto abruptly dissipates. It vanishes as swiftly as a wisp of smoke in the wind. However, the void left by this disappearing memory is quickly filled by a disconcerting sight. It is as though an inky black substance begins to ooze from the ceiling, gradually coalescing into a sinister figure that takes form on the wall just behind me.

As I stand there, rooted in both fear and curiosity, I can't tear my eyes away from the reflection of this looming entity in the bathroom mirror. With each passing moment, it grows darker and taller, its ominous presence steadily intensifying. It is a sight that defies rational explanation, leaving me with a growing sense of unease.

In response to this eerie manifestation, I pivot around, pressing my back against the bathroom door. This action is both a subconscious attempt to distance myself from the unsettling presence and a conscious acknowledgment that I can no longer ignore its existence. The room pulses with an otherworldly energy, and I can't help but wonder what this foreboding entity might signify or what ominous purpose it serves.

Feeling unusually small as the darkness expands above me, distorting the perception of the ceiling's height, I bow my head, as if surrendering to a force that has seemingly controlled my life for as long as I can remember when sounds invade my thoughts.

Pound, pound, pound

I startle at the persistent knocking at the door behind me that beats against my back. However, I pay it no attention, as I am rendered helpless, incapable of moving or reacting to the crowd's concern for my well-being.

The pounding on the door intensifies, with my friends' voices growing increasingly urgent, pleading for me to respond. Yet, I remain unable to do so. Fear grips my throat, leaving my mouth agape in shock as I watch a formidable presence enter the room before me.

"Someone just open the door!" I scream out loud.

But when I finally lift my hand up to fumble for the door handle, I find it to be locked. Not just locked but almost sealed.

"Did I lock it?" I try to recall.

I don't remember locking it, I think to myself while staring down at the handle by my side.

I finally locate the latch to unlock the door, but it stubbornly refuses to open. Panic sets in as I begin to yank on the handle, only to realize the door is inexplicably jammed. Desperation takes over as I try to force it open, pulling with all my strength and pounding on its surface, all the while knowing the darkness billowing behind me continues to intensify.

With my head resting against the door, eyes squeezed shut in defeat, I dread opening them again—fearful of what lies ahead, yet even more unnerved by what might be lurking behind me. Summoning a sliver of courage, I slowly open my eyes. In an instant, terror grips me—it's right there, directly behind me. In the mirror, I see the dark mass, fully manifested, its cloak flowing like a relentless black shroud cascading downward, engulfing the ground beneath my feet.

With what appears to be its arms raising to either side, elbows bent and elongated fingers pointed directly at my back, the figure swiftly lunges its hands into my sides. The sensation is immediate and horrifying, as if its fingers are reaching deep inside, seeking my very core. The pain is excruciating, an intense twisting sensation that feels like my insides are being wrenched and torn apart by a malevolent force. My breath catches, my vision blurs, and a primal scream escapes my lips as the figure's icy grip tightens, pulling me further into the darkness. The pain is immediate and excruciating, a searing agony that spreads through my body like wildfire. I gasp, my vision blurring as the darkness threatens to consume me entirely.

Everything changes rapidly as a sick panic settles in the pit of my stomach, a warning from my body that something was terribly wrong. I can feel myself losing consciousness, but I desperately cling to every shred of sanity, hoping this is all just a product of my imagination. It feels like I am trapped in a never-ending nightmare, a terrible movie I wish would come to an end.

My grip on reality begins to slip, and though it feels like this should be a dream, I am acutely aware that I am very much awake. I can feel the icy grip of Death inside me as my breathing slows and my heartbeat fades to a faint rhythm. My vital organs, having persevered as long as they can, are now sequentially undergoing a final shut down procedure. Control slips away from me; I can no longer see clearly or even stand. The dizziness overwhelms me, pushing my body beyond its limits. The bitter taste of bile rises from my stomach, and I cough and spit it out, struggling to hold on.

Was that blood? I wonder, trying to focus on the thick substance I just spewed out, splattered across the floor. The sour taste burns my throat, and my parched mouth yearns for water to rinse away the unpleasant sensation. Desperation grips me as I realize the severity of my condition, each moment bringing me closer to the brink.

Collapsing to the floor, I turn my head to the side and find immediate relief in the cold touch of the tile beneath me, a small reprieve as a single tear rolls down my cheek, a silent testament to the despair and helplessness that has taken hold.

Without a moment's pause, the black figure begins to encircle me, starting at my legs and winding its way around my body, resembling a serpent positioning its prey for consumption. The sensation is suffocating; the air around me grows colder as its dark, sinewy form tightens its grip.

The presence evokes memories of the same haunting black shadows I tried to escape from in the other room. It feels like the same darkness that obscured my thoughts when I first heard the murmurings of Death by my ear. This presence mirrors the inky chasms that haunted my room in childhood nightmares, shadows that seemed to come alive and whisper my deepest fears. The darkness now feels alive, pulsing with a malevolent energy that seeps into my very bones.

I can almost see the darkness swallowing the light, the dim glow of the bathroom light becoming feeble against the overwhelming blackness. My heart pounds in my chest, each beat slower than the last, as if the darkness is drawing the very life out of me. The figure's encircling motion is hypnotic, its presence a sinister dance around my prone form.

My vision blurs, and the edges of my sight darken, the world around me narrowing to a tunnel of oppressive black. Desperation claws at my mind, the primal urge to escape warring with the paralysis of pure terror.

"You have to get out of here!" I say in fear at the awareness of what is happening.

"I'm not ready, I'm not ready to die!" I declare in terror, my words causing further fear to rise up at the recognition of what I now admit.

Overwhelmed by sheer desperation and adrenaline, I extend my trembling hands toward the sink, mustering the last of my strength to hoist myself up one final time before the encroaching darkness completely consumes me.

Fumbling my weak body up, I brace my elbows against the countertop and, with one last thrust, manage to lift myself to the sink. Splashing water on my face in a desperate attempt to wake up from this nightmare, I look at myself in the mirror. In that instant, every last shred of hope vanishes like a flame snuffed out by a sudden gust of wind.

My once-vivid blue eyes are swallowed by a glossy, abyssal blackness. The inky darkness begins to drip from my eyes, sliding down my cheeks like thick, oily tears. Each drop leaves a sinister trail on my skin, stark against the pale background. The blackness oozes relentlessly, turning my face into a canvas of creeping darkness. The transformation is unsettling and grotesque, with the black liquid seeping from my eyes and pooling at my chin before dripping to the floor. It feels like my very essence is leaking out, the blackness continuing its relentless descent, furthering the horrifying spectacle.

My trembling hands instinctively reach up to rub my eyes, desperately hoping for some semblance of normalcy upon a second look. The mirror reflects back the same eerie void, intensifying my fear and dread.

"Those are not mine! They aren't mine!" I yell out, pressing my hands firmly against my eyes.

Panic sets in as the realization hits me: there is no escaping this; no chance of running down the hall to the safety of my parents' warm embrace. Not even a whisper of prayer escapes my lips, bound by an invisible force, leaving me incapable of pleading for help.

Fear and uncertainty wash over me like a tidal wave, drowning my thoughts and senses in a deep, foreboding abyss. The darkness, wrapped tightly around me and refusing to let go, continues to tug at me, battling against the last remnants of strength in my arms clinging to the edge of the countertop. It pulls relentlessly, threatening to drag me into an abyss that feels far deeper than the tile beneath my feet.

Suddenly, a torrent of questions inundate my mind, and an insatiable thirst for answers engulf me. I find myself compelled to discern truth from the lies, to unravel the mysteries of existence, and to comprehend the very purpose of life itself as if my life now depends on it.

"No! No! I'm not dying, there is still time," I reassure myself. "This is all in my head, just a hallucination from everything I've taken tonight." But as I close my eyes, hoping to wake up in the warmth of my bed and find the nightmare over, a startling voice pierces my ears, more audible and foreboding than before: *"It's too late!"*

I look in the mirror again, hoping for any resemblance of normalcy. My face appears completely colorless and deathly pale, eyes still black as the night sky when the realization finally sinks in.

"You just killed yourself," I quiver out loud.

How could I have been so foolish all these years? I think.

"What were you thinking?" I spew once more, condemning myself as I witness the horrifying scene reflected in the mirror, all the while reluctantly beginning to embrace the enveloping darkness that surrounds me.

As I peer deeper into the emptiness within my eyes, my sorrow over impending doom is evident. The darkness ascends higher, uncoiling as it reaches my head. It emits a cloak of shadows that drapes over me like a heavy garment, holding me upright as my body struggles to support itself.

I can feel the darkness coursing through my veins, spreading like poison, tightening its grip on my body. Each breath becomes a struggle as the oppressive force squeezes tighter and tighter, unwilling to let me draw in another gasp of air. The pressure mounts, compressing my chest and constricting my throat, leaving me desperate and gasping for relief that never comes. I cast one final glance at my reflection in the mirror as life slowly drains out of me. My arms lose strength and fall to my sides, my legs giving way beneath me.

Then, as if slow motion defies gravity, I watch my defeated reflection in the mirror change as I fall toward the toilet, unable to halt my descent. An excruciating pain erupts in my head upon impact, sending shockwaves through my entire body. With each breath, I feel the darkness seeping into my mouth, descending within me, extinguishing everything it touches. It flows down my esophagus, infiltrating my organs with a chilling ease. My lungs strain and finally forfeit their fight, my heart beats its final rhythm. My insides feel afflicted and withering as the darkness spreads, turning everything it touches to void. I lay there for a brief moment, but it lasts only an instant before everything fades to black.

CHAPTER 3

The Dream

1 Peter 1:24

*All people are like grass, and all their glory is like the flowers of the
field; the grass withers and the flowers fall, but the word of the Lord
endures forever.*

Joel 3:13-15

*Swing the sickle, for the harvest is ripe.
Come, trample the grapes, for the winepress is full
and the vats overflow—so great is their wickedness!*

*Multitudes, multitudes in the valley of decision!
For the day of the Lord is near in the valley of decision.
The sun and moon will be darkened, and the stars no longer shine.*

Psalm 37:1-2

*Do not fret because of those who are evil or be envious of those who
do wrong; for like the grass they will soon wither, like green plants
they will soon die away.*

Job 10:21-22

*Are not my days almost over?
Turn away from me so I can have a moment's joy before I go to the
place of no return, to the land of gloom and utter darkness, to the
land of deepest night, of utter darkness and disorder, where even the
light is like darkness.*

"Christopher," a voice whispers, my name resonating through the air like a familiar melody. As I stand amidst a serene wheat field, the soft light gently caresses the colors that dance along the edges of each golden stalk. It's as though the world itself is orchestrating a symphony of hues and gentle breezes.

The voice calling my name carries a sense of warmth and recognition, and I can't help but feel a smile tugging at the corners of my lips in response. It's the kind of smile that emerges from a deep sense of connection and comfort, as if reuniting with an old friend.

Intrigued, I embark on a delightful pursuit, chasing after the subtle displays of light that bounce off the wheat stalks. Each glimmer creates a mesmerizing, golden path through the soft, waist-high grass. The swaying motion of the wheat, guided by the whims of the wind, adds to the enchantment of the moment.

The atmosphere is one of leisure and contentment, casting a spell of relaxation and inviting me to recline amid this tranquil scape. It's as if the very essence of the field yearns for me to embrace its serenity and become one within its natural symphony.

"Christopher," the voice calls once more, accompanied by a soft, almost playful giggle that dances on the air like a mischievous breeze.

Filled with curiosity and a child's playful spirit, I can't resist taking a leap forward. Laughter, faint yet inviting, appears to originate just beyond my line of sight, pulling me closer like an irresistible magnet.

"Oh, how fun!" I say, frolicking merrily as I used to as a young boy. Laughter trickles through my body, infusing me with buoyant energy. Joyfully, I start running in the opposite direction from where I hear my name being called. Glancing back over my shoulder, I catch a glimpse of a smiling face partially concealed by the sun's radiant glare. Even with the dazzling sunlight, I can see the soft, familiar smile playing on her face, and I immediately recognize her.

"Mom," I say, the word forming on the tip of my tongue as I recognize her familiar mannerisms.

She giggles and mirrors my movements as we playfully weave through the stalks of wheat in our game of chase. Between the rays of sunlight glinting off of the golden highlights of her warm, silky brown hair, I look back and notice the light creating a shimmering halo around her. Fueled by childlike delight, I skip ahead faster in my pursuit of play.

"Christopher," she calls out in a sing-song voice, her arms outstretched as if about to catch me. My laughter grows as I run my fingers through the soft tufts of wheat, plucking some of the long stems along the way.

"Christopher," she calls again as I skip ahead in joyful anticipation. I can't contain my laughter, which turns into cackles of excitement, eagerly awaiting her to catch me in her arms and twirl me about, while the golden wheat in my hands dances around me.

Skipping joyfully through the golden wheat, I glance back, expecting to see my mother chasing me with outstretched arms and a warm smile. But suddenly, the air grows cold, and an eerie silence envelops the field. The wheat, once dancing in the breeze, now stands ominously still. I turn to see my mother, but she is no longer there. In her place looms a shadowy figure, dark and foreboding, its presence chilling my very soul.

"CHRISTOPHER!" the voice thunders, no longer the gentle tone of my mother but something otherworldly, filling me with a cold dread. The darkness pulses and grows, engulfing the space where my mother once stood. I freeze, my heart pounding in my chest, as an inexplicable terror grips me. The playful game of chase has turned into a nightmare, the once familiar wheat field now a labyrinth of shadows and unknown horrors. My instincts scream at me to flee, but I'm rooted to the spot, the sinister darkness drawing closer with every passing second.

As the whispering hiss of my name slithers out from the engulfing blackness, a cold dread seizes me. The voice, unrecognizable and sinister, crawls under my skin, making every hair stand on end. Panic and confusion spiral within me like a whirlwind, obliterating any sense of reality. The wheat field, once a place of joy and laughter, morphs into a scene from a nightmare.

"What's happening? Where is my mother?" I mutter to myself, each word laced with disbelief and growing terror. My mind races, desperately seeking answers in this maze of fear and darkness. The choice before me is paralyzing: do I plunge into the terrifying abyss to find her, risking being swallowed by whatever malevolent force lurks within? Or do I flee, driven by the raw instinct to survive, abandoning any hope of saving her?

The voice roars again, "You cannot escape me!"

Its malicious tone vibrates through the very air, wrapping around me like chains of fear. The hatred in those words is tangible, a physical force pressing against me, trying to crush my will. In a burst of fear-fueled clarity, my decision crystallizes. I turn and run, every fiber of my being screaming for survival. The dark entity's malevolence chases me, but I push forward, driven by the primal and unyielding instinct to escape this nightmarish reality.

The sky above, once a canvas of blue, is rapidly devoured by a menacing black cloud, casting an apocalyptic shadow over the land. The sun, once a beacon of warmth and light, fights a losing battle, its rays dimming to a mere whisper on the distant horizon. Driven by a primal urge for survival, I sprint towards that fading light, my only hope in this rapidly darkening world.

Glancing back at the wheat field, the sight that unfolds is nothing short of surreal. The once golden stalks of wheat transform before my eyes, becoming a whirlwind of black dust, swirling and churning as if alive. The wheat I clutch in my trembling hands crumbles to ash, slipping through my fingers like the last remnants of a forgotten dream, joining the chaos of the wind-swept field.

The wind, now a gale of fury, assaults me with particles of the disintegrated earth. I shield my eyes, coughing violently as the dust fills my mouth and lungs. With my vision obscured by the swirling dust and the overwhelming darkness, I press forward, each step driven by a deep, instinctual need to escape this nightmare. The faint glimmer of light on the horizon serves as my beacon, a symbol of hope amidst the engulfing chaos. Each step is a battle against the relentless force of the wind and the encroaching darkness, my child-like innocence begins to shatter from the terror of the moment. The world around me has become unrecognizable, a scape of fear and despair, far from the tranquil field I initially encountered.

In the distance, an ominous rumble grows louder, akin to thunderous roars that shake the earth beneath my feet. A lone tear rolls down my cheek as I instinctively call out for my mother's help, the words of a frightened child.

"Mom! Please help me! Where did you go? How do I find you?"

My heart races with mounting fear. The relentless black cloud advances, seemingly winning the race to consume the faint light on the horizon. But a glimmer of hope emerges as a single ray of light forms a clear path within the encroaching darkness.

"I can reach the horizon! I can beat the darkness!" I stutter in self-encouragement, though lacking absolute confidence.

As I race desperately towards the fading light, time seems to slow to a crawl. My foot, in a cruel twist of fate, snags on something sinister lurking unseen on the ground. My body lurches forward uncontrollably, arms flailing in a futile attempt to regain balance. The world tilts and spins as I fall, the encroaching cloud of darkness consuming the last slivers of light, plunging everything into an abyss of black.

In that suspended moment, I brace for the harsh impact of the ground, but it never comes. Instead, there's a startling void, an eerie absence of reality.

Suddenly, with a sharp intake of breath, I'm torn from the nightmare. I jolt upright, heart racing, skin slick with cold sweat. My eyes snap open to a room bathed in shadows, unfamiliar and disorienting. Panic courses through me like electricity, my heart pounding against my chest like a drum of war. Every sense is heightened, every nerve on edge, as I struggle to distinguish reality from the remnants of the dream. The oppressive darkness of the room envelops me, a tangible echo of the nightmare that still clings to the fringes of my consciousness. My breath comes in ragged gasps, each inhale a struggle against the lingering panic. I try to anchor myself in reality, whispering a mantra of reassurance, "It was just a dream."

But the unfamiliar surroundings do little to ease my unsettled mind. Shadows lurk in every corner, transforming ordinary objects into sinister shapes. The air feels thick, heavy with an unspoken menace, as if the remnants of the nightmare have seeped into the room, blurring the lines between dream and reality.

My eyes dart around, straining to make sense of this strange place. Each unfamiliar detail sends a fresh wave of anxiety coursing through me. The unfamiliarity of my surroundings only amplifies the disorientation, leaving me to wonder how I arrived here and what might be hidden in the shadows. The normalcy of waking up in a known environment is cruelly absent, replaced by a deep sense of unease and vulnerability.

"What happened?"

The question echoes in the stillness of the room, carrying with it a weight of confusion and unease. The sense of foreboding from the dream lingers like a shadow, refusing to be dispelled by the simple realization that I'm awake.

"Where am I?"

The words sound strange to my own ears, as if they belong to someone else. This unfamiliarity with my own voice adds another layer of disorientation to the already unsettling situation. For a moment, I'm caught in a spiral of doubt and fear, questioning the reality of everything around me.

Despite the overwhelming sense of confusion, I force myself to focus, to push aside the creeping dread and the unnerving strangeness of my voice. It's crucial to regain composure, to anchor myself in the here and now, no matter how unfamiliar it may seem.

"It was all just a dream," I repeat over and over, trying to reassure myself that everything is fine.

As my senses gradually return to me, I'm greeted by a strange, acrid odor hanging in the air. The fumes have a sulfurous quality that burn my eyes and throat. The atmosphere feels oppressively heavy, making every breath a laborious effort. Swallowing, I notice an odd taste lingering in my mouth.

With my head throbbing, I lower it between my legs, arms wrapping protectively around the back of my neck as I attempt to collect my scattered thoughts. Brief flashes of the dream's unsettling images dart through my mind. I want to shake off this disconcerting feeling, but when I make an effort to move, I'm met with a deep, excruciating ache that seems to radiate from the core of my being, extending into my limbs. So, I remain seated, my body limp and sagging, struggling to comprehend what my body is going through and why.

Attempting to push myself up once more, the unfamiliar pain shoots through me anew, eliciting a gasp of agony. Tears well up in my eyes as I sit there, cradling one arm with the other and gently rubbing it as if it were the primary source of pain. Yet, I sense a profound discomfort that runs deeper than the physical sensations of burning skin, throbbing head, and aching limbs. It's an emptiness, a void, a profound sense of lack that gnaws at my very soul.

I recall my family's time in Canada, where sudden, frigid winter storms would engulf everything in relentless blizzards. I used to watch the blowing snow from the warmth and comfort of my parents' home, thinking, "I'm glad I'm not out there looking in."

But now, I feel as though I am on the outside, peering in. Somewhere, the doors seem to have closed, locking me out, and I'm left wondering why. This emptiness creeps up my spine like a flame's caress on a dry, grassy field, seeping into the very core of my bones. My thoughts drift back to the latter part of my dream, where I fell into the consuming darkness. I can't shake the feeling that something is missing, that something has been taken from me.

I attempt to survey my surroundings, hoping to find myself still in the bathroom where I passed out at the party, but the searing pain in my eyes radiates throughout my head. Every attempt to open them feels like awakening inside a furnace, aggravated by an acidic mist in the air that stings and irritates my eyes, making focus impossible.

After some time, I manage to shield my face with my hands in a way that allows brief, albeit blurry, glimpses of the room I'm in.

"I need to find the door. I need to get out," I mutter aloud, the putrid smell in the air burning my lungs and evoking memories of the chaotic night that led to this disorienting state.

As colors gradually transform into shapes through my hazy, hungover eyes, I realize that the bathroom no longer resembles the one I remember from the previous night. I fumble to locate the sink, intending to use it to steady myself and wash my face, but my blurred vision can only make out smooth walls devoid of any fixtures. There's no sink, no toilet—this doesn't look like a bathroom at all. The small, cramped room features amber-red tile floors that appear aged and weathered, as though rusted.

With my vision clearing, I notice shadows stirring on the floor, and my gaze follows them as they travel upward. The walls seem to ripple as if shadows are trapped within them, swaying back and forth in an unsettling rhythm. They beckon me, almost hypnotically, and for some inexplicable reason, I find myself drawn to move in sync with their eerie dance.

I gaze upon the enigmatic sight before me and wonder, *What is this that I am looking at?*

My body sways in slow motion as the dark crimson reds blend into indistinct blues, until the realization strikes that this isn't a wall—it resembles a flame!

"A flame! As in fire?" I exclaim with a mix of alarm and disbelief, wondering if the room I passed out in had suddenly become engulfed in flames, and no one had rescued me yet.

I scramble to my feet and cry out, "Help! Fire!"

But instead of a swift ascent, I fall backward onto the rusted floor from which I initially rose. I quickly extend my hands to brace for impact, but the fall proves to be hard, as though I tumbled from an unthinkable height.

In agony over my legs' inability to support me, I watch the flame expand upward as far as my eyes can see. As I press my hand into the "ground" and shift my body onto my knees, I turn around once more, only to realize that I am entirely encircled by fire. There seems to be no way out, and the flames appear to imprison me. At first, sheer terror grips me, the thought of the fire closing in and burning me alive consuming my thoughts.

However, I soon recognize that this is no ordinary fire. It seems to feed solely on the red earth beneath it, emitting neither smoke nor the acrid scent of burning. It moves serenely, like silk billowing in the wind, encircling me but never drawing closer.

A deep fear takes root in the pit of my stomach as I desperately attempt to comprehend where I am. Questions flood my mind: *Who could have placed me here? How did this happen? Am I still dreaming?*

"Hello?" I shout. "Hello!"

The flames shift uneasily in response to my panicked cries, but no one answers. I stretch my hand toward the fire, partly out of curiosity, hoping for a rational explanation. Another part of me is desperate to test whether the fire is real and what pain it might bring if I were to attempt to jump through it. But as I cautiously reach out, I notice something else—the grotesque appearance of my own hand. How could I have missed this before? Examining the rest of my exposed skin, I am increasingly alarmed by each boil, raw, burnt area of flesh, and sickly discoloration. The more I see, the more the pain intensifies. My hand begins to tremble from the newfound agony, and I ponder, *How am I still alive?*

I delicately raise my fingers to my face, feeling boils protruding from my cheeks and along my hairline—or at least where my hair used to be, for it has been completely burned off. All that remains are the stubs, marked with scars and burns from something I can't even remember happening. My lips feel swollen, chapped, and burnt, with my body threatening to go into shock from the overwhelming pain. I swallow hard, a desperate need for water overtaking me.

"Who would do this to me?" I wonder aloud.

As I sit hunched over in agony, a faint memory begins to swell within me, as if Death himself has entered my fiery cell to remind me of his victory over me. The memories from that night when darkness overcame me washes over me. However, these memories are not as I initially recalled; they are far more terrifying.

Despite the searing heat from the flame, an icy coldness courses through me as I relive the last moments before I lost consciousness. The haunting words, "You just killed yourself," echo through my mind, reverberating with chilling clarity.

Unlike the misty blackness I remembered from my drunken stupor, I am now left with a much more horrifying image of the events that unfolded, as if I am seeing them through someone else's eyes.

In this new memory, I can see myself standing before the small mirror, my eyes as black as the night, panic swelling within me. Strangely, I observe myself in the third person, as if watching the scene play out before me. However, there is no black mist forming behind me as I initially remembered. Instead, I see Death himself entering the bathroom through a dark void that opens beneath me.

Death, a towering figure shrouded in flowing black robes, moves with an otherworldly grace, casting an eerie stillness over the room.

His presence is both mesmerizing and terrifying, embodying the void itself. I watch as my former self examines my black eyes in the mirror, oblivious to the approaching doom.

With deliberate and almost tender motions, Death drapes his black garments across my shoulders, the fabric cold and heavy like a burial shroud. His touch presses down upon my former body, the heaviness evident in my mannerisms. Then, with sudden brutality, he sinks his hands deep within my sides. Pain radiates through my body, a pain that still resonates even now as I recall the events and continue to watch him tilt me backward, far beyond the capabilities of any human, with my spine bending at an unnatural angle.

Death's grip is unyielding, his hands like icy talons inside my body as I watch myself fight for every remaining breath. Hopelessness washes over me as I witness him release his right hand from within my body, the coldness leaving a hollow, aching void in its wake. With cruel precision, he pries open my jaw, forcing my mouth wide open.

With a slow, deliberate breath, I witness Death exhaling a deep, inky substance into my mouth and my body reacting violently to it as he forces it down my throat. Terrified by what I am recalling, because it is not how I originally remembered it, I feel an unsettling fear as the memory continues to unfold.

I watch as my body undergoes a transformation in Death's elongated arms. My clothing withers away, and my skin takes on the appearance of a third-degree burn victim. The screams of agony emanating from me could shatter glass as burns and scars are etched into my being. Death, after stripping my old body, clutches it tight and waves his hand at his side as the portal opens back up beneath him with both bodies sinking into the darkness below the room where I died. As he descends into the abyss with my newly altered body, I briefly glimpse the toilet, where I can now witness the lifeless corpse of my former self. My head is submerged under the rim of water, and my familiar body lies stiff and pale, like a corpse that has been dead for hours.

"Why? Why?" I scream, the horror of the memory overwhelming me. I swallow hard and turn away, not wanting to witness any more of what I had just seen.

"I won't let my mind go there. Death cannot look like this for me! How is this possible? Why me?" I mutter in frantic panic, the reality of my situation sinking in.

As I grapple with this chilling new reality, a primal fear surges within me, compelling me to take immediate action. I can't bear the thought of being imprisoned in this nightmarish realm, treated like a mere animal. The air around me grows dense, and my attempts to draw breath are met with futile coughs.

Summoning every ounce of courage I possess, I resolve to break free from this torment. I charge headlong into the wall of fire, driven by the desperate hope that I might return to the comforting embrace of reality.

But my efforts prove in vain. The fiery barrier rejects my passage, sending me reeling backward, my body wracked with pain. As I lie crumpled on the floor, I lift my gaze to the wall of flames, my vision blurs and senses dull. The line between the nightmare and the tangible world blur further, and I can't help but wonder about the extent of the damage I inflicted upon myself.

As my strength wanes, my body tattered and broken, I find myself surrendering to the emptiness that surrounds and envelopes me, leaving behind the tormenting flames and the chilling enigma of my otherworldly predicament.

CHAPTER 4

The Remembrance

Matthew 13:41-42

The Son of Man will send out his angels, and they will weed out of his kingdom everything that causes sin and all who do evil. They will show them into the blazing furnace, where there will be weeping and gnashing of teeth.

Psalms 9:16-18

The Lord is known by his acts of justice; the wicked are ensnared by the work of their hands. The wicked go down to the realm of the dead, all the nations that forget God. But God will never forget the needy, the hope of the afflicted will never perish.

"Father," the word echoes in the quiet of the distance, carried by a soft breeze. "Father, I will always stay faithful to you."

I hear again, my body stirring out of a restless slumber.

"Father."

I hear it again as I shift to one side; a profound sense of familiarity washing over me, leading me to ponder the origin of this voice and why it evokes such a strong feeling of recognition within me.

"Father, I love you so much."

It continues as I sit up, grappling with the possibility that I might be hallucinating or trapped in a never-ending dream. In the eerie silence that follows, I strain to hear the familiar voice, but it vanishes.

I glance around, hoping to wake up in my own reality, believing this torment might be a byproduct of the drugs and alcohol from the previous night. However, my gaze is inexorably drawn to the swaying colors before me that, just as before, confirm I'm still within this . . . Hell.

"Hell," I murmur softly, the word seemingly hanging in the air around me with its malevolence. Suddenly, my throat constricts, and I struggle to breathe. The word stands on the edge of my mind as it rolls off my tongue and lingers, deepening the palpable stillness. Fear takes root in me as I contemplate the word and the revelation it may hold over my current situation. The wall of fire changes, adopting a dark, eerie blue hue, its movement languid and unsettling.

"Father . . ."

The voice returns, interrupting my thoughts and fears about my current state.

"Thank you for sending . . . to die . . . my sins," the voice murmurs, the words fragmented as if transmitted through a malfunctioning radio. "Please help those . . . not know . . . find you."

The words bring forth a powerful memory, forging a deep connection to a distant time when I existed as a completely different individual, in an era far removed from the present. During that time,

I had spoken these very words in earnest prayer. As the flames sway and dance before me, an irresistible force compels me to observe, surrendering to their mesmerizing allure. Gradually, my airways open up, allowing me to release a profound exhale, as if I'd been holding my breath for ages.

As I observe, the flames mesmerizingly transform, pulling me into a memory, transporting me to a different world and era. Like gazing into a mirrored surface, I see a vivid image in the flame before me: a young boy, kneeling in reverent prayer, engaged in heartfelt communication with a God I once intimately knew. The evocative scene stands as a powerful reminder of a previous version of myself, hailing from a forgotten era.

"Thank you for sending your son to die for me, Father," the boy utters. *"There are those who have not yet discovered you. Aid them in finding you as I have, so that they too may find salvation."*

As I continue staring into the mesmerizing dance of the flame before me, memories wash over me like a distant tide. The colors within the fire gradually engulf the recollections, blurring the lines between past and present. My heavy eyes begin to droop, and I find myself transported back to a pivotal day etched in my memory, when I still believed in a merciful God.

In those days, I was a different person, a younger version of myself, brimming with unwavering faith in the potency of prayer. In this moment of hazy uncertainty, I can't help but feel the chasm that had grown between me and the God I once held so dear.

I can still vividly recall the night that was the catalyst for my swift descent into chaos: the night I was arrested at my church after I attempted to run over a youth pastor who had shattered my trust. After that, I had taken a dark and treacherous road, seeking acceptance through violence and crime, molding my identity into something that was the antithesis of Christian values. In the process, I had cast aside everything I had once known about living a life devoted to God, and had, in essence, rejected God Himself. My life spiraled out of control with FBI investigations, cage fighting, and a spree of other offenses that drastically shifted my moral compass. I morphed from a child celebrated for my devout spirit, once honored with the "Best Christian Character Award" in middle school, into a monster I never imagined I could become.

"That was a dark chapter," I whisper to myself, attempting to rationalize my actions as though there could ever be a valid reason for attempting to end a life.

Questions swirled relentlessly within me, forming an internal storm of doubt and contemplation. *Why should I believe in a God who remained hidden, unproven? How could I have faith in a God who allowed pain and death to persist?* The stark contrast between the God who proclaimed to be love and the world filled with hatred and malevolence challenged my faith to its very core.

The existence of a loving God seemed inconceivable in a world where suffering and violence ran rampant, especially the world He claimed to have created. Eventually I reached a point where the pursuit of something that professed itself to be love no longer made sense. So I relinquished everything I had gained through my early encounters with the Lord—through my church, my baptism, my prayers, and my service during church retreats—because no matter what, evil appeared to overshadow the good. Darkness had a more prominent presence in my life than light, and hatred seemed to yield greater results than love.

I abandoned everything I once knew about God in favor of a belief system that made more rational sense to me, one that, at its core, simply did not include God. I no longer wished for His existence to be a part of my reality.

The weight of my realization hits me like a sledgehammer, and I find myself voicing a chilling admission, "Maybe that is why I killed myself."

In that moment, I fully grasped the depth of my intentions that fateful night, realizing they extended far beyond mere attempts to escape the surrounding chaos and turmoil. I had been resolute in my determination to end my life, to bring an end to whatever twisted game had ensnared me.

However, now, removed from every remnant of the life I once knew and free from the influences that once defined it, it feels as though a crucial part of myself has been forcibly torn away. In this newly awakened state of pain, an unexpected terror begins to creep in—the chilling thought of God's nonexistence. Deep inside, I come to recognize that although my beliefs about God might not have been completely accurate, I never truly considered the possibility of His complete absence. If God didn't exist, then the place I find myself in now could potentially be the ultimate destination for all humanity, both believers and non-believers. Contemplating this possibility is profoundly unsettling.

A sense of hopelessness surges within me, hollowing out my heart. As I watch, the flames dance and morph, casting shadows that seem to paint another memory in the air before me. Suddenly, I find myself standing in the church my family once frequented—a sacred space where I had poured out my heart in fervent prayer to God.

I see my brothers playfully racing out of the building, me following behind. But then, I halt and turn to gaze back at the front stage of the church, where a cross stands prominently displayed. Try as I may, I can't remember why I stopped. As I continue to watch the shifting colors within the flames, a heartfelt "thank you" escapes the lips of my younger self, and the memory vanishes abruptly within the fire.

Continuing to reminisce, I remember the times when I used to express heartfelt gratitude to Jesus for sacrificing Himself to redeem me from my past and future sins. Those were different times, filled with faith and hope, when the concept of salvation and divine forgiveness had a profound impact on my life. Back then, I believed His death was necessary to save me from the sins that plagued our world.

But sitting in this fiery abyss, I begin to grasp a different facet of His sacrifice. It wasn't solely about saving me from the sins of the world; it was also about rescuing me from this perilous abyss. He had died for me, and yet, here I am, having knowingly chosen this path.

Oh Jesus, what have I done? I internalize. The weight of my rejection of Him presses upon my conscience at the realization that I willingly, consciously turned my back on Him.

Is this truly Hell? I wonder. *Had I indeed perished and awakened in a place devoid of His presence?*

The hopelessness that has taken root within me grows like the ominous cloud I glimpsed in the bathroom before arriving here. The vivid memories replay in the wall of fire leaving an ache deep within me. It intensifies my sense of despair, as if someone is delivering a message: I once had a choice, an opportunity, but now it was irrevocably gone. No more choices lay ahead that would ever involve or include God again.

In my mind, I beseech God, pleading for Him to awaken me from this nightmarish dream. I promise to mend my ways, to cease the violence, crime, and drugs that have come to consume my existence.

"Please, just get me out of here!" I implore, desperate to alter the grim reality that I am slowly coming to accept.

How I long to bask in the warmth of the sun's embrace again, serenaded by the sweet melodies of birds, and unburdened by worry or doubt, free to make choices that might one day lead to redemption if only there was enough time left to still make a difference.

"Please, let there still be time," I pray fervently, clinging to a glimmer of hope.

But nothing around me changes. There's no sign of a response. Only an empty, hollow shiver courses through my scorched and blistered skin, finding its dwelling place in the depths of my mind, where it murmurs words of doubt, despair, and fear into the recesses of my soul.

It whispers that no one can hear me, that none have heeded my prayers. It insinuates that I crossed the threshold into damnation, far beyond the reach of God's ears.

"No!" I cry out. "This is just a dream!"

Panic surges in my throat, akin to the fear I felt as a child when strange noises would wake me in the dead of night; the kind of fear that makes you believe something else is present in the room, watching you. Yet, you can do nothing but pull the covers over your head, keeping the terror bottled inside, hoping not to be noticed by whatever your imagination has conjured.

I clench my fists tightly and shut my eyes, taking deep breaths in an attempt to escape this nightmare. Yet, with each breath, I feel myself spiraling further into a state of uncontrollable chaos.

"That's enough! I need to get out of here! No more hiding!" I resolve, determination surging through me.

I find myself engaging in an act I never imagined I would witness myself doing. It starts innocently enough with a small pinch on the arm, an attempt to wake myself from what I hope is just a dream. I feel ridiculous and, above all, desperate. Quickly, my actions escalate from mere pinching to violently tearing at my own flesh in a frantic effort to escape this nightmare. I stare in horror as the skin on my arms splits, revealing raw, bleeding muscle beneath. Each rip sends a shock wave of intense, burning pain through my body. Despite the agony, a relentless drive within me refuses to yield. I cannot accept that this is my reality. I am resolved to wake up or die trying.

As I witness my own flesh hanging off my body and blood pooling around me while I kneel on the ground, an unimaginable realization dawns upon me: my flesh regenerates right before my eyes. I can inflict unimaginable agony upon myself, but I can no longer die. I can no longer feel anything other than this unrelenting pain.

"NO!" I scream in despair.

Tears stream down my face as my hands continue their relentless assault on my own flesh. Between sobs, I chant, "Wake up! Wake up! WAKE UP!" in a desperate plea to escape the nightmare enveloping me.

My voice echoes into the abyss, a desperate plea to escape this tormenting nightmare.

Time hangs suspended between the ceaseless pain and the crushing realization that nothing will alter this nightmarish reality. Claustrophobia tightens its grip on me, driving me further into a frenzy. The fiery walls encircling me seem to close in, their intensity and ferocity growing. The red, rusted ground beneath me feels unsettling, as I notice a crimson substance oozing through the cracks, seeping between my toes. It taints the air with the sickening scent of blood and decay, each breath of its putrid aroma triggering involuntary gagging and dry heaving.

"If I am in Hell," I gasp in short, shallow breaths, "then that would mean I must have died first. And I am clearly not dead!"

I cry out, attempting to push aside the haunting memory of my last moments alive and the final words the specter of Death revealed to me.

"Therefore, I am not in Hell," I mutter in an attempt to reassure myself, to impose reason upon this irrational nightmare, to drive away the demons that now torment my thoughts with an air of irrevocable finality.

I pinch my nose, resisting the urge to vomit from the overpowering stench of blood, and squeeze my eyes shut, chanting that this is merely a dream.

Just then, from beyond the searing confines of my fiery prison, an otherworldly, spectral scream pierces the air, tearing through the fabric of my existence. The sound plunges deep into the core of my being, paralyzing my mind in a submissive stillness. My breath catches in my throat, held captive by the sudden terror. Even the flames before me halt, crystallizing like eerie shards of glass, as if they too sense the profound dread enveloping me. In that exact moment, a chilling realization takes root within me, sprouting like a seed of despair in the barren soil of my consciousness—I am not alone.

CHAPTER 5

The Awakening

1 Corinthians 3:11-17

*For no one can lay any foundation other than the one already laid,
which is Jesus Christ. If anyone builds on this foundation using gold,
silver, costly stones, wood, hay or straw, their work will be shown for
what it is, because the Day will bring it to light.*

*It will be revealed with fire, and the fire will test the quality of
each person's work. If what has been built survives, the builder will
receive a reward. If it is burned up, the builder will suffer loss but
yet will be saved—even though only as one escaping through the
flames.*

*Don't you know that you yourselves are God's temple and that
God's Spirit dwells in your midst?
If anyone destroys God's temple, God will destroy that person;
for God's temple is sacred, and you together are that temple.*

Romans 2:5-8, 12

*But because of your stubbornness and your unrepentant heart, you
are storing up wrath against yourself for the day of God's wrath,
when his righteous judgment will be revealed.
God "will repay each person according to what they have done."
To those who by persistence in doing good seek glory, honor and
immortality, he will give eternal life.
But for those who are self-seeking and who reject the truth and
follow evil, there will be wrath and anger.
All who sin apart from the law will also perish apart from the law,
and all who sin under the law will be judged by the law.*

In the midst of my fiery prison, a deep and ominous rumble emanates from the unfathomable depths of the unknown, shaking the very ground beneath me in a sudden and unexpected explosion. Instinctively, I prepare for the worst, uncertain of what might unfold. Large pieces of debris collide with the outer boundaries of the flaming wall, prompting me to seek cover, bracing for the inevitable. As a sizable object crashes nearby, I hunker down, avoiding the potential danger it heralds.

Attempting to peer through the fiery barrier into the abyss, I find my view obstructed by shifting colors and the relentless dance of flames, causing my eyes to smolder and sting. Reluctantly, I divert my gaze to spare myself further discomfort, dreading the thought of being rendered blind and defenseless in this dark and malevolent realm.

From a distance, beyond the confines of my flaming prison, I discern the anguished cries of others in the throes of agony. As I strain to make sense of the situation, my imagination begins to weave a horrifying reality for the people behind those blood-curdling screams. I picture others trapped in the throes of terror, their faces contorted in sheer horror, their voices strained from the intensity of their fear.

Are they being chased by something? I think. *What could it be?*

Yet, before I can ascertain the source or nature of their torment, a thunderous roar reverberates, overwhelming their voices. I shrink closer to the ground, hidden from view, trying to make myself as small as possible against the flames. I'm not even sure if I emit a scent that could give away my whereabouts.

To say I am terrified is an understatement. I feel like trapped prey, exposed and vulnerable with very little understanding of my surroundings or what could be lurking in the shadows beyond my flame. Then, a disconcerting thought dawns upon me—*You're already dead.*

Why am I afraid if I can no longer die? I wonder to myself.

Giving no more thought to my previous question, my senses remain on high alert as I bear witness to the explosive tumult from beyond my fiery confines. Holding my breath, I strain to listen and wait, my heart pounding in the stifling silence. Suddenly, as abruptly as it began, the cacophony subsides, leaving an eerie quiet in its wake. I feel like someone or something may be observing, waiting, and listening for the slightest sign of vulnerability.

Abandoning all doubt about the authenticity of my nightmarish situation, I realize this is no mere dream. It is evident that I am not alone in this infernal abyss. Whatever lurks beyond my confines waits in anticipation for anyone foolish enough to make the slightest peep.

Indeed, I must share this hellish realm with countless others—perhaps millions—condemned to eternal torment alongside me, I think to myself.

The tumultuous emotions from the recent chaos have hardly begun to settle when another wave of terror crashes over me. The frantic footsteps and agonized screams of another person pierce the air, cutting through the atmosphere like a knife. It is as if the very ground beneath me quivers in response to the urgency of the situation.

My heart, already racing from the previous commotion, now pounds in my chest like a relentless drum. I feel a surge of adrenaline coursing through my veins, propelling me into a state of heightened awareness. *What is happening out there?*

In the midst of this new turmoil, I find myself torn between the instinct to flee and the desire to help.

Flee where though? I wonder. *There's nowhere to go, nowhere to hide and no way to help!*

Before I can finish my thought, the ground trembles again, sending shockwaves of panic through my body. It feels as if the chaos is intentional now, in relentless pursuit. The patterns of movement that shake the earth are erratic and sudden, as if chasing something or someone it has sensed or seen.

There is no time to dwell upon the fate of the others, though; no sooner has the thought entered my mind, then another eruption of chaos surges from beyond the confining walls, punctuated by a scream—no, a roar—that shatters the very air around me. Stumbling forward and then recoiling from the explosion and the deafening noise, I seek refuge by covering my head with my arms, desperate to shield my ears from the shriek.

The earth trembles and fractures, emitting sounds of splitting rocks from beneath me, as if the ground itself is preparing to engulf me whole. Although the idea of a catastrophic earthquake briefly crosses my mind, there is something eerily unnatural about this seismic activity—an orchestrated quality that seems to defy the natural laws. This unsettling sensation suggests a manipulation of the earth's movements, hinting at forces beyond the usual tectonic shifts. It feels controlled, directed toward a specific target. While I can't be certain if I am the intended focus, I can't shake the nagging suspicion that I am ensnared in the midst of this turmoil. The precise and deliberate nature of these disturbances suggests that they are not random occurrences but rather targeted actions, potentially with me at their center.

The sounds that assail my senses fill me with an unearthly fear, inciting every primal instinct to flee. Yet, I remain trapped and defenseless, awaiting the arrival of whatever looms on the horizon.

An entire world seems to exist beyond my fiery prison, and it now reveals itself in a wrathful crescendo of impending obliteration. I yearn to know more about it. As I stand there, torn between the desire to retreat from the chaos and the inexplicable pull drawing me deeper into the unknown, a profound sense of unease settles again in the pit of my stomach. The overwhelming reality that I am not alone in this turmoil is both disconcerting and intriguing.

The whispers, barely audible over the backdrop of chaos, call out to me, their ethereal nature creating an eerie and surreal atmosphere. It is as though the very winds that carry them conspire to beckon me forth, promising safety in the midst of the storm.

I struggle to reconcile this enticing promise with the unsettling familiarity of those voices. They echo the same haunting whispers that had plagued my restless nights when I was still alive, invading the sanctuary of my dreams with their enigmatic messages and unsettling presence. Now, they found their way into the waking world, blurring the boundaries between reality and the surreal.

The temptation to follow those whispers, to seek the source of their siren call, is undeniable. It is as if they hold the key to unraveling the mysteries that have haunted me since the night before. Yet, a nagging doubt lingers, warning me that this allure might conceal dangers of its own, that the promises of safety could be nothing more than a deceptive mirage in the midst of the tumultuous winds.

As I grapple with these conflicting emotions, I can't help but wonder if I am on the verge of uncovering a deeper truth about the world beyond my sight or if I am descending further into a realm of darkness and uncertainty from which there may be no return.

"Did death follow me here?" I voice my fears aloud, succumbing to anxiety as I realize that the malevolent presence responsible for bringing me to this place is now in relentless pursuit, its alluring whispers echoing upon the winds that reluctantly carried its empty promises across the land.

What would happen if he found me? I ponder, consumed by trepidation.

The shock waves from the distant destruction reach the ground beneath my feet, causing me to lose my balance and tumble onto my hands and knees once again. I attempt to rise, determined to confront whatever lurks out there, perhaps unveiling the face of the shadow that haunted my life. Yet, no sooner have I regained my footing than I am forcefully thrown down once more, my body meeting the floor with a resounding thud. It feels as though I stand no chance against the phantom creature responsible for this devastation, if it even happens to discover my presence behind these fiery walls. In a world utterly unfamiliar to me, I feel doomed and forgotten by the world I once inhabited.

"But what help could anyone give me here, even if they remembered me," I ask myself.

"Who could rescue me from this nightmare, who . . . who?" I whisper through my tears.

Closing my eyes in an attempt to find solace, I am swiftly reminded that there is no respite here. THERE IS NO REST FOR THE DAMNED! Fear grips me as though something holds sway over my thoughts. My mind races, conjuring every nightmare and horror I have ever envisioned. In a cruel twist of fate, the flames before me project my fears into tangible forms, as though I am giving life to my own terrors and nightmares.

I exhale the terror that has consumed me from within, allowing it to permeate the air around me. Left to my imagination, I can only wonder what lies beyond the walls of flame.

"What kind of creature has caused this sudden and violent upheaval from the outside?" I wonder to myself in the aftermath of the screams, the violent tremors and the eerie voices that can be heard upon the brief moment of silence that offer safety and rest. I attempt to compose my thoughts, seeking a plan of action, yet am promptly reminded of my status as a prisoner, devoid of any apparent means of escape. Once again, my contemplation is shattered by a deafening eruption of explosions.

What in the world could be happening out there? I ponder with increasing dread.

For now, there's a slight relief that my immediate surroundings remain intact. Nevertheless, the ongoing chaos beyond sends shockwaves across the land, with each tremor strong enough to send me tumbling to the ground, rendering me little more than a loose bag of bones. My skin begins to bruise and blister from the relentless battering. The skin on my arms scrapes away easily each time I crash to the ground or get pushed closer to the flamed walls. My blood smears the floor, painting it a sinister shade of red. After repeated falls, I decide to abandon my futile attempts to stand. I lay there on my stomach, arms outstretched, fingers digging into the earth, desperately trying to anchor myself. I frantically clutch at anything in the hopes that the ground won't split open, sending me plummeting into an unknown chasm or burying me alive for eternity—a fate I dare not even contemplate right now.

If there are others out there, I cannot hear them anymore amidst the deafening crumbling of earth. I can scarcely hear my own screams that escape my throat in fervent pleas for this torment to cease.

The wall of fire seems agitated and disturbed by the events unfolding on the other side, billowing above me in fits of rage. I feel as though the fire is alive and that it may consume me at any moment.

Of course, that's if the ground beneath me doesn't shatter and swallow me whole first, I think.

Clearly Hell has taken note of my presence, but for some reason, the unseen forces appear unaware of my exact location, growing frustrated at their inability to locate me. While I am somewhat amused by the notion that I remain concealed from the entities roaming the outskirts of my fiery prison, I am also gripped by an ever-expanding emptiness within me. It feels as though it's carving a hole in my chest—a growing sense of hopelessness. What terrifies me even more is that I fear the absence of hope now more than the destruction I hear unfolding outside my prison walls. I'm haunted by a pervasive fear, sensing it deep within as it whispers relentlessly that all that awaits me is further indescribable terror. This constant murmur in my mind leaves me with a dread that there is nothing to look forward to but escalating horror.

No nightmare could compare to the profound hopelessness and horror that gave birth to this place. It's not the Hell my pastor once described, a place where sinners were punished with fire and brimstone. This emptiness, this sense of lack, is far more agonizing than any physical injury or burn I might endure.

What has been stripped from me that causes such inner pain? I ponder.

The pain within me is excruciating, and it hardly compares to the open wounds that now expose bones protruding from my skin—wounds that must have occurred during the last violent upheaval. Yet, the pain I endure isn't merely physical; it's a pain of separation. This place is suffused with an emptiness that one can only feel deep within, where you come to realize that in life, no matter how dire things seemed, there was always a glimmer of hope. Here, that glimmer is utterly absent. Without hope, there is no life.

How could I have been so foolish with the life I was given, to throw it all away so easily? I contemplate, my fingers clenching the ground, digging deeper into the red earth as another unearthly roar tears through the air, causing the ground beneath me to tremble. I squeeze my eyes shut, then force them open once more, noticing that even the flame seems weakened by the force of the monstrous outcry. It quivers, shifting through a kaleidoscope of colors, its searing heat bearing down upon me. I huddle my head between my shoulders and the ground, silently wishing I had a prayer to offer for this torment to end.

The unrelenting tension in my muscles begins to zap my strength, and my hands loosen their grip of the earth out of sheer exhaustion. I can feel that my body is not designed to endure this hostile environment; it's as though my muscles are decaying right before my eyes.

Tears leak from my tightly closed eyes, but they bring no sense of relief from the pent-up stress. These tears, as they trace down my face, feel like little rivulets of acid, searing my already wounded cheeks along their path. It's as if the sulfurous, acrid air around me has permeated my skin, escaping through my pores and ducts. My emotions threaten to surge forth as I'm overwhelmed by the rapid succession of horrifying events I've experienced in such a short span. But I swallow hard, suppressing my emotions, unwilling to let them rise and consume my already fragile mind. The harsh reality I must confront is a bitter pill to swallow. So, I lie there, until finally, the ground beneath me ceases its convulsions, the flame stops its searing assault, and the eerie silence allows me to hear my own breath once more.

I raise my gaze and observe the fiery wall gradually settling, its familiar rhythmic swaying resuming. Overwhelming relief washes over me as I dare to believe that the worst has passed. I hear the tremors and movement of the enormous creature receding, and while the earth still rumbles, it's no longer as intense as before. The unsettling energy slowly diminishes, as if the creature has been satisfied by the chaos and destruction it wrought.

I loosen my grip on the dirt, a wave of relief flooding through me as I can finally draw a breath without the immediate threat of impending doom. I lie there, lifeless and exhausted, the blood-soaked soil beneath me, hoping and praying that nothing else will disrupt this day.

"I am so tired, so exhausted," I murmur to myself as I lie there, my head turned to one side, inhaling the red dust particles rising from the ground. The movements of the fire in front of me captivate my fading consciousness. My eyes, heavy as lead, succumb to the weight, and I don't reopen them.

Thoughts of what might befall me in this forsaken place flicker through my mind as I drift deeper into my own subconsciousness. I know I shouldn't yield to the flame's power over me, but I can't resist. I'm so weary, so utterly exhausted. I can feel the heaviness settling over me, permeating my thoughts and clouding my vision.

As I feel myself surrendering to the enigmatic influence of the flame, a haunting memory from my youth begins to take shape amidst the flickering shadows. It is a recollection of a time when I was much younger, a night when the demon of my past had returned with relentless intent, nearly snuffing out my life. The memories surfaced like ghostly apparitions, their presence growing stronger with each passing moment.

I recall the chilling darkness of that night, the same darkness that now envelopes me. It was a night where my vulnerability was an appetite that could no longer be ignored. The malevolent entity had tormented me, its sinister whispers echoing in the confines of my mind, driving me to the brink of despair.

But there was a glimmer of hope amidst that darkness, much like the allure of the flame that now captivated me. In my memories, I saw a flickering light—a candle's flame, casting a warm and protective glow, as warm as a mother's embrace. It had been my sanctuary, my refuge against the encroaching malevolence. It was a symbol of resilience, a reminder that even in the face of unspeakable terror, there was a flicker of light, a sliver of hope.

As these memories coalesce within me, I begin to ponder the grip that both the flame and the memories have over me. There's a compelling force in how they beckon and control, even in the darkest moments. It's as if they have a life of their own, shaping my thoughts and guiding my actions with an almost magnetic pull. This influence, mysterious and profound, leaves me questioning not only their origins but also their intent and my own resilience against them.

My head dips, and I gently rest my cheek on the blood-soaked earth below. The flame's irresistible allure holds me captive. Within its searing embrace, there is no relief—only the unyielding grip of torment and persistent memories that refuse to fade. As I lay my head down, transfixed by the dancing inferno, another memory forcefully takes shape before my eyes, more vivid and insistent than the last. The flames crackle and roar, engulfing me completely in its fiery grasp, closing the chapter on my haunted reverie with a blaze that sears both mind and soul.

CHAPTER 6

The Demon

Job 4:12-17

*A word was secretly brought to me, my ears caught a whisper of it.
Amid disquieting dreams in the night, when deep sleep falls on
people, fear and trembling seized me and made all my bones shake.
A spirit glided past my face, and the hair on my body stood on end.
It stopped, but I could not tell what it was. A form stood before my
eyes, and I heard a hushed voice:
Can a mortal be more righteous than God?
Can even a strong man be more pure than his Maker?*

Proverbs 18:21

*The tongue has the power of life and death,
and those who love it will eat its fruit.*

James 1:13-15

*When tempted, no one should say, "God is tempting me." For God
cannot be tempted by evil, nor does he tempt anyone; but each
person is tempted when they are dragged away by their own evil
desire and enticed. Then, after desire has conceived, it gives birth to
sin; and sin, when it is full-grown, gives birth to death.*

*T*he eerie sound of shattering glass pierces through the silence of my bedroom, abruptly yanking me from the depths of my slumber. My heart races with fear as I jolt awake, the remnants of sleep rapidly fading into the recesses of my consciousness. A disconcerting, abrasive noise crawls along the windowpane, resembling the unsettling scrape of claws belonging to a formidable, unseen creature. Panic washes over me, leaving me paralyzed in the inky darkness of my room. I dare not reach for the bedroom light, fearful that any movement might attract the attention of whatever lurks beyond the glass.

Then, as if the very fabric of my reality has ripped apart, the room explodes into chaos. It sounds as if an immense force has smashed through the window right next to my bed, the deafening impact echoing in my ears. The noise is so thunderous that it feels as though the entire window has been reduced to shards. Trembling with fear, I muster the courage to peek cautiously from above the safety of my bedsheets at the window.

To my utter disbelief, the glass remains perfectly intact, a barrier between me and the enigma that has invaded my room. Panic surges through me, and I frantically scan the bedroom for any signs of intrusion, yet everything appears strangely untouched, as though nothing has happened at all.

"What the hell was that?" I wonder aloud, my heart still pounding in my chest.

Scanning the room, I scrutinize my window, desperate for any rational explanation for my abrupt awakening. But once again, there's no sign of damage or any indication that something has tampered with it. However, my gaze is inexorably drawn to a particular corner of the room, where darkness seems to pool and intensify, as if an unexplainable void is forming—an unsettling, ever-deepening abyss reminding me of a similar unsettling darkness from my youth.

"It's all in your head! Go back to sleep. He's not back, He's NOT BACK!" I chant to myself, trying to muster the courage to banish the lingering fear. I refuse to revert to the scared little boy I used to be.

Moments drag on, and I remain still, my fingers now tapping nervously on the side of the bed. An anxious anticipation simmers within me, as if I'm waiting for some unknown threat to make the first move.

Thoughts race through my mind, and my fingers continue their rhythmic tapping—tap, tap, tap—a subconscious coping mechanism to help me organize my turbulent thoughts.

I can still feel the lingering fogginess of sleep, but my mind refuses to grant me the solace of rest. Something about the events of the previous night, just before I retired to bed, gnaws at me. I remember the peculiar sensation that washed over me as I entered my room—a heaviness in the air that seemed to constrict my breathing. It was a feeling I hadn't experienced in years, reminiscent of the dread I felt as a child when confronted with a similarly menacing, demonic presence in my bedroom. It was the same fear, the same sudden anxiety, and the same instinctual fight-or-flight response, all rushing back to me as I crossed the threshold into my bedroom.

"That was a long time ago!" I yell defiantly into the darkness, my voice heavy with anger and frustration. "I am not the little child you used to torment!" My words ring out, echoing in the stillness of my room.

Adrenaline courses through my teenage body, an unfamiliar hormone compelling me to rise against something that once scared me. The shadows of my past loom, but I stand firm, challenging them with newfound courage.

"Just as I thought!" I mutter under my breath after the silence stretches on, uninterrupted. "You can come after a little boy, but now that I'm not so little anymore, you refuse to show yourself?" I say aloud, my voice tinged with defiance.

My verbal challenge serves to banish the old fears, to persuade myself that I've matured past the shadows that once dominated my youth. My words, bold and challenging, are thrown like gauntlets at the feet of whatever haunts me, daring it to confront the person I have become.

"What was it I used to say aloud when I was little?" I try to recall, my memory reaching back into the past. "Oh, that's right, I used to try and call out Jesus' name, as if that ever worked. If you think you can frighten me, you're mistaken!" I declare, my bravado slowly building.

"You want me . . . come and get me! You did nothing but taunt me, harass me, and scare me when I was too little, too weak to do anything to stop you!" I shout in exasperation, the memories of childhood fears resurfacing. "You're nothing but a coward, a little coward that likes to scare children! Why don't you come scare me now if you think you can!" I challenge, throwing my hands outward in the air in a defiant gesture.

It feels empowering to stand up for myself against this "spirit of fear" that haunted me throughout my childhood. Yet, I can't help but feel a bit childish after my outburst, realizing how absurd I must look, talking to myself and making empty threats to nothing but the darkness of my room.

"Ah, who cares how I look," I reassure myself, brushing off any embarrassment with a dismissive wave.

An hour drifts away, but just as I surrender to sleep once more, I'm rudely awakened by a sudden scratching on the window next to my bed. It sends a surge of fear through my veins, and I can't help but wonder if my earlier words might have triggered this eerie response.

"It's just another dream. Go back to sleep." I tell myself as I lay my head back down.

Shaking off the unease, I flip over to the other side of my bed, hoping to find comfort in my exhaustion. I close my eyes and try to dismiss the entire incident as a product of my imagination. However, an unsettling feeling persists within me, as though I'm being watched. I can't shake the overwhelming sensation that I am not alone in my room.

That's when I hear it again—a long, deliberate, drawn-out sound of fingernails running down the glass pane of the window in my room. My eyes widen in fear as I shoot back up in bed. This time, I know it wasn't my imagination. A paralyzing fear courses through me, making me hesitate to even steal a fleeting glance at my window. The dread of coming face to face with whatever might be lurking just beyond the glass holds me in its icy grip. I find myself utterly immobilized, my body locked in a state of terror, rendering me incapable of any movement. In that harrowing moment, I remain seated, a silent and trembling witness to the eerie stillness that envelops my room.

With each passing second, the obscurity of my surroundings becomes more palpable, and my imagination runs wild with the ominous possibilities of what could be concealed within the shroud of darkness or worse—just beyond the pane of glass.

In the moment of anticipation, I hear something heavy and solid approaching, as though it is dragging itself along the carpet of my floor, from the far corner of my room. I gradually pivot my head toward the source of the sound. My gaze fixes upon an unsettling sight unfolding before me. A sinister silhouette as black as the deepest abyss sprawls across the floor, its long, outstretched limbs and torso creeping ominously in my direction. Its presence is so engulfed in darkness that even amidst the pitch-black room, its eerie silhouette remains chillingly distinct. I hold my breath as panic sets in, and I question myself in desperation—what do I do?

And then, from a different source, as if from a higher power, I audibly hear the words, "Shut your eyes, child!" I can feel a heavenly presence protecting me, ready to defend me. But this is not so much a presence of peace as it is one of urgency. I immediately do as the mysterious voice says, thinking to myself that I have never heard so clearly the voice that I can only imagine belonging to God or to one of His heavenly hosts. I fall back into bed and pull the covers over my head, wondering why I deserve to be defended when I have already long rejected Him.

I squeeze my eyes shut just in time before I feel the bed sink to one side and then to the other. The spirit of fear has taken me up on my challenge and has come back ten times worse than I could have ever imagined. Whispering threats and taunts fill the room, each word dripping with malice.

The air grows colder, as if the very essence of dread has seeped into the room. I can feel its presence looming over me, a suffocating weight *pressing down on my chest. The spirit conjures visions in my mind of my deepest anxieties, amplifying my doubts and insecurities.*

My body trembles, my mind teetering on the edge of panic.

There's a profound humility in being reduced to your most vulnerable self, cowering beneath the bed covers like a child once again, face-to-face with the same monster that haunted my boyhood. This isn't about whether monsters exist; it's about admitting that I am being haunted and tormented by the same indefinable fears that plagued my childhood. This spirit of fear transcends simple fright; it feels malevolent, sinister—as if evil itself has taken form.

During my teenage years, an unnoticed transformation occurred within me. My understanding deepened, inadvertently exposing me to new evils and darker realms that I naively embraced, not realizing the authority and obligations I was accepting.

After all, they're just harmless movies and music, right? I thought.

But clearly, they were not, as they unknowingly opened doorways and forged pacts I was blind to. These were not mere entertainments but agreements signed with my own hand, endorsed in the spiritual realms, my signature unwittingly granting the rights that allowed this nightmarish reality to unfold.

Now, the once minor menace of my childhood has grown into a relentless behemoth, casting a vast, ominous shadow across my life. It looms over me, its breath of disdain pressing ever closer to me, daring me to confront it, to test my resolve against its overwhelming presence.

"Keep your eyes shut!" I hear once more, the voice urgently insisting that I must not, under any circumstances, surrender to the taunts. The only confidence I have rests on that voice not abandoning me in this moment. I muster all my strength to keep my eyes shut, despite the overwhelming urge to bolt out of bed and run.

Then suddenly, the mattress sinks next to my right shoulder, and then my left, as if arms are being pressed into the mattress on either side of me. Laying there motionless, not wanting even the slightest breath to escape my mouth, I cannot help but think a demonic force is taunting me, almost as if it is challenging me to open my eyes; challenging me to look straight into his.

"Look at me!" The words echo menacingly in my mind, carrying with them an unmistakable tone of mockery and challenge.

"You think you're strong enough? Well, let's find out!" I can almost discern its taunting words as its eerie presence exerts itself, applying pressure to the bed around me as though daring me to face it head-on.

A heavy, labored breath escapes its unseen form, brushing against my face with a nauseating warmth that carries an unmistakable, putrid stench. It's an odor that transcends the realms of earthly unpleasantness, as if a noxious fog has engulfed my senses. My trembling hands press firmly against my eyes, responding to the heavenly voice's command to not yield. The very air feels charged with an unsettling malice as I struggle to block out the looming horror.

This is a confrontation unlike any I have ever experienced—a dark spirit on the prowl, seeking any reason, any opening, to unleash its wrath upon me. The hatred and disgust that emanate from it seems to saturate the room, penetrating the very essence of my being. In its contemptuous intent, I can feel the weight of its loathing presence, and I tremble in the shadow of this dark and sinister entity. The grip of desperation tightens around me, squeezing at my very core, as I hang onto every moment, convinced it may just be my last.

The predator-prey analogy weighs heavily on my mind. When prey feels safe, it carries on with its life, oblivious to the lurking danger. It's precisely when the prey's guard is down that the predator strikes, seizing the opportunity to attack. It seems that this evil force chose to reveal itself only when I was most vulnerable, caught in that delicate space between slumber and wakefulness.

In that fear-stricken moment, it becomes painfully evident that I have gravely underestimated the authority that now encroaches upon my very existence. Cowering beneath trembling hands, I lie flat as a board on my back, my blood running cold as the room reverberates with the relentless cadence of my racing heart. It is as though we stand on the precipice of an impending showdown, an eerie silence hanging in the air, each heartbeat filling the room with dreadful anticipation.

The entity that has materialized in my room seems to await my inevitable surrender, poised to seize its authority and unleash its viciousness upon me once I succumb to its relentless psychological warfare. I struggle to maintain my composure, my mind locked in a torturous battle between terror and defiance. The weight of the unseen presence presses upon me, as if it seeks to force my compliance through sheer willpower.

Just as thoughts chase each other in and out of my frantic mind, a subtle shift in the atmosphere signals a moment of fleeting reprieve. The weight that had settled on my bed lifts off the mattress, and a heavenly voice resounds in my consciousness, commanding me to run. With no hesitation, I bolt out of bed, driven by sheer survival instinct. Time is of the essence, and I waste no precious seconds.

As I sprint through my bedroom door and into the dimly lit hallway, my thoughts return to previous hauntings, where the comforting presence of my parents had held authority over these demonic spirits. In their presence, these entities would cease their relentless assault, recoiling in submission to the powerful force my parents seemed to emanate.

A single thought dominates my mind as I run down the hall towards the staircase—I must reach my parents if I am to survive this. My footsteps echo through the silent house, punctuated by the unsettling sound of picture frames crashing to the floor behind me, and my mother's *cherished trinkets being hurled from their shelves in a chaotic frenzy as the spirit is in hot pursuit.*

Panic fuels my desperate ascent, and I skip two steps at a time, then three, my feet a blur on the stairs. The main floor of our house beckons, and I round the corner, gripping the banister tightly to swing myself around.

My eyes lock onto the direction of my parents' room, where a sight both astonishing and comforting meets me. My mother stands in the doorway, as though she was expecting me, ready to embrace me and offer the sanctuary of her presence. It leaves me in wonder, how she knew in that precise moment that I would come running to her.

With each stride, I close the distance to her, hope surging within me. Her eyes hold a profound calmness, radiating a sense of security and assurance that everything would be all right. I can almost feel the safety of her arms, almost feel her protective embrace.

But then, just as I leap toward her, a chilling sensation grips my right ankle, and I am yanked backward, crashing into the stairs. Except, what awaits me is no longer solid ground. The stairway beneath me seems to shatter, and I plummet into an abyss of pitch darkness, consumed by an insatiable void.

A piercing scream escapes my lips, echoing through the crimson void. The sensation of falling lingers, my legs kicking out involuntarily as I emerge from one restless reality and plunge into another. The floor beneath me is a sea of red dirt, its lighter particles dancing in the air like spectral phantasms. Gasping for breath, I struggle to sit up, trying to regain my bearings as the vivid memory before me fades. It feels as though I have tumbled from one terrible dream into another, as if I've been forcibly ejected from one realm of existence into another, each transition leaving me more disoriented and breathless than the last.

In this eerie place, memories swirl like specters, distant yet agonizingly near. The shadows around me stir, and colors shift in a grotesque ballet. The noxious air fills my nostrils once more, a constant reminder that I remain imprisoned within the confines of Hell itself. Here, there is no refuge, no escape, not even from the harrowing memories I desperately try to repress. I can't even take solace in the warmth of my mother's embrace, for the recollection of that fateful night is etched vividly in my mind.

Why am I being compelled to relive this traumatic experience? The question gnaws at me as I struggle to make sense of the unfolding events and why the flame deems it necessary to confront me with this memory at this moment. *How had my mother known I was ascending from the basement to her second-floor bedroom?* The rational explanation was that she had heard my footsteps, but the more I ponder it, the less likely this seems. *If she had, why had she not appeared alarmed, as though she already knew who was approaching and why?*

Irrespective of unknown circumstances surrounding her, there my mother stood, waiting at the entrance of her bedroom, as if she had been anticipating my arrival. The moment I rushed into her arms, the door closed behind us, shutting out the world beyond. It was clear that she had sensed something ominous was pursuing me that night. She knew, or else she wouldn't have been there, ready and vigilant.

In perfect harmony with her, my father was already out of bed, preparing himself for whatever was to come. It was as though they communicated without words, understanding the gravity of the situation. I watched as he moved with urgency, his actions deliberate and filled with purpose. He anointed each door with a small amount of oil, his prayers carrying the weight of scripture as he passed by every frame. The image of my father in that moment was etched in my memory—hair tousled from sleep, shuffling in his slippers, robe hastily thrown on, squinting against the darkness as he navigated our home.

A tender smile graces my lips as I cherish that memory. I remember my thoughts at the time, how I had seen it as just another instance of my dad being his usual "Mr. Righteous" self. But now, looking back, I understand that he was doing it all for me, to protect his terrified son. He was still striving to be my hero, even in the face of the unknown. It warms my heart to realize this, though it also saddens me that it took me this long to fully appreciate my parents' love and unwavering dedication to always be there, ready to embrace and protect me.

The fading smile on my face mirrors the recollection of those challenging nights. I often find myself wondering why these trials appeared to single me out. *Why was I the one grappling with these evil forces, enduring sleepless nights haunted by nightmarish visions?* Tornadoes, plummeting to my doom, and the ghastly specter of my family's demise were recurring themes in my nocturnal terrors, interwoven with occasional episodes of physical torment.

Why did they only manifest themselves to me? I muse inwardly, a question that had plagued my thoughts.

Were there other people, I wonder, *somewhere else in the world, grappling with similar demonic forces or experiences?*

"What had I done to deserve such torment?" I voice my inner thoughts aloud.

In that instant, a peculiar notion begins to take shape in my mind. Perhaps the purpose behind these nightmarish trials was to divert my focus from those who loved me. Maybe it was because God had called me to a great purpose, and the Devil, recognizing it, sought to thwart this awakening within me. Perhaps it was a calculated effort to instill such profound fear in me at a tender age that it would ultimately turn me against the very people who cherished me the most. Or it might have been intended to keep me perpetually consumed by fear, leaving me with nothing else to motivate me but fear itself.

No matter the reason, I was never content with just being myself; I constantly felt the need to prove my worth. From a young age, I knew my parents had hoped for a girl. And so being the youngest of three boys, I struggled to carve out my own identity. My oldest brother became a worship pastor and was considered the "perfect son," while my middle brother stood at 6' 5" and was a star athlete. Thus, I sought alternative paths to gain the recognition I craved from my family. It was only when I strayed from the path of righteousness, drawing the attention of law enforcement and school authorities, that I felt like my parents finally noticed me.

How foolish I had been to allow rejection and fear to dictate my choices. *How many people had I unintentionally and intentionally hurt as a result of my misguided decisions?* My heart aches as I think of my dear mother. I put her through so much, and yet, her arms always remained open when I needed them the most. But not here, not now, and perhaps not ever again.

I can still hear her voice in my mind as she used to recite Bible verses to me. Words about how God didn't give us a spirit of fear but one of love, peace, and a "sound" mind.

Whatever that meant, I muse with a wry smile. Back then, I often brushed her words aside, not fully comprehending their significance.

But now, here in this place, those words take on a newfound weight and meaning. I start to grasp their true significance, and I begin to appreciate the impact they could have had on my life. The words from that book weren't just empty phrases meant to make you feel good. Each syllable was meticulously crafted to resonate like music, stirring the spiritual air in the room, concealing its speaker from the darkness, and holding immense power. Some words concealed, others healed; some warned, while others encouraged. If only people knew the incredible power contained within the verses they left neglected on dusty shelves, their lives battered by sickness and chaos, oblivious to the answers and remedies hidden within their own homes.

However, speaking those words in this place feels perilous. I dare to mutter a few passages I remember, but an unsettling feeling washes over me as I do so. It seems dangerously unpredictable to utter those words here. Even the flame that surrounds me reacts uneasily to any spoken words from that sacred book.

I can't risk it. I can't risk what I don't fully understand. So, I remain silent, choosing caution over potential consequences in this enigmatic realm.

The place I now find myself reminds me that fear reigns supreme, amplified to its utmost potency. Here, it doesn't just consume you; it strips away every trace of love and peace, leaving you bereft of humanity. In this realm, your rights and privileges are replaced with an overwhelming sense of fear and hopelessness.

As I grapple with this newfound understanding of my own condition, I can't help but wonder why this revelation came to me now, when I feel utterly powerless to change anything. *Is it yet another layer of torture, an additional torment meant to break my spirit?*

"Did it mean that I was cursed from the very beginning?" The frustration and resentment in my voice are palpable as I seek answers in the midst of my anguish.

There was a time when I believed in God, and I remember reading in the Bible about Jesus dying on the cross to offer salvation to all. Back then, I thought I was saved, and that salvation would always be mine. But I eventually turned away from that faith, searching for my own belief system which wasn't just a neatly packaged explanation that I could pull out when needed to justify why things unfolded the way they did. I didn't want to grapple with the idea of a God who claimed to be love yet allowed so much evil into the world.

Now, as I find myself in this desolate place, I realize I have no answers. I must confront the truth that it wasn't God who cast me here in wrath and judgment, but my own choices and the rejection of His presence in my life. I hadn't passed through gates of judgment; I simply woke up here alone, left with my thoughts to grapple with the realizations about my past and the unknown entities lurking in the fiery abyss. *What awaits me next? What new affliction will be introduced to me in this place?* It seems like this realm was meticulously designed to maximize pain in every aspect of one's existence. My body is engulfed in relentless agony, my mind tormented by fear, and my memories tainted by regret.

"What awaits that could possibly be worse than this reality?" I muse aloud, trying to find a shred of hope.

Yet, as I search for any form of solace, the oppressive silence around me grows even more deafening. Desperately, I yearn for something—anything—to shatter the suffocating stillness. But the eerie, hellish atmosphere remains unyielding, not even a whisper disrupting its dominion. The silence invades my mind, a relentless force that magnifies my sense of isolation, plunging me deeper into solitude than ever before.

As the stillness deepens, it drags with it a creeping insanity that weaves itself deeper into the fabric of my reality. With each passing moment, the lines of my mental clarity blur, inching me closer to the brink of madness.

CHAPTER 7

The Madness

Jeremiah 13:15-16

Then I said, listen. Listen carefully: don't stay stuck in your ways!
It's God's message we're dealing with.
Let your lives glow bright before God before He turns out the lights,
before you trip and fall on the dark mountain paths.
The light you always took for granted will go out
and the world will turn black.

2 Peter 2:17-19

These people are springs without water and mists driven by a storm.
Blackest darkness is reserved for them. For they mouth empty,
boastful words and, by appealing to the lustful desires of the flesh,
they entice people who are just escaping from those who live in error.
They promise them freedom, while they themselves are slaves of
depravity—for "people are slaves to whatever has mastered them."

Psalms 88:3-12

I am overwhelmed with troubles
and my life draws near to death.
I am counted among those who go down to the pit;
I am like one without strength.
I am set apart with the dead,
like the slain who lie in the grave,
whom you remember no more,
who are cut off from your care.
You have put me in the lowest pit,
in the darkest depths.
Your wrath lies heavily on me;

you have overwhelmed me with all your waves.
You have taken from me my closest friends
and have made me repulsive to them.
I am confined and cannot escape;
my eyes are dim with grief.

I call to you, Lord, every day;
I spread out my hands to you.
Do you show your wonders to the dead?
Do their spirits rise up and praise you?
Is your love declared in the grave,
your faithfulness in Destruction?
Are your wonders known in the place of darkness,
or your righteous deeds in the land of oblivion?

"**W**hat have I done?" The weight of that question bears down on my heart as I grapple with the horrifying reality of where I find myself. I feel utterly foolish, realizing how simple-mindedly I lived and squandered my days.

"I wasted them, every single one, and now they amount to nothing—absolutely nothing!" The words escape my lips in a despairing yell.

Reaching the end of myself, my reward is the unending torment of this infernal abyss. The silence surrounding me mocks my thoughts as they whirl in chaos.

"It's all so painfully clear now. Why didn't I just believe when I had the chance?" I wonder, reflecting on my choices.

I knew exactly what I should have done, and yet, now I can neither rectify my actions nor return to the realm of the living to make amends.

"I'm an empty vessel, a decaying husk, a part of the living dead. My soul yearns for a second chance it can never have. I've made my bed, and now I must lie in it, eternally haunted by the consequences of my decisions."

"Damn you!" I shout with fiery indignation in my voice. "You lied to me! You promised myself and countless others that you didn't exist, and yet, here I am! You've taken on so many disguises, hidden behind so many falsehoods that belief didn't matter. But here we are—you, cloaked in your deception, and I, having believed every word of it!"

In the midst of my tormented existence within this bleak realm, I come to a solemn realization: it wasn't hell that had ensnared me or forced me into this wretched state. It was my actions and my decisions that led me here. Hell itself, devoid of life and consciousness, bore no capacity for deception. I had unwittingly "dug my own grave." But a profound question gnawed at my soul, unsettling me deeply: could a supernatural force be concealing the truth of this place, only to unveil the stark reality that our own choices might lead us here? This notion disturbed me, suggesting a manipulation of reality so subtle yet so profound, implicating our very agency in the unfolding of our fates.

"Could there be something, or perhaps someone," I whisper into the nothingness, "cloaking this realm from the watchful eyes of those traveling down the winding roads that converge here?" This thought also haunts me, leaving a chilling suspicion that an unseen hand shrouded this abyss from mortal perception. Like an impenetrable veil, it's as though demonic scales have been gently placed over the eyes of the blind, rendering them not only incapable of seeing light but also offering an eerie, supernatural protection against the piercing effects of truth.

With an ache in my heart and an overwhelming sense of regret, I long for the chance to extend a lifeline to any living soul still treading the path of life.

"If only I could convey to someone still alive of the horror of this place," I muse, my voice trembling with fervent yearning. "I would implore them to unveil their eyes to the truth, to awaken to the profound reality that looms before them, and to seek salvation before it's too late.

My words echo through the bleak expanse, resonating with passionate conviction.

"It's not worth it," I fervently declare, as if speaking before an audience of the condemned. "Not even a fleeting moment should be squandered in the clutches of material gain. From dust we were created and to dust we return."

"I beg of you," I plead, hoping someone might hear me. "Turn away from the flesh. You have the strength; He gives it freely. Seek the truth—seek it as if your life depends on it!" As I earnestly speak these words, a heavy burden of regret weighs upon me, for I know all too well that I once ignored such counsel in my own history.

The agonizing truth is that hope has become an elusive phantom, a distant specter that I can scarcely imagine. Yet, I yearn for it with an intensity that eclipses the abyss that surrounds me. This longing is akin to the tender caress of cool water upon parched lips, a fleeting glimpse of a future that promises to be more than the nightmarish reality that holds me captive. It is a thirst for hope, an ache for salvation, a desperate plea for deliverance from the darkness that clings to my soul.

Tears flow from my eyes like caustic rivers, their acidic touch etching deep, painful furrows into my flesh as they sear their path towards oblivion. These scalding droplets never linger, many evaporating upon my parched skin before they can escape the confines of my face. The oppressive silence of this place wraps itself around me, whispering softly in a voice as cold as an arctic winter.

"Weep, my child; unburden your soul. Let your mournful cries scatter upon the winds, where neither living soul nor silent void shall ever bear witness to them," it echoes, a cruel reminder resounding relentlessly within the confines of my mind.

There is no salvation to be found, no solace to quench the unyielding thirst for the pain that gnaws at my very core. Loneliness has become my unwavering companion, a relentless tormentor that shows no mercy.

"I am utterly alone," I admit, my voice trembling with despair. *I will forever yearn for something I can never have,* I think, as a shimmer catches my eye from the tear left upon the edge of my nose, reminding me of how significant tears used to be.

Everyone, at some point in their existence, sheds tears, but few recognize that the ability to shed tears is gifted to us from the divine, whether or not we recognize Him as such. And these tears are, in essence, prayers cast into the ethereal plane like arrows descending with hidden messages to a creator who awaits to read them. They are collected and studied by this higher power, a deity often unknown yet ever-present, listening and waiting to embrace us on the other side, whether good or bad and whether or not we accept His presence.

Now, reflecting on this truth, it becomes clear how we often underestimate the power and significance of our tears. In those moments of vulnerability, when tears stream down our faces, we unknowingly communicate our deepest emotions, fears, and hopes. Now that I am here, these truths become even more evident in the absolute lack of relief my tears now have.

"How could I have been so foolish not to see how powerful tears were and the significance they carried with them?" I question aloud, my voice laced with frustration, each defeated word hanging heavy in the air, thick with disappointment. The realization of having overlooked the importance of these moments of emotional release fills me with regret at having missed an essential connection with the divine, a connection that was always there waiting to be acknowledged and embraced.

Yet, in the dismal realm of Hell, such solace is an unattainable dream. Here, hopelessness reigns supreme, and our tears evaporate or fall answerless to the barren ground below, stripped of the prayers they once carried within. It is a place where the very essence of hope has withered and died.

Like many, I was unaware that understanding the significance of tears doesn't require religious beliefs. They were simply there, a testament to the link I once shared with God—a promise of relief, even though I never credited the source.

It is clear to me now that the scars I bear are not just marks of past wounds; they are etched reminders of what was once taken for granted: a "human experience" that I now understand was a precious gift, carelessly forfeited by my own choices and lack of acknowledgment to the One who was always there to bring comfort and peace.

Reflecting on my past, I recognize that these experiences, both joyful and painful, were integral to my growth and understanding. The power to love deeply, to find joy in laughter, and to endure through difficult times reveals the intentionality our Creator had through something so small and seemingly insignificant.

I see now how precious life truly was. The scars become symbols of resilience and reminders of the lessons learned. They represent the strength to overcome adversity and the wisdom gained from each struggle. In understanding this, a deeper connection to the divine becomes more and more clear.

I am reminded of the bittersweet recollection of the events surrounding the loss of my best friend in the seventh grade. My tears, and the support of my family, walked me through this journey.

When I received the devastating news of my friend's passing and that of his parents in a car accident, my world was turned upside down. The pain and void left by their absence were overwhelming, and I found solace in shedding tears and expressing my anguish during those lonely nights. Despite the profound sorrow, I sensed that my tears held a purpose, that they were not shed in vain.

This subtle reassurance, through the process of mourning, allowed me to heal naturally over time, without the need for medical treatment or therapy. Healing, it seemed, found its way to me, embracing me gradually, regardless of my conscious efforts or beliefs.

The trip my dad and I took to Canada to revisit my best friend's final resting place marked a significant moment in my healing journey. As I stood before my friend's grave, tears in my eyes, I felt a sense of resolution and renewal. I found hope that something new and positive could emerge from the pain and sorrow I had endured, and a belief that my friend and his parents were in a better place brought me a measure of comfort and closure.

This touching narrative underscores the resilience of the human spirit and its capacity to find meaning and healing even in the face of profound loss. In that moment standing before his grave, death didn't seem so absolute. It was as if my tears had transformed into tiny, unspoken messages, tenderly carried by an invisible hand to my friend, carrying with them a promise of a future reunion. In that inexplicable connection, I found a glimmer of hope amid the overwhelming pain of loss.

The questions lingered in my mind like persistent echoes. How had I once possessed the power to tame my pain? And from where had the wellspring of peace and comfort flowed? These were mysteries beyond my grasp now.

As I lower my hands from my face, attempting to rekindle the memory of that long-lost sensation, I realize that the relief, the serenity after grief, has slipped away. It serves as a stark reminder that in the absence of hope, there exists only unending, gnawing anguish deep within the chest—a torment that can no longer be alleviated through alcohol, substance abuse or even suicide.

I observe the final tear I can summon as it trickles off my nose and descends to the ground, disappearing before it can moisten the parched earth below, vanishing in the sweltering heat. I weep for myself in vain, for there is no one left to catch my tears. There is no promise, no escape from the relentless grip of Death.

I am now a part of Death and Death a part of me. With each passing moment in this realm, I feel myself slipping further into the abyss. The darkness deepens, the silence grows more deafening, the loneliness more suffocating, and the horrors of the unknown more vivid.

I pace restlessly within my cramped confinement, desperate to escape the suffocating feeling of being trapped. Suddenly, distant screams resound from the depths of Hell once more. These anguished cries rise from a place even deeper than my own, causing me to freeze at the edge of the towering inferno. I strain my ears, hoping to discern a hidden message that might be meant for all who can hear. The screams sound distant yet oddly intimate, their origin obscured by the oppressive silence of this dark realm.

These voices seem to transform into ghostly echoes, haunting my mind and crying out from the memories of their former selves. They plead not to be forgotten, but I can sense that the all-encompassing darkness is already erasing any trace of their existence. It's as though the memory of my own existence is slowly fading as well, destined to be swallowed by the eternal void, lost in this abyss.

In this cursed place that seeks to negate life's meaning and reduce it to nothingness, the value of life becomes strikingly clear. Life, once seemingly common and ordinary, now feels sacred and precious in the face of absolute loss.

Sinking to my knees, my body tensing as the distant cries continue to echo, the encroaching blackness drapes over me like a thick, ominous wool coat. It carries with it the weight of eternal doom. I gaze up into the empty, hollow spaces within the flame, desperately clinging to their fading light. Shadows dance and swirl around me, seemingly synchronized with the shrill rhythm of the screams.

The notion crosses my mind that these tormented spirits might be beckoning me into their anguish, ensnaring me in an eerie, ritualistic dance that foreshadows what awaits. Fear and paranoia grip my heart as the weight of my previous thought lingers, causing my pulse to race. Worse yet, I begin to question my own sanity, unsure of what is real and what is a product of my unraveling mind. I'm left vulnerable to the unknown dangers lurking in this ever-encroaching darkness, lost in the haze of my own thoughts and fears.

Like a fleeting whisper, a distant memory surfaces, slicing through my turmoil. I clutch this memory like a lifeline in the barren scape of my current existence. It emerges unbidden, a shimmering oasis in the arid desert that my life has become. I recall the sensation of water, how it flowed like liquid silk through my fingers, its coolness kissing my parched skin. The memory is vivid, almost tangible, igniting within me a profound yearning.

In my mind's eye, I see the ripples on a serene lake, the gentle waves lapping against the shore. I remember the mesmerizing dance of water droplets on a rainy day, the joy of catching them on my outstretched palm. It's a reminder of the simple yet extraordinary wonder that water used to be.

But now, as hard as I try to recall its refreshing embrace, the once commonplace element of water eludes me completely. It's as though water has turned into a myth, a legend from an era long gone. I reminisce about the carefree days of my childhood in Texas, diving into the bayous without a second thought. The joy of immersion, the sensation of being enveloped by its liquid embrace—these are sensations I yearn for with every fiber of my being.

Water, once so commonplace, has transformed into something sacred and mystical. It is a symbol of life itself, a reminder of the world I once knew.

I close my eyes, drawing deep breaths as I call forth the memories, letting them envelop me like a tide of mixed emotions. Each recollection swells and recedes, leaving behind traces of both sweetness and sorrow, akin to waves gently lapping at the shore, reshaping the sands of my mind with their persistent ebb and flow. In this new world where water has become an unattainable dream, I hold onto these recollections as if they are the last remnants of a lost paradise. The past becomes my solace, my sanctuary, and a testament to the beauty and necessity of something so simple, yet so extraordinary—water.

"How foolish I was to care so little about my life," I utter aloud, my voice quivering with a mix of disbelief and regret.

In life, our senses are gratified daily, moment by moment. Whether it is the joy of tasting a delicious meal, the pleasure of inhaling a fragrant flower, the comfort of a warm embrace, or the wonder of witnessing a breathtaking sunset, we are blessed with the constant opportunity to experience life's incredible attributes. They come one after another, without cost or sacrifice.

But in this place, my senses have become my tormentors. They were never designed to endure an environment of perpetual scarcity, depletion, and suffering. It's as though they've turned against me, a reminder of the life I once had, the life I thoughtlessly discarded.

Reflecting back, it would seem as though life was meant to be lived like an artesian well, naturally and continuously replenished by some hidden source. Just as wells are designed to continuously fill, our souls are meant to be deeply nourished, highlighting the similarity between how water sustains our physical bodies and how God nurtures our spiritual selves. This analogy underscores the essential role of water in our physical survival, paralleled by the divine grace that enriches and sustains our spiritual existence, reflecting a harmonious balance between our earthly needs and our heavenly connections. This relationship brings a profound realization of how water not only sustains our bodies but also serves as a divine conduit, connecting us to God and nurturing our spiritual selves. Through water, we see a tangible expression of divine care, a reminder of our creator's presence in the essential sustenance that flows through all aspects of our lives.

Yet, the choices we make can cause contaminants to enter in or our wells to run dry, poisoning or draining away the spiritual sustenance that shapes our eternal destiny. This depletion reflects the profound impact of our decisions on both our immediate and everlasting well-being, underscoring the importance of nurturing our spiritual resources with as much care as we attend to our physical needs. We often seek to fill ourselves with anything other than the clear, life-giving water from which we were created to draw strength. We yearn to be full, to satiate our desires, to find purpose and meaning in the world. What kind of well would we be if we were empty, after all? It's a question that should echo within each of us.

Yet, sadly, in our pursuit of fullness, we sometimes choose paths that lead to contamination. We allow impurities to seep into our wells, tainting the quality of our essence. We fill ourselves with material possessions, fleeting pleasures, and distractions, thinking they will quench our thirst. But these substitutes only leave us thirstier, emptier, and more disconnected from our true purpose.

When we become dried up, our potential to overflow with goodness and compassion diminishes. We find ourselves in a state of spiritual aridity, where the serpents and devils of despair and emptiness thrive. These inner demons feed on the dust of our deserted lands, perpetuating a cycle of discontent and longing. It is as if the kingdom of darkness's purpose is to dry us up so that we may be consumed.

Yet, there is hope. Just as a well can be cleansed and refilled with pure water, so can our souls find redemption. It requires a conscious choice to return to the source, to seek the springs of water that sustain us. Only then can we overflow with the abundance of love, joy, peace, kindness, and self control that we were meant to share with the world. In that overflow, we delve into the profound essence of fulfillment, replacing the voids within our hearts that remained empty in spite of every worldly possession and false promise. In their stead, we embrace the life-affirming waters graciously bestowed upon us by the Almighty God.

This act of embracing our inherent makeup is akin to acknowledging our true essence, aligning ourselves with the divine blueprint meticulously crafted by our Creator. It is a transformative journey, one that allows us to discern the genuine desires that resonate with our Maker's intent, the secret petitions, while simultaneously dispelling the counterfeit yearnings that are incongruent with the destiny set before us by God. In this sacred quest, we unveil the magnificent tapestry of our existence, woven with threads of divinity and adorned with the blessings bestowed upon us by the Creator, thus connecting us more deeply to a generational inheritance and treasure within Heaven long awaiting the few whose hearts are fully committed to Him. For the worldly treasures fade away, back to dust, where moth and rust destroy and where thieves can break in and steal, but the treasures in Heaven, moth nor rust can destroy; thieves cannot break in and steal.

Oh, how my heart longs for the gentle kiss of water upon my parched lips once more. To feel its cool embrace coursing through me, infusing life into my fragile bones with every precious sip. I am a vessel, desirous and empty, my very essence scorched and desiccated. My soul echoes with hollowness, craving the touch of anything, anything to bring me back to life. In this merciless domain, there exists no water to sate my unquenchable thirst, no sustenance to replenish my weary form, and no divine presence to provide comfort and inspiration.

I find a place to recline on the floor of Hell's blood-infused soil, my chest hollow and expanding with an overwhelming emptiness. It's as though I'd be better off vanishing, becoming nothing, just like the lifeless, soulless earth beneath me. But perhaps that's the very purpose of this encroaching emptiness: to strip away our humanity until we can no longer feel, until we forget that we once possessed a soul—a soul that bore the divine fingerprints of our Maker.

I hadn't realized that it was those divine fingerprints that defined my identity on Earth. They carried within them the essence of joy, allowing me to experience happiness; peace, granting me the ability to find solace; love, empowering me to create connections; self-control, offering me clarity of thought; and goodness, enabling me to receive the beauty of existence.

My Maker, my Creator, my God, how I now bow before Your absolute greatness, my face pressed to the ground in my absolute nothingness, as it is now abundantly clear that what made humanity truly remarkable was, in fact, You.

I choke on yet another sob, overwhelmed by the weight of my newfound regret. I am a cursed man, trapped in mournful reflection, fully aware of what I possessed and the opportunities I squandered. Now, I feel as though I've been robbed of the very essence that once defined me, giving me purpose and identity. Falling to the ground, stripped of everything, my only companion is shame, which erases any trace or reminder of the One who created me. This profound humiliation leaves me isolated, disconnected from my origins and the divine spark that once defined my existence.

My vulnerability leaves me gasping in the rusted particles, stirred up from my descent, and the surrounding abyss, shrouded in eerie silence, recognizes that my protective covering has been removed. It's as if this place fully comprehends that I can no longer choose life, and it surges forward with the grim awareness that God exists, but not here, not to save me from the encroaching darkness that looms.

The sun will never rise again, and the possibility of another chance, of a new tomorrow, has been irretrievably lost.

Tomorrows were meant for more than just a new day; they were bestowed as opportunities for redemption. I now comprehend the countless tomorrows God had granted me, waiting patiently to see if today would be the day I finally took a chance with Him. But I denied Him time and time again. The sun ceases to rise, and all my tomorrows dwindle away. Even if I were to flee to the farthest corners of this forsaken realm, I will never again experience that sense of new beginnings, nor find solace in the knowledge that today offers a fresh start to rejoice and be glad in. The comforting promise of renewal has vanished, leaving behind only the echo of what once was.

As I lay my head upon the ground, my tears mingle with the crimson dirt, creating a somber mixture of ash and blood. Amid this melancholic tableau, a peculiar phenomenon catches my eye. Within the fiery dance of the inferno before me, there is a stirring, circular motion that echoes the mysterious movements of ethereal spirits above. This mesmerizing spectacle draws a stark contrast between the chaos at my feet and the celestial choreography overhead.

Suddenly, a heightened awareness washes over me, and I realize that the tormenting screams from the depths have been stifled by an oppressive stillness that pervades this eerie realm. Something has shifted; as I rise to my feet, anticipation courses through me, heightening my senses as I await the revelation of this altered reality. I stand poised, ready to face whatever may emerge from beyond the silence, eager to uncover the mysteries it holds.

A faint whisper grazes my ear in a swift, sudden rush, sending goosebumps skittering along my arm as fear wraps itself around me. Heart racing, I spin around, my eyes darting across the empty space, only to find nothing—leaving me to wonder if I truly heard anything at all. Then it returns, a subtle presence flitting from side to side behind me in rapid succession, as if it's starting to encircle me from every direction within the blazing vortex. It's at this moment that a distinct shadow starts weaving in and out of the walls of flames, enveloping me, its form shifting in enigmatic patterns that defy explanation.

It whispers once more, and I strain to catch the single word it repeatedly utters, its high-pitched, hushed tones slicing through the oppressive silence.

My gaze remains fixated on the fluid shadow, its movements growing increasingly deliberate, almost as if it has transformed itself into a serpent, slithering along the perimeter of my confined space, intermingling with the rapid undulations of the flames.

"*Mors…* " it hisses, the Latin word unfamiliar to my ears, yet its profound meaning resonates with an eerie familiarity. In an instant, a torrent of memories rushes forth, engulfing my mind and transporting me back to that fateful night when ominous shadows relentlessly pursued me. They had invaded the confines of that small bathroom, their chilling whispers echoing in my ears, repeating the very word—"Mors"—as I felt the precarious grip of life slipping away from me.

I never learned Latin, yet somehow I comprehend its meaning in this inexplicable place. The paradoxical nature of this understanding fills me with wonder and unease as I grapple with the mysteries of this surreal realm.

In sheer horror, I watch as the shadow morphs into an elongated figure with grotesque features, circling around me, shifting in and out of its original form. It weaves in and out of the fiery wall, filling my enclosure with the relentless repetition of that haunting word, "*Death,*" now spoken in the English tongue. Each utterance serves as a sinister reminder of the perilous reality that surrounds me.

"*Deatthhhh.*"

Its whispers coil around me, and the shape before me stretches into a towering, faceless entity, reaching further into the flames above. The paralyzing fear it infuses in my soul overwhelms my imagination, envisioning a fate far more sinister than a mere shadow.

Tremors seize me once more, originating from my fingertips and rippling through my body. I steal a fleeting glance back up towards the evolving figure as it descends upon me in one final, swift swoop, plunging into the ground below. Its final words to me echo with a dread-filled utterance that blankets my cell as it physically dissolves from my sight, sinking into an abyss below. Yet, its voice persists, perhaps haunting others unbeknownst to me who are also trapped. It audibly reverberates through hollow voids and deep chasms, originating from depths I had merely speculated upon before this harrowing encounter.

I stifle a scream, my eyes locked on the spot where the shadow vanished, as a chilling fear courses through me. My instinct to cry out is suppressed by the terror of potentially awakening something worse lurking in the outer realms of this hellish place. However, as the shape-shifting shadow disappears, I begin to hear another mysterious sound emanating from the very place it had vanished.

It's a muffled sob, a wailing cry, a pitiful whimper—a sound that carries a distinctly human quality in stark contrast to the eerie cries of the unfamiliar entities that I've heard in the distance. This soul's cries seem to denote an awakening or a descent into deeper affliction, and they resonate with a desperate, frantic edge that chills me to the bone.

Continuing to fixate on the ground where the shadow submerged itself, a sense of unease grips me. Reluctant to confront the disturbing truth that I fear might be unfolding, my gaze remains locked on that spot, my heart heavy with trepidation. It's as if the enigmatic, shadowy figure paid me a visit, taunting me with its capabilities, as though only to dredge up childhood fears of being buried alive. The thought crosses my mind, *Could someone truly be trapped beneath me, fully conscious and aware of their dire predicament? Are those muffled cries the result of the encroaching dirt, squeezing the*

life out of them as they gasp for one final breath, pleading for salvation?
It's a horrifying image that haunts my imagination.

Pressing my ear against the earth below, hand covering my mouth, I can hear the ominous crackling of flames drawing nearer. The oppressive heat of the approaching fire bears down on me, intensifying the urgency of my situation. The cries grow louder, as if the trapped soul strains to pierce the barriers of their entombment.

I scramble backward in dread, the realization sinking in that I am sitting atop someone's grave—another unfortunate soul who once stood where I am now, ensnared beneath me. A sickening feeling takes hold as I contemplate the possibility of suffering the same fate. I clamp my hands over my mouth, stifling the screams that threaten to escape, when suddenly, the whispers return, the ominous murmurs of the shifting shadow of Death enveloping me once more.

Pressing my hands over my ears, scalding tears flow down my face, their heat searing my flesh. The pain and despair engulf me as I try to block out the overwhelming sensations surrounding me. I raise my gaze, peering upward into the hollow flame, gripped by an overwhelming and profound sense of dread.

"Is this shadowy entity here to bury me alive as well, or has it somehow latched onto my own fears of becoming buried in a similar state as the person beneath me?" I ask.

The thought of someone trapped underground, utterly immobile, fills me with horror. Just as I'm imprisoned behind the wall of flames, this tormented soul is buried alive and condemned to endure the anguish of isolation within a nightmarish coffin. The idea of being unable to move, to be utterly helpless, is too dreadful to contemplate for long, for fear of unearthing a torment even worse than the one I currently endure—a torment that may soon become my own as a sickening punishment.

I press my hands harder against my ears, attempting to block out the insidious whispers of the shadow's taunts, which blend with the sobs of the trapped soul beneath me.

"*Come, come, come,*" it chants from all directions, as though it's trying to lure me into a deeper abyss of despair. It's as if it wants me to descend further, to explore depths beyond even my current ordeal.

Despite knowing it's a deception, I feel the temptation to give in, if only to escape the ceaseless screams and the tormenting whispers. In this chaotic moment, my weakness threatens to overpower me, and I fear I might succumb to the false promise of a quieter, better place that this shifting shadow of Death seems to offer. I'm afraid that, in my vulnerability, I will end up in the same grave as the unfortunate soul beneath me.

"*Come,*" whispers the shadow of Death, extending a hand of invitation from within the flames. I find myself instinctively reaching out, entertaining the notion that the earth might not burn me as agonizingly as the flames do, and perhaps it could be a better place. But how can I ignore the agony in the cries I hear from below? Why am I considering what I know to be my worst nightmare?

With a jolt of resolve, I pull my hand back and retreat as far as possible from the shadow without scorching myself against the relentless flames behind me. I sit there, paralyzed by terror, tears continuing to stream down my face, the agony of their acidic nature unnoticed by me in my fear.

"O God!" I cry out in desperation, my voice suddenly ringing out with a loudness that startles even me. "PLEASE! Save me!" I plead, my voice carrying my profound fear and anguish into the darkness, a plea for deliverance from the abyss that surrounds me.

Suddenly, the shadow's whispers come to an abrupt halt. The air hangs eerily still while the flames flicker violently, as if they are responding to something I said.

With cautious trepidation, I lower my hands from my ears. The silence makes a feeble attempt to regain control, as if it wishes to suffocate the muffled cries from below once more. But the tormented soul beneath me remains relentless in its wailing, and the air seems to shift, nearly robbing me of my breath, as I sense the swift departure of the shadow, as though it is fleeing in haste. Simultaneously, the arid earth beneath me stirs with a soft, unsettling tremor, synchronizing with the spirit's hasty departure. The cries from the abyss below become abruptly snuffed out, leaving behind an unsettling, eerie hush that cloaks me like a shroud. Suddenly, a final, solitary, and haunting plea pierces through the oppressive stillness that envelops me, leaving me in dread of what just transpired below.

As I dwell upon the fate of the individual beneath me, the dire foreboding of what is to come gnaws at my soul.

Then, as though the abyss itself had unleashed a nightmarish wail, a deafening, demonic howl shatters the silence. It echoes through the infernal abyss, reverberating like a symphony of torment, sending tremors of dread racing through the very marrow of my bones. A piercing, otherworldly roar reverberates in the far distance, and a chilling realization dawns upon me.

"It was my desperate cry for salvation, my plea to the Almighty, that unwittingly stirred the demonic beasts from their restless slumber," I mutter to myself, condemning my own foolishness which inadvertently draws further attention to my precarious situation.

Rising from their infernal lairs, drawn by my call, the atmosphere grows increasingly heavy with their presence and the weight of the powers of the air they command as their ominous scouts rush forward across the scape in search for the one foolish enough to utter His name.

Hell's beasts have been summoned, and in this dire moment, I keenly feel the weight of my own foolishness. It is my own actions that have become the beacon of my impending destruction. Their savage presence draws ever closer to my location, where I remain imprisoned and helpless, unable to flee from the relentless pursuit.

The flames crackle, devouring everything in their path, their fiery maws hungry for my demise. Desperation surges within me as I realize the magnitude of my predicament. The deafening roars of the approaching beasts echo through the inferno, each step pounding in my chest like a thunderous drumbeat, announcing the relentless march of my doom.

I can feel the searing heat closing in, the very air around me blistering with intensity. The scalding tears on my face evaporate as quickly as they fall. I press my trembling hands tighter against my ears, desperate to block out the horrifying sounds, but there is no escape from the impending cataclysm.

As the flames lick closer and the beasts draw nearer, I know that my fate is sealed. My heart pounds in a final wave of dread, each beat echoing in my ears like a drum signaling the end. Desperation takes hold, and I again press my hands against my ears, trying to block out the terrifying reality unfolding around me. The heat of the flames scorch my skin, and the guttural growls of the approaching beasts vibrate through the air. As the fear and panic crescendo, I squeeze tighter and tighter, the pressure building within my skull until, mercifully, all fades to black. The world slips away, leaving me in a void of unconsciousness, a brief escape from the nightmare that approaches.

CHAPTER 8

The Outworld

Job 18:5-18

Surely the light of the wicked will be snuffed out.
The sparks of their fire will not glow.
The light in their tent will grow dark.
The lamp hanging above them will be quenched.
The confident stride of the wicked will be shortened.
Their own schemes will be their downfall.
The wicked walk into a net.
They fall into a pit.
A trap grabs them by the heel.
A snare holds them tight.
A noose lies hidden on the ground.
A rope is stretched across their path.

Terrors surround the wicked
and trouble them at every step.
Hunger depletes their strength,
and calamity waits for them to stumble.
Disease eats their skin;
death devours their limbs.
They are torn from the security of their homes
and are brought down to the king of terrors.
The homes of the wicked will burn down;
burning sulfur rains on their houses.
Their roots will dry up,
and their branches will wither.
All memory of their existence will fade from the earth;
no one will remember their names.

They will be thrust from light into darkness,
driven from the world.

Ecclesiastes 10:1

As dead flies give perfume a bad smell, so a little folly outweighs
wisdom and honor.

2 Corinthians 2:15-16

For we are to God the pleasing aroma of Christ among those who
are being saved and those who are perishing. To the one we are an
aroma that brings death; to the other, an aroma that brings life.

Ephesians 6:12

For our struggle is not against flesh and blood, but against the
rulers, against the authorities, against the powers of this dark world
and against the spiritual forces of evil in the heavenly realms.

In the depths of the desolation, a diminutive demonic creature, hardly more than a grotesque distortion of life, scuttles forward as a sinister scout for its malevolent masters. It traverses the jagged rock faces with uncanny agility, its sinewy limbs writhing in eerie grace as it navigates the treacherous terrain. Its leathery, ashen skin clings tightly to its skeletal frame, like a tattered shroud draped over Death himself.

With each step, the fleeting interruptions in the flames unveil to me its beady eyes, gleaming with hatred and intent, radiating like crimson embers, casting an eerie glow in the dim, hellish light that sporadically bathes the surrounding cliffs. Its gnarled claws scrape against the unforgiving rocks, producing an unsettling cacophony that reverberates through the desolation.

As it inches nearer, the creature's approach is accompanied by the anguished wails of the unfortunate souls it encounters. Seemingly drawing answers from their tormented forms through an unearthly, cruel ritual, every stride toward me thickens the atmosphere, like a dense fog descending upon the forsaken realm. An eerie and foreboding aura envelops it, darkening the already nightmarish surroundings, intensifying the unsettling dread that emanates from its relentless pursuit.

Now perched upon what appears to be a ridge just beyond my protective barrier, its malevolent gaze scours the desolation below in search of any sign of life or vulnerability. The surrounding atmosphere tightens, each heartbeat echoing like a distant drumbeat. The creature emits a series of steady clicks, akin to a form of echolocation, all the while creeping closer to me.

My heart races, and cold sweat clings to my trembling form as I desperately seek refuge within the feeble circle of flames that surrounds me. The demon's malevolent gaze fixes on mine, and its grotesque facial features contort and twist open into a sinister expression, revealing rows of jagged, serrated teeth.

In a horrifying moment, not even seeing the creature descend from its perch, a clawed hand darts through the flame with grotesque swiftness, seizing me in an iron grip of torment. Agony courses through my veins as its bony fingers dig into my flesh like hot coals; its inhuman strength overwhelms me, ripping my flesh as it clamps down upon my bones.

Desperation and terror surge through me as I am forcibly pulled away from the meager safety of the flames, my flesh singed from the fire's impact upon it as I penetrate its protection, all the while being dragged deeper into the nightmarish abyss.

My cries for mercy are met only by the creature's gleeful cackling, echoing through the hellish scape as a reminder to others of its superiority. The malevolent glee in its eyes intensifies when I realize that my torment has only just begun as it drags me closer to the looming figures of its masters, their ominous forms casting eerie silhouettes in the flickering, blood-red light of the flames in the background.

Before I can fully grasp the situation, the menacing creature hurls me at the feet of the dark lords towering above. This abrupt encounter leaves me feeling as though I am trapped in a nightmarish dream state, unable to comprehend how I was captured and brought here so swiftly.

As the towering demonic principalities loom overhead, their monstrous hands poised for a devastating strike as they descend swiftly toward me, I am abruptly jolted awake. The nightmarish realm, with its concoction of demonic beings dragging me into the outer reaches, shatters like fragile glass, and I am swiftly pulled from the nightmare by a cacophonous roar that mimics the sound of a thousand beasts echoing through the empty chasms of hell.

A wave of relief washes over me as I realize it was all just a dream. Yet, the thunderous cries echoing just beyond the flames serve as a stark reminder: *the nightmare might be a chilling glimpse of what's to come.*

"Perhaps the dream was a warning," I remark aloud, pondering the events of the possible vision while carefully controlling my breathing, trying not to make too much noise or draw any unwanted attention to myself from whatever might lurk just beyond the reach of my flames.

The roars continue, resonating through every depth, cutting through the air like serrated blades, piercing eardrums and deafening all who bear witness. Their outcries echo from the distant reaches, and the sound seems to emanate from all directions, furthering my fear in anticipation for what is to come.

The sound of hurried footsteps races past my fiery refuge, accompanied by eerie scratches and labored breathing. A vivid image of the nightmarish entity that captured me in my dream haunts my imagination, urging me to remain as silent as a mouse, blending into the earth beneath, to avoid drawing any attention to myself. So, I lie there, trapped amidst the flickering flames, gripped by fear like a helpless schoolboy, my mind racing with uncertainty about what to do or where to flee. Yet, I remain steadfast in my resolve to stay absolutely quiet and still.

The flames shift and quiver around me as the relentless roars of the beasts echo through the blackened atmosphere, piercing through the fiery barrier. Their hunger-filled cries reverberate like a chilling prelude to imminent violence, as if they are poised to kill and savor blood once more.

Instinctively, I huddle in a defensive posture, rising to my knees, my hands cradling my head in a futile attempt to shield myself from the impending terror. There's no refuge, no rock to hide behind, no stick to futilely swing in defense. It's here for me, and no form of concealment, prayer, or resistance can protect me this time.

Fear overwhelms me, pressing upon my very being like thousands of pounds of iron chains meticulously wound around my body, each link heavier than the last. These chains, cold and unyielding, anchor me to the earth below with a relentless, suffocating weight. They dig deep into my flesh, leaving indelible marks of dread and despair.

As I attempt to move, each advancement feels like an agonizing struggle against this invisible but palpable burden. The ground beneath me sags and buckles under the colossal weight of my fear, as if the very earth itself conspires with my tormentors to keep me tethered to this nightmarish reality. Every breath is a labored effort, as if I must contend with the gravitational pull of a world that wants to devour me whole.

In the midst of my inner turmoil, I find myself engaged in a heated debate with my own thoughts.

Maybe I should just show myself and be done with this already, I argue with myself, the notion of surrender tugging at my consciousness. *Perhaps if I stand up and surrender, they might show some mercy or simply leave me be,* I contemplate, as one of the beasts settles dangerously close to me.

As I sit alone, my thoughts and fears playing before me of what lay just beyond my fiery walls, my father's words echo through the silence: "Always face your fears."

I wonder if he could have ever imagined those words leading me here, to confront fear in its purest form. Did he foresee a time when my surroundings would turn prayers into echoes of despair? As he imparted that advice, did he truly have faith in my courage to endure such trials?

Now, as a sense of despair begins to seep into my voice, I long for his guidance more than ever. I can't help but wonder, with a heavy heart, if he is thinking of me right now, in my darkest hour.

Visions swirl in my head, each one a poignant tableau of how my family might have reacted to the news of my death. I see their faces, marked by shock and grief, as they grapple with the harsh reality in quiet living rooms and hushed conversations. I wonder about the emotions that gripped them at my funeral, the grief and sorrow that must have filled the air, and the questions that may linger in their hearts.

Who even came? I wonder, my mind lingering on the disquieting thoughts of the ceremonies that were undoubtedly unfolding.

Contemplating the events surrounding my funeral, the values instilled in me by my father randomly pop into my mind. He was the kind of man who raised fighters, not quitters. Were he here, he wouldn't surrender so easily nor give in to whatever was awaiting him. He would rally me to fight alongside him and stand our ground.

Strengthened by his values and the memories of my childhood, I resolve not to surrender to the obstacles that lie ahead or to any demonic force that might attempt to drag me from my current plight, as possibly foretold in my dream. Beginning to muster my courage, I hear a sudden, eerie cry for help—abruptly silenced in a chilling, forceful manner, as if something had just snuffed out the very breath from another soul.

No sooner do I muster the resolve to confront the unseen, than a torrent of doubt begins to seep into my thoughts. *What hope is there for me in the face of something so large that it shakes the earth beneath me?* I question internally.

As additional screams slice through the darkness—only to be cruelly stifled—I'm further compelled to cower to the echoes that bear witness to the terrifying force skulking just beyond my light.

What chance is there for me? I ponder, grappling with my fears and the encroaching shadow of despair.

"Hide Chris," I say aloud, attempting to bolster my own resolve, convincing myself that there is no shame in it.

"You can't hide forever," I argue with myself.

"Nor would I want to," I respond, as if engaging in a dialogue with my own conscience.

"Face them," I challenge myself, the words escaping my lips with determination, as if I'm trying to summon the courage to reveal myself and confront the monster head-on.

I'm sorry, Dad, I think to myself as I muster every ounce of courage I have left in the wake of what is to come. *I'm sorry I let you down. I'm sorry I gave up. I'm sorry I lacked the courage you believed I had. I'm sorry I gave up so easily in life without recognizing how valuable it truly was. I'm so very sorry.*

If I had one more chance to see my father, I would ask for one more hug. Those embraces always made me feel safe, as if nothing could harm me in his presence. I recall with a slight smile the night of the encounter with the demon in my room. I remember the fear etched on the demon's face when my dad walked through the door—it was a priceless sight.

"Sure, he was startled by the demon's very existence, but he didn't even hesitate!" I relive aloud, as if recounting the event with someone. "He remained composed, as if he had faced countless battles before and now confronted a familiar adversary. Except, he knew he could conquer it, and the demon knew it could be conquered."

After allowing a few moments to pass, I gather my thoughts and prepare myself for the impending events. I stand up, slightly favoring my right leg and positioning myself further back, ready to defend against any swift attacker. I ensure that whatever comes my way understands that I won't go quietly; I'll fight with all I have.

"There's no more running. There's no more hiding. As God is my witness, it's you or me!" I declare with a newfound determination, resolving to face my ultimate destiny.

But just as I'm about to shout, something unexpected and mysterious occurs: a woman's voice pierces through the wall of flames with precision, startling me to a standstill. I find myself unable to process what just happened or even comprehend who or what spoke to me. *Could it be that the flames, my eternal captors, now possess a spirit of their own and are trying to communicate with me?* I stand there, perplexed, scrutinizing the fiery barrier, half-expecting it to morph and unveil its true form.

"Hello?" I whisper in bewilderment.

"Cicho, ty głupcze!" the woman's voice speaks out, leaving me certain that it's not the flame or a spectral entity, but a real person, much like myself.

I'm so bewildered by the idea that another human being may be just on the other side of the flames that I'm at a loss for words or how to respond. My instincts, honed by fear and solitude during my time here, have left me unprepared for human interaction. It feels strange to have any form of contact, especially with another person. After all, it seems like an eternity has passed since my last encounter with a fellow human. Despite my efforts to respond, all I can manage to stammer out is, "Wha—a . . . What!?"

"You are an imbecile!" the woman's voice scolds me, making it clear that she's addressing me directly.

"I don't . . . I—don't understand," I stutter, as our conversation is halted by a deafening roar that reverberates through Hell, a grim reminder that the principle of Death himself is dangerously close, rapidly closing the distance between us.

"I know it was you who uttered those words!" she hisses disapprovingly at me, cautioning me against revealing our location through any reckless actions.

In this moment teeming with fear and curiosity, I feel strangely alienated. For the first time since arriving here, an unfamiliar presence has approached me, and to my surprise, it doesn't exude an aura of threat. If anything, she seems like she's hiding just as I am.

Could she have been right there all this time? I mull over in my thoughts.

The question of why she isn't ensnared by the flames, while I am, puzzles me. It leads me to wonder if my predicament is either strangely advantageous or horrifyingly worse than I had initially believed. I start to entertain the notion that perhaps I'm intentionally imprisoned by someone or something, and that entity will soon return to claim me.

"You are a coward," she asserts, cutting through my thoughts. "You think you can spout whatever you want just because you have flames to hide behind? Who the hell do you think you are? Don't you realize you can't say such things here? Your stupidity might just condemn us all to their wrath!" Her words hang in the air, sharp and accusatory.

I stand there, taken aback by the unexpected confrontation. It's an awkward introduction, given our circumstances—both of us trying to hide from a fierce, demonic creature that's rapidly approaching.

The creature must be extremely close by, and yet she's condemning me for speaking a few words out loud, I argue silently with myself, attempting to rationalize my actions in comparison to hers.

"What do you mean?" I whisper, confusion threading my voice to a near inaudible murmur. "You were talking just as much as I was." Frustration mixes with my bewilderment. "Aren't you being just as much of an imbecile?"

"Are you stupid?" She lashes out at me. "I'm not referring to speaking in general, you fool! You spoke HIS name down here!" she points out, her tone dripping with condemnation. "Just uttering His name, or words from that book, or any kind of prayer to Him sends out . . . you know . . . why do you think they're coming after you now, all of a sudden? Don't you know anything?" she says, speaking down to me as if I were a child. She's accusing me of calling out to God.

"You listen here," she says, cutting through my thoughts. "Let me in, and I won't reveal that you were the one who said it."

As I take a step back, trying to process her words, she urges me to share my secret so that she can hide as well.

"Let you in?" I say aloud, my voice trembling with confusion.

"Enough with your stupid games! They're approaching. Quickly, tell me your secret so I can hide too!"

"You don't understand," I reply quickly, a sense of desperation creeping into my voice. "It's not like I chose to be in here and have the ability to come and go as I please. I awoke here. I can't get out—I've tried!" I reason with her, trying to make her understand. "How can I let you in when I don't even know how I got here in the first place?"

"You liar!" she spits out at me. "No one has the means to hide here, let alone the privilege of concealing themselves within fire. What are you? A sorcerer?" She interrogates me further. "What master do you serve that would give you such authority over fire that it conceals you from even them?" she asks. "Our master doesn't grant that kind of power to just anyone. You must be worth quite a lot to him to send such a force after you."

"What? Of course not!" I exclaim, denying any betrayal.

"Of course you didn't!" She mocks me bitterly. "Because even a varmint, those pesky little hellions, know better than to utter such words as you did and draw their attention upon yourself. No one is that stupid unless they are trying to get caught!"

Desperate for answers and to know more about our predicament, I plead, "Please, tell me—where did you come from? How did you get here? How did you know I was here?"

"Keep it down, you fool!" she hisses, warning me once again. "They're coming this way. There will be consequences for your mistake if they find you."

"Who are they?" I inquire, feeling weak in the knees at the thought of revealing myself to those malevolent creatures.

"I have to go," she declares abruptly. "One of them is nearly upon us! I have to go. I won't risk being caught for you."

"Wait!" I half yell in a whisper. "Don't leave me! Please come back!" I beg.

"Hush!" she hisses at me. "You can make all the noise you want once I'm gone but don't think for a minute you're going to lure them to me. I'm on to you."

"On to me?" I question, utterly confused by her accusations. "I don't know what you're talking about. I'm not playing any games. What are those monsters you keep referring to?" I plead for information.

"Reapers!" she says with a shrill in her voice. "Now lower yourself and hide! NOW!"

I heed her instructions, bending down to press my cheek against the ground, the acrid fumes assaulting my eyes as I listen to her fading footsteps rapidly retreating into the distance. It's undeniable now: there is a vast world outside my fiery prison, and for some unfathomable reason, I seem to be the only one trapped behind these walls of flame.

The ground trembles beneath me, and the haunting voices of the damned grow hushed in the presence of one of the creatures that now looms over me—a Reaper, as she called it. I ponder what in all of Hell a Reaper might be, hoping I won't soon find out. I can feel the immense power and weight of the beast with every thunderous step it takes. Its movements grow slower and more deliberate as it draws nearer to my hidden flame, seemingly puzzled by the abrupt absence of scent or any sign of concealment. The air is thick with tension, and the creature's uncertainty hangs palpably in the atmosphere as it cautiously advances, its movements echoing like the ominous drumbeat of an impending confrontation.

I forget to breathe, biting my lip until it bleeds as a nervous response to the impending danger. I lie there, pressed against the dirt, as still as I can be, eyes wide open in fear as I catch an obscured silhouette of the beast through the wall of my flame. As I strain to discern the approaching creature, its form gradually becomes more distinct. It appears to be a four-legged entity, its body elongated and sinuous, with a serpent-like tail trailing behind it. Horns jut out from its head in various directions, reminiscent of dragons, their mythical and fearsome visage now taking on a horrifying reality before my very eyes. The sight of this nightmarish being leaves me awestruck and trembling, as I grapple with the sheer magnitude of the surreal encounter.

I watch its shadow flicker upon my wall as its head lowers toward the earth, taking in deep breaths, trying to pick up my scent. The earth quivers in the presence of the dragon, which begins to slowly encircle my confinement, its guttural grunts exhale the thick sulfuric air around me.

There's a deep-throated rumble emanating from it, resonating through the dimly lit space. As I peer through the veil of my flickering flames, which obscure most of my view, I can just make out the dark silhouette of something monstrous beyond. Its large, elongated mouth opens at the very spot where the phantom girl had stood moments earlier, swallowing the shadows around it. Suddenly, a deafening roar bursts forth from the creature, sending a shockwave that forces the surroundings to tremble in submission. My wall of flames bends and shudders above me, casting an erratic dance of light and shadow, while a flurry of sparks showers over me, each spark fleeting yet intensely bright against the darkening gloom.

I close my eyes and dig my fingernails deep into the earth, summoning every ounce of strength within me to refrain from screaming as the flame collapses upon me under the dragon's breath. It melts my flesh, turning it almost into wax as it drips across my chest and onto the soil beneath me.

Don't let go, I hear inside my head. *Keep. Holding. On!*

The dragon's deafening roar finally subsides, leaving the air heavy with anticipation. Its massive form trembles as it forcefully stomps the ground, sending tremors through the earth. The surrounding terrain seems to quiver in response to the dragon's immense power, and for a moment, a tense stillness fills the air.

In the wake of the dragon's fury, the world seems to hold its breath, as if bracing for what might come next. My heart continues to race, the echoes of the dragon's roar reverberating in my ears. I can't help but wonder if the creature is truly gone or merely biding its time, waiting for the opportune moment to strike.

My senses remain on high alert, and I strain to listen for any signs of movement or danger. The sulfuric fumes linger in the air, casting an eerie pall over the ill-fated scape. The flames that surround me dance with uncertainty, casting long, wavering shadows that seem to taunt me.

As I lie there, hidden behind the veil of fire, I can't shake the feeling that the nightmare is far from over. The oppressive atmosphere and the unknown forces that lurk beyond the flames keep me in a state of perpetual dread, unsure of what horrors may await me in this unholy realm.

I finally release the breath I have been holding, the dust particles swirling around me in agitation to my exhale. Finally blinking my eyes, a tear catches in the corner and rolls down my cheek as the pain well up inside me from the boils and scorched flesh, trying to repair itself after such intense trauma.

Before I can even begin to evaluate the extent of my injuries, a terrible, sly voice hisses through the air. The sound pierces through my pain, sending a jolt of adrenaline coursing through me once more. It's a stark reminder that this nightmare is far from over.

My heart pounds in my chest as I strain to identify the source of the voice. It comes from all directions, an eerie echo that reverberates through the hellish scape. The words themselves are incomprehensible, a sinister language that sets my nerves on edge.

"**Silentium!**" I suddenly hear piercing the thick air, the dragon quieting itself as though submitting to another authority.

"**Te mihi revela aut meam iram patere,**" intones the ominous voice, its words cryptic yet filled with an unsettling command. As it speaks, the outline of a dark, hooded figure gradually materializes atop the imposing beast that stands before my flickering flame. With an eerie fluidity, the figure dismounts, dissipating into smoke-like tendrils that drift downward to the ground.

These vaporous wisps then coalesce, and the hooded figure takes form again, moving with deliberate steps toward the edge of my flickering fire. The entire process unfolds like a surreal dance between shadow and substance, leaving me in both awe and dread at the unearthly spectacle before me.

"Do you recognize my voice?" I hear the figure hissing once more, this time with a complete understanding of the language it speaks.

"I have been waiting for you. Do you believe you can cry out to your God as if He can hear you anymore? I will track you down. I WILL FIND YOU! This is my dominion you're in, and no god can come to your aid now," he proclaims with authority.

"My legions have been summoned, my power courses through their veins. It is only a matter of time," he taunts.

"You will belong to me before the third moon wanes," he declares with unshakable confidence, his voice resonating across the land as if a multitude of voices all speak as one.

As the Reaper's proclamation reverberates across the scape of the land, it becomes abundantly clear that all those under his dominion are completely subject to his will. Their voices serve as conduits of his wrath, echoing his commands in eerie unison, while he proudly stands upon the territory he claims as his own.

Curiously, though, the Reaper and its dragon appear oblivious to the fact that I am cowering just a few feet away from them, concealed behind the flickering flames that offer me an illusory sense of safety. As I briefly revel in the irony of the situation, my pride is short-lived. The nightmarish creature upon which he rides suddenly emits a loud snort of contempt and raises its head high above me. It releases a dreadful cry, instilling both fear and respect throughout the eerie expanse and commanding the attention of all who behold it.

Despite the intensity of the moment, I remain hidden in the shadows, my heart racing from the recent encounter. The scent of sulfur lingers in the air, a constant reminder of the hellish scape that surrounds me. I dare not move or make a sound, for I know that the Reaper's malevolent power is not to be underestimated.

As the Reaper and its dragon appear to leave, distracted by the voice of a creature that came forth, I am left to assess the injuries I sustained. My skin is charred and singed, clinging uncomfortably to my burned flesh while I struggle to peel it off to start the regenerating process once more. Every movement is met with a sharp reminder of the agony I am in. I realize that I am fortunate to have survived the Reaper's assault, but the scars, both physical and emotional, will remain with me.

A heavy, oppressive silence settles around me, thick with tension. The dragon's presence—or its absence—remains uncertain, obscured perhaps by my own painful reckoning with my injuries. This ambiguity sharpens the edge of every quiet moment, leaving me wary and watchful in the unsettling calm.

Each inhalation comes in quick, shallow bursts, my chest heaving with effort as the searing agony from my scorched flesh relentlessly surges through my body. My acrid tears, heated by the intensity, boil and scald my eyes with each blink. Crying means risking the loss of my sight, and in the midst of such agony, that is a fate I cannot bear.

As I struggle to make sense of the situation, my thoughts deceive me into believing it's safe once again. I begin to piece together the fragments I recall from the Reaper's threats: the Reaper spoke as if he knew me intimately, as if he has always known me. It's as if this enigmatic force possesses knowledge of my existence, even during the lapses of my consciousness within the realm of the living, and now he relentlessly searches for me in the land of the dead.

Perhaps the dark figure, concealed beneath his hood, is fear incarnate, an unrelenting presence that has stalked me since my earliest days. He seems to be the very entity that had lurked in the shadows of my childhood room, his ominous presence fueling my nightmares. He feels like the malevolent force that had pursued me on that fateful night when despair had driven me to the brink. The idea that he has been with me throughout my life brings clarity to his recognition and threats, as I contemplate the relentless nature of this eerie and maleficent being.

Despite my fervent reluctance to acknowledge him, the words of the hooded figure carry an unsettling weight of undeniable truth. The figure asserts dominion over these regions, and the unmistakable evidence of his power manifests in the haunting and eerie voices that permeate the scape. These voices echo the Reaper's proclamation with a persuasive force that reveals the depths of his power and dominion over those he enslaves.

With each echoing voice, the feeling of helplessness and dread within me deepens. I grapple with the disconcerting realization that I am ensnared in a realm where my control is nonexistent, and the rules governing this place are dictated by forces far beyond my comprehension. The revelation leaves me with a profound sense of vulnerability, as I come to terms with the stark reality that I am at the mercy of powers I can neither understand nor defy.

The figure's chilling declaration echoes in my mind, his words a sinister reminder that there was no escape, no divine intervention to rescue me. My feeble cries to a God who could no longer hear me or offer assistance laid bare the fragility of my mind. Like a thread stretched to its limit, it is ready to unravel at any moment, a tenuous lifeline in the face of the overwhelming darkness that surrounds me.

Just as I start to regain a semblance of composure, my fears finding a momentary respite in the returning silence, a new, unsettling declaration shatters the calm once again.

"I can smell your filth," the ominous figure proclaims once more, his whispers filled with an intensity that reverberates through the very land itself.

In the midst of this eerie declaration, the dark figure remains shrouded in mystery, his presence concealed in the shadows.

"Reveal yourself and kneel before me," he bellows, every word oozing with malevolence.

"There is no God but me in this realm. There never was anyone capable of saving you from my grasp. I shall find you, and when I do . . ." His words abruptly cease, lingering in the air, heavy with an unsettling obscurity that leaves me shaken and tentative, my confidence wavering under their ominous weight. The image of the Reaper as a commanding principality, a master of a terrible dragon that speaks through the voices of countless subordinates, hangs in my thoughts like a nightmarish tapestry woven with threads of dread and despair. I grapple with the chilling reality of the situation, overwhelmed by a sense of impending doom.

I squeeze my eyes shut, the temptation to obey and reveal myself to the commanding voice gnawing at me. But the words *Hold on!* echo persistently in my mind, and I cling to them, even if all I can grasp are the loose particles of dirt in my trembling hands. A sense of unease washes over me as I wonder why this ominous figure, referred to as the "Reaper" by the phantom woman, has yet to disclose his knowledge of my presence and capture me. He stands mere feet away from my prison walls.

Can he not sense my presence within the fiery glow? Is he blind to the cylindrical flame that betrays my hiding place? I wonder. *Why does he hesitate?*

And then, in a sudden and eerie turn of events, I glimpse through the wall of flames the hooded figure's fragmented movements. He whirls something above his head, uttering incantations that seem to summon an unseen force.

"It's over; he's found me," I say aloud as the Reaper's movements coalesce around me, seemingly now aware that I am within the fire."

A sharp crack slices through the air, the whip's lash cutting through the very fabric of the acrid fumes and sulfuric vapors that surround me. I know, with a sinking feeling, that he found me. He's aware of my hiding place.

Inwardly, I utter my final goodbyes to my father and family, a secret prayer clinging to my thoughts, hoping against hope that somehow, through one last miracle, my farewells will reach them.

As I summon the last shreds of my resolve, preparing to surrender to my seemingly inevitable fate, a chilling sequence of events unfolds before me. Simultaneously, a blood-curdling scream pierces the air, followed by another swift crack of a whip. My eyes dart towards the source of the commotion, and I catch a partial glimpse of the hooded figure, accompanied by his fearsome dragon.

A deafening roar erupts from the dragon, its ferociousness directed at the screams that echo just feet away from me, in the opposite direction of where I face. I can hardly fathom how anyone hearing the pitch and resonance of this monstrous creature's cry could do anything but freeze in sheer terror, fearing that they might be the next target of its wrath.

"No! No! Not me, my lord. Not me!" The desperate, blubbering cries resonate from just beyond the veil of flames. The cruel lash of the whip finds its victim, and by some miraculous twist of fate, I come to the staggering realization that the victim is not me.

The hooded figure remains silent, a sinister puppeteer manipulating the soul with the entangling whip. The dragon at his side snorts with a raging, reptilian fury, its screech tearing through the darkness, anticipating the fate of the captured victim. I strain to hear the soul's anguished pleas, their futile struggles against their impending doom. It's a harrowing spectacle, and I can't help but wonder about the gruesome fate that awaits the unfortunate soul at the hands of this ominous figure.

I crouch back down, my heart pounding in my chest, my head angled ever so slightly upward as I strain to decipher the ever-shifting shadows cast by the dancing flames. My mind races with a multitude of scenarios, each playing out in my imagination as I struggle to distinguish the unfolding events from the ominous silhouette painted upon the wall of fire. Fear and uncertainty grip me as I bear witness to this nightmarish scene, my senses on high alert, and every nerve in my body tingling with trepidation.

Abruptly, the cacophony of the soul's struggle ceases. Through the flickering, thinner portions of the fiery barrier, I discern the soul now lying prone upon the ground, helpless at the feet of the menacing dragon. The Reaper descends, the whip still entwining around the person as if it were a living entity, constricting like a snake coiled around its prey, squeezing out every last ounce of breath before devouring it. The scene is suffused with an overwhelming sense of dread, as I helplessly watch the soul's fate hanging in the balance, a grim tableau of impending doom.

"Please, have mercy, my lord," the soul implores, his breath labored from constriction. "What am I but a peasant in your sight? I pose no threat to you, my lord."

The tall, shadow-draped figure remains silent, staring down upon the soul as though he is pondering his next move, or perhaps realizing that the captive before him is not the one he sought.

Gradually, he lifts his hand, extending a pointed finger toward the prisoner, and bellows two words, which reverberate within the mouths of all those nearby.

"Judicium Exspectat!"

Without a moment's pause or any chance for a response, the dragon arches its massive head backward and swoops down upon the defenseless soul with devastating force. Its jaws snap shut around the hapless victim, a final, agonizing cry echoing into the depths of darkness for all the mindless souls nearby, ensnared under its control, to hear. I grimace, squeezing my eyes shut and clamping my hands over my ears as the gruesome sounds of bones breaking and flesh tearing emanate from the beast's gaping maw.

With a grotesque grace, the creature fully extends its wings, and takes flight into the upper realms of hell, obediently following the command of its rider. The horrifying spectacle leaves me in a state of shock and revulsion, a witness to the unspeakable horrors that unfold in this nightmarish realm.

As the sound of the dragon's powerful wings begins to fade into the distance, the atmosphere around me settles back into its normal stance, the resounding echoes of feet fading with them as I can only imagine the scouts or others under its control returning from whence they came.

The faint cries of the damned take up their sorrowful song of mourning as the commotion fades, and suddenly, I feel as though all has gone back to "normal" once more; all except for my horrified realization of what I almost surrendered to and realizing that the demonic entity—the Reaper—was looking for me.

I fear his inevitable return, but wonder with a deep sigh of relief how he was unable to see me through my prison of flames. How was the dragon unable to discern my scent? The Reaper summoned something as if he was very much aware of my state and ready to strike down the flame concealing him against his prize. The unexpected revelation of the other person must have thrown the Reaper off guard.

"Who do you think you are?" I spit out loud at myself. "Do you think you are something special for hell to merit a search party after?" I quickly chastise myself, condemning my own arrogance.

"You are a nobody! A foolish kid who took his own life!" I remind myself, my self-loathing intensifying.

"What worth could you possibly have here to entertain the ridiculous thought that something as powerful as that creature would care about your whereabouts?" I conclude, berating myself for even entertaining such a foolish notion. I convince myself that the Reaper had clearly come for the other person, and I had simply been fortunate enough not to be caught in the crossfire.

The familiar tendrils of loneliness envelop me once more, settling upon my shoulders and encasing me in their ever-expanding void, which deepens with every passing moment. My sense of self-worth diminishes further as I sit back on my knees, defeated in my posture. A heavy ache tightens my chest, and I place my hand over it to confirm that I am still breathing, a grim reminder of my existence in this cursed place.

Has my heart also abandoned me, lost interest in beating? I wonder. Glancing down at my hands I notice the muddy, reddish substance caked around my fingers and beneath my fingernails.

How odd, I think. *There's no moisture in the dirt to have created this mud-like texture, yet my hands feel sticky with this stuff smeared between my fingers.* Curiosity prompts me to reach down and touch the ground to investigate further, and to my surprise, the dirt actually feels moist.

It's at that moment I realize that I've been sitting in a stream of dark, viscous liquid that has been oozing from under my fiery wall, pooling next to me without my awareness. My eyes widen in shock as I look at my hands, then back at the peculiar liquid. I inhale sharply, sucking in a breath of air as I come to a horrifying realization:

the substance is blood, the fresh, warm blood of the forsaken soul devoured by the beast moments ago. I shiver and recoil in horror from the gruesome truth of my surroundings.

I scramble away from the spreading pool of blood, which continues to seep in and encircle the perimeter of my cell. It creeps from under the flaming wall, flowing around my feet, and the sharp scent of iron mixes with the sulfuric fumes, filling the air. My throat tightens, and I gag, dry heaving repeatedly, though there's nothing left in my stomach to expel, but the instinct to retch persists.

I'm next, I think to myself, a shiver of dread running down my spine. *It's only a matter of time before it's my blood that will coat the floor.* I bury my face in my arms, suddenly acutely aware of how fragile and deteriorated my skin has become on my arms and legs, and how intensely they ache.

With no place to rest my head, not even a spot to lie down, I am haunted by the grim reminder of the unfortunate soul's blood—a stark foreshadowing of my impending fate. Despair engulfs me as I realize there exists another world beyond my flames, one I am only just beginning to perceive. Amidst this deepening misery and hopelessness, a faint stirring outside my walls snatches my attention. In the throes of despair, a glimmer of hope flickers to life. Through the roaring blaze of my barrier, I hear a faint whisper. The stranger has returned.

"Are you still there?" she asks.

CHAPTER 9

The Stranger

Matthew 10:28

Do not be afraid of those who kill the body
but cannot kill the soul.
Rather, be afraid of the One who can destroy
both soul and body in hell.

John 15:6

If you do not remain in me, you are like a branch that is thrown
away and withers; such branches are picked up, thrown into the fire
and burned.

Hebrews 10:26-31

If we deliberately keep on sinning after we have received the
knowledge of the truth, no sacrifice for sins is left,
but only a fearful expectation of judgment and of raging fire that
will consume the enemies of God.
Anyone who rejected the law of Moses died without mercy on the
testimony of two or three witnesses.
How much more severely do you think someone deserves to be
punished who has trampled the Son of God underfoot, who has
treated as an unholy thing the blood of the covenant that sanctified
them, and who has insulted the Spirit of grace?
For we know him who said, "It is mine to avenge; I will repay,"
and again, "The Lord will judge his people."
It is a dreadful thing to fall into the hands of the living God.

A whirlwind of questions floods my mind as I realize that she has indeed returned.

"Hello," she calls out once more, "are you still there?"

"Yes," I respond, relief washing over me. "I am. I am still here."

"If you don't mind my asking, I must know. What are you?" she immediately inquires. "What powers do you possess?" she whispers through the flames, her voice tinged with bewilderment.

"I do not understand," I quickly reply, my confusion growing with each question.

"Uh," she sighs in frustration, evidently not receiving the answers she sought. "Are you mortal? Or are you of another kind—are you an elementalist?"

As I sit there, still utterly befuddled by her questions but immensely grateful for the conversation, I begin to answer her.

"No," I begin, "I am no…" But she cuts me off abruptly, seemingly having predicted the entirety of my response.

"Don't play with me," she snaps with impatience. "Are you a sorcerer?" she demands.

"No! No," I hurriedly reply. "If you think this is some kind of power I possess, then I guess I don't know how to use it because I'm trapped here! I feel like I'm dying over and over again but without the relief of death!"

"Are you human then?" she asks, her voice taking on a grave tone. "Can you feel your soul burn from within that flame, like flesh would burn a body, similar to when you once lived?"

"Yes, of course," I answer, perplexed by her line of questioning and wondering what else she might suspect I could be. "What do you mean, 'like flesh would burn a body?' It's my own flesh and bones that I feel burning under the heat of the flame—my skin has turned into blackened scars and gaping wounds, burns beyond the third degree, but regenerating in a repetitive cycle of torment ever since I arrived here," I explain, my voice trembling with the memories of unending suffering. "There are boils all over my body, so sensitive to the touch that when they rupture, I can see layers of my own skin, muscle, and sometimes even bone."

"As real as it looks," she begins to explain, her voice taking on a solemn tone, "as real as it feels, your body did not come with you to hell, my friend."

I listen intently, hanging onto her words, my curiosity mingling with a profound sense of dread.

"What you feel is the abortion of your soul and your mind's inability to comprehend what has transpired. Your soul has been stripped of its body, and it is exposed for the first time. It longs to feel again, but pain is the only thing that it responds to now that it is no longer connected to . . . never mind." She backpedals, her voice slightly quivering, as if she has said too much, revealing her own emotional scars from this place. I can only wonder how long she has endured here, how many days and nights, weeks and years.

"The pain of the soul is far greater than any physical pain your body could have endured on Earth," she continues, her words carrying an intensity. "Because the soul was never meant to be exposed—it was never meant to be so vulnerable to such darkness.

So . . . defenseless without its protector shielding you from every word, hex or vex that you were once protected from when you were in the land of the living." She pauses with an abrupt realization, as if she had momentarily forgotten something important, and it is only now dawning on her once more. The weight of her words hangs heavily in the air, and I can't help but wonder what she's remembered, what she's withholding.

Encountering another soul, much like myself since arriving here, has shifted my perspective dramatically. It has illuminated just how much this place, this realm, this dimension, takes from you. It's a relentless thief, stripping you of everything you once knew about this existence and leaving you worse off than you could have imagined. This realization has deepened my concern about what lies ahead because I still know so little about this place. I've only scratched the surface of the outer realm and the lower realms that the ominous spirit below introduced to me not too long ago. Despite the flame separating us, I suddenly feel profoundly connected to this stranger through the shared pain that we both endure.

I look down at my hands, no longer recognizing them as the hands I grew up with, yet unmistakably mine. I ask out loud, not really intending to be heard, "Why can I still see my hands if my body no longer exists?"

As my question lingers, I notice, in my peripheral vision while still gazing at my own hands, a dimly lit, shadowy figure approaching the flame, gradually revealing her obscure silhouette.

"Because that is how your soul remembers them to be," she interjects. "Your soul has not let go of the memory of its body yet, but trust me when I say your body has already let go of you."

She pauses, collecting her thoughts, before continuing, "Had you remained in your original body, the flames would have consumed you instantly. Yet, if some miracle had spared you, your body would have instinctively begun its natural healing process, striving to save you from your current agony. Alternatively, after enduring such extensive trauma, your body might have allowed you to pass away—easing your pain permanently by drawing its final curtains. But since you've crossed those final thresholds—because you are here, still 'alive' in a sense—it is only our bodies on Earth that are freed from suffering, not our souls."

I look down at my hands once more, feeling the weight of her words. I examine them as if seeing them for the first time, a sense of disconnection washing over me.

"These hands, my very own flesh and blood, the things I've gazed upon countless times before, now feel strangely foreign to me," I say aloud as the idea of being separated from the essence of my own body leaves me with a profound sense of loss and violation.

In this distorted moment, where a myriad of emotions burns under the heat of the flame alongside me, for the very first time,

I no longer recognize myself. Imagine losing a close friend and then hearing they've come back, but they're completely changed and unrecognizable. This transformation is jarring and confusing because it shakes the foundation of how you knew and connected with them. The comfort and familiarity you once shared are now replaced with a strange, unsettling uncertainty. It's like you're trying to connect what you once knew so well with something entirely new and unknown, creating a deep feeling of discomfort and confusion.

Perhaps that's why the apostles didn't immediately recognize Jesus, I contemplate, surprised by the unexpected thought that crosses my mind.

Regardless of my personal feelings or understanding of the situation, this is the new me, whether I like it or not.

She is right. If I still had my body, its inherent defenses would have already initiated a battle to protect me from the pain, agony, and torture I am currently enduring.

However, something within me remains passive during the most horrifying events, taking no action to combat the pain I face. It merely sits there, observing, waiting for help that would never come, enduring and absorbing more and more suffering from within and around itself. Perhaps it's this emotional abortion that is so unsettling within me. I grapple with the confusion of my soul and spirit without considering the impact the absence of God plays on each. Perhaps that is what is "passively" troubling me.

As I reflect on my journey, it becomes painfully clear just how negligent I've been. I failed to recognize the profound beauty of His creation—the intricate design, the subtle nuances, the artistic expression delicately woven into every fiber of my being. His craftsmanship is evident in the vessel He meticulously crafted for me, a vessel I shamefully mistreated.

During my lifetime, I neglected this precious gift, heedlessly poisoning it with carelessness. I pushed it beyond its limits, demanding more than it could bear, without a second thought for its well-being. In my shortsightedness, I failed to appreciate the sheer marvel of its existence.

I never truly valued this body, this vessel of life and experience. I didn't see it for what it truly was: a marvelous creation, a masterpiece of divine artistry. It is a spectacular entity, a living testament to His boundless creativity and love. And yet, I overlooked its magnificence, blinded by my own ignorance and indifference.

Now, as I come to terms with my past neglect, I am filled with regret and remorse. How could I have been so blind to the beauty that surrounded me, so callous in my disregard for His handiwork? It is a sobering realization—one that humbles me and serves as a stark reminder of the importance of gratitude and reverence for the gifts we've been given.

In the beginning, as the sacred texts tell us, God fashioned humanity from the very dust of the Earth. He sculpted our bodies with utmost care, each intricate detail a testament to His divine craftsmanship. With a breath, He bestowed upon us the gift of eternal life, and we became living beings, a harmonious blend of the physical and the spiritual.

Yet, as I reflect on this ancient truth, a profound question takes root within me: *What happened to that divine bond that Adam and Eve once had? What shift occurred from their eternal existence to the mortal state we all share in today?* It's as if we've undergone a transformation, a metamorphosis from the timeless beings of Eden to the fragile, fleeting creatures we are now.

In the Garden of Eden, our ancestors enjoyed a direct connection with the Creator. They walked in His presence, unburdened by the limitations of mortality. Their bodies, while physical, were infused with an eternal essence. It was a state of perfection, where life knew no end, and suffering was a foreign concept.

But something changed. A moment of disobedience fractured that perfect union. As Adam and Eve tasted the forbidden fruit, the consequences rippled through their existence and ours. The divine bond was severed, eternal life replaced by mortality and the awareness of good and evil.

Our bodies, once resilient and untouched by decay, became subject to the relentless march of time. They grew frail, susceptible to illness and aging. Death, once a distant notion, now loomed as an inevitable reality.

As I ponder this transformation, I can't help but wonder about its purpose and meaning. What lesson lies within this shift from eternal to mortal? Is it a test of our resilience, a trial of our faith, or a reminder of our humble origins? Or perhaps, it's a reminder that while our bodies are temporal, the spirit within us still carries the spark of the divine.

God must have recognized the inherent vulnerability of these earthly vessels to the exposure of sin and graciously gifted us with remarkable defenses and unique characteristics that aided in our survivability. He must have understood that without certain safeguards and protections, we would be exceedingly fragile in the face of the world's challenges. To ensure our well-being, He established a series of intricate systems and mechanisms within our bodies. These built-in defenses shield us from harm, disease, and the elements of the external world.

Even my skin was a remarkable creation, I think to myself, reflecting on how it possessed an extraordinary sensitivity to touch while also providing a gentle shield against the world. It was not merely a superficial covering but a remarkable barrier meticulously designed to protect me from my environment. It served as a shield against harmful pathogens, chemicals, and physical injuries. Beneath the surface, my immune system stood as a vigilant guardian, constantly patrolling for invaders and swiftly launching counterattacks when threats were detected.

Similarly, my organs and bodily functions must have also been finely tuned to maintain internal balance to sustain my mortal life. My heart tirelessly pumped oxygen-rich blood throughout my body, while my lungs continuously exchanged gasses to keep me breathing. Even my complex digestive system broke down food to nourish my cells, and my nervous system processed information and responded to external stimuli.

God's creation, including these intricate protective mechanisms, reflects His divine wisdom and care for His creatures. He knew that without these safeguards, our lives would be fraught with constant peril. In acknowledging our fragility, He instilled within us the ability to heal, adapt, and thrive in a world teeming with challenges, even in light of the original sin.

Ultimately, the adage "from dust to dust" serves as a reminder of our humble origins and our mortality. It underscores the cycle of life, where our physical bodies return to the Earth when our time on this plane ends. Yet, during our earthly sojourn, our bodies are a testament to God's divine craftsmanship, designed to withstand the trials and tribulations of life while allowing our souls to experience the beauty and wonder of His creation. Each intricate detail, from the complexity of our cells to the resilience of our immune systems, reflects the Creator's wisdom and care.

As I journeyed through life, I often took these protections for granted, treating my body as a mere vessel for my desires and ambitions. I failed to recognize the profound significance of the safeguards that shielded me from harm, both seen and unseen. My existence was intertwined with the physical and spiritual blessings bestowed upon me by the Creator though I didn't ask for it nor was it ever hinged upon my acceptance or belief in Him. However, now realizing the weight of her words, I understand how my actions unwittingly severed that connection that had sustained me throughout my existence.

In this place, I have grown even more adrift, both emotionally and mentally, stripped of the divine solace and strength that once anchored my being. Anxiety, despair, and a relentless sense of purposelessness now shroud my thoughts, casting a shadow over my very existence. Deep within my being, a profound longing stirs—an ache that pulsates within my chest, a relentless reminder of what has been stripped from me. It's a rhythmic ache, akin to the steady heartbeat that used to course through my veins.

All that is left now is to further my knowledge and understanding of the things to come that I may be better equipped to handle them. So, not wanting to miss the opportunity to gain more insight, and so incredibly grateful for an opportunity to commune with another person, I gently urge the woman to share further information with me.

"What does the soul look like?" I finally gather the courage to ask, although the answer terrifies me. "What should I expect to see one day when my soul finally lets go of the only image it's known of myself?"

There's a prolonged pause, during which I watch the dim, shadowy figure slowly circling the perimeter of my fiery prison, as if debating whether to reveal more.

"Have you ever seen a lifeless body after days of decay?" she responds with a question of her own. "Have you ever smelled the putrid rot of skin, hair, and organs, all exposed and twisted in ways they were never meant to be? Have you ever heard the mournful cry of blood-soaked earth, or tasted the stagnant air that surrounds it, realizing that the work of death's decomposition and disfigurement had only just begun?"

I gulp, the gravity of her words sinking in, and I suddenly realize that what she described is eerily similar to what I've been experiencing within my own body since arriving in this dreadful place.

"In life, no," I begin to answer hesitantly. "But since being here, I feel like I've been enduring some of what you describe within my own body."

"Well, just as a lifeless body transforms into something unrecognizable through the process of decay," she continues, "so does the soul undergo similar effects when severed from its physical and spiritual vessel, but the soul's experience is far more harrowing. It cannot disintegrate into dust to conceal its former torment as the body can."

She continues with a somber tone. "You and I, we are both doomed without another form of protection." You'll reach the end of your endurance and succumb eventually. Everyone does; no one is immune. Not even your safeguards you have within these flames can shield you from him! You will require his covering, just as you required your former covering." She finishes, letting me absorb her words as the flames dance in slow, fluid movements beside the shadowy figure, who continues to circle around them.

"Gradually," she carries on, "your mind will come to terms with the fact that there is no life flowing through what you once believed was your body but is, in reality, your soul.

"You will begin to experience the sensation of gasping for air around you, only to find that there is none to actually breathe. You will feel the blood cease its flow through your veins, for that is typically the last thing the mind comprehends when the body is dying. The memory of that feeling, your life-source draining from your body, will replay itself in your mind when you realize your soul has departed from it. Soon, you will accept the fact that you need no air to breathe and no blood to live in this realm." Her words lingered in the air with a profound sense of despair washing over me as they began to be absorbed.

I couldn't help but reconsider my previous perceptions of my condition. The constant state of disrepair and regeneration in my skin took on new meaning in light of her explanation. What I once believed to be torment might now be the natural state of a soul detached from its physical and spiritual protections.

I wonder what she means by "you will require his covering, just as you required your former covering." *Does this mean that unless I pair myself with another deity, I will remain in a constant state of decay until I too lay within the earth as that poor individual had underneath me?*

Questions race through my mind, and I find myself searching for answers in the dimly lit, flame-encircled space that has become my prison. The weight of my situation presses down on me, and a sense of vulnerability and hopelessness settles within me like a relentless storm.

Even the souls that followed the Reaper must have actually done so willingly and not as merely enslaved. The connection with it must have spared further deterioration, if what she says is true, I reflect, considering the implications of her words.

"Is there no escape from this cursed existence?" I finally manage to utter, my voice barely above a whisper.

"No," she replies to my unintended question. "The longer the soul is without its covering, the more it begins to mirror whomever or whatever it serves. Transformation takes various forms for each of us down here. No two demonic principalities are the same, and as a result, no two souls respond identically to their influence.

"The Reapers strive to ensnare you before being summoned by their masters. Devoid of a voice to advocate for themselves, they require a following of the damned to proclaim their judgments upon those sought by their masters. Just like all demonic principalities, they seek to ascend in rank and earn favor with our lord. The longer they can conceal you, the more you'll resemble them, making you less appealing to other deities.

"Early susceptibility renders you vulnerable to lesser demonic entities, many of whom you'd never wish to serve. You transform into something entirely alien to your former self, transfigured to the point of no longer resembling human qualities or attributes. You become a reflection of a self you were never meant to be—naked and empty," she concludes, leaving me with a haunting realization.

Her words echo in the confined space, each sentence laden with the weight of despair. I listen intently, realizing the dire predicament

I'm in. The idea that my very essence can be altered, warped into something unrecognizable and devoid of humanity, paints an entirely new perspective of life I had not considered.

"Tell me more about yourself?" she asks nonchalantly, as if nothing she just revealed was all that profound.

As I contemplate my response, she interjects, "Though you may feel tormented by being trapped within the flames, what you don't realize is that your soul is still being shielded by something, protecting you from the creatures of Hell whose mission is to collect specimens like yourself to present as trophies before our lord." She pauses again, deep in thought as though just coming to the realization of something momentous.

"It's curious," she continues, "not even the Reapers could detect you."

"What are the Reapers?" I ask not wanting to miss the opportunity to learn more about the beings that nearly enslaved or consumed me, should they return and she depart again.

"What do you think they are?" she answers sharply, ignoring my question and pressing further. "Who are you that the Reapers are in such disarray in their search for you? Who are you to be audacious enough to invoke that Name—the Name above all names—in a realm that despises it, in a realm that seeks to eradicate it? You should have known that the divinity associated with that Name cannot perceive your presence in this realm. Yet, you cried out to it anyway.

"Who are you that your soul is still receiving a covering, despite the separation of your body, while the rest of us are left exposed, just within the Reapers' grasp through our stench of utter vulnerability and weakness?" Her questions resonate with intense hatred in her voice.

Her comments weigh heavily on my mind, sowing fear amidst the uncertainty they bring. I assumed the Reapers found their target, or perhaps I hoped they had, to shield myself from the unsettling thought that they might still be searching for me.

I draw in a deep breath, pondering her earlier words. She mentioned the sensation of gasping for air, the longing to breathe, but explained that such actions were mere reflexes of living, no longer necessary in this realm.

Then, my mind latches onto another question: *what about blood?* I recall the gruesome scene when the dragon devoured that man and the blood that soaked the floor afterward. If blood and breathing are no longer necessary here, why do we still bleed? Why do we continue to regenerate flesh, yearn to breathe, and experience pain beyond the limits of our earthly bodies?

A revelation dawns upon me as I consider these thoughts. Hell has been perfected to keep its denizens in a perpetual state of hatred, despair, misery, complaining, coldheartedness, malevolence, faithlessness, incivility, and self-indulgence.

My soul might be catching on to the notion that it doesn't require air to breathe in a dimension designed for death, just as she explained. However, I'm not prepared to accept that I could ever become a mere fraction of what I once was, submitting to some demonic principality. I yearn for air in my lungs to dispel the fear, to breathe, and to feel alive again. But fear relentlessly infiltrates my being once more, making it increasingly difficult to catch my breath and hold onto the semblance of the life I once had, the life I still yearn for. My heart aches as I gasp for any semblance of relief from my torment.

"I am a nobody," I gasp, my heart racing. "There's no reason for these Reapers to be searching for me!"

"But you are," she voices enigmatically, her anger evident. "The Reapers heard your cry, and now they know you're here. It's by some chance or miracle that you weren't captured by them this time, but that's precisely what I mean: your covering is your flame—they couldn't see you because of it!" Her voice rises.

"This is a prison!" I shout back. "It's not a covering; it's a prison! It's my Hell!"

"No one is that fortunate to have escaped the Reapers' relentless scrutiny," she retorts, denouncing my outburst. "No one!"

I gulp, feeling the heat of this moment rising into the very thing I had been fearing. I take a moment to recompose myself with the question that has been gnawing at my core since witnessing the consumption of the unfortunate man just moments ago.

"If—if they did see me," I begin, my voice shaking, "and they did capture me, what would have happened to me? Would I not have just been consumed by them?" I am full of fear as I recall the soul's agonizing screams while the dragon's bone-breaking jaws clamped down upon him and consumed him.

"You would have—," she pauses and then corrects herself, "No!" She lashes out abruptly. "You're not getting any answers from me until you answer some of my questions!"

I close my eyes and drop my head in defeat, so desperate for her just to believe me when I say I neither remember nor know anything she continually asks me.

"So," the woman starts up again with her interrogation, "are you gonna tell me who you really are? Or, shall I go tell my master what I found?"

CHAPTER 10

The Transfiguration

Joel 1:4

*What the locust swarm has left
the great locusts have eaten;
what the great locusts have left
the young locusts have eaten;
what the young locusts have left
other locusts have eaten.*

Revelation 9:3-5

*And out of the smoke locusts came down on the earth and were
given power like that of scorpions of the earth. They were told not
to harm the grass of the earth or any plant or tree, but only those
people who did not have the seal of God on their foreheads. They
were not allowed to kill them but only to torture them for five
months. And the agony they suffered was like that of the sting of a
scorpion when it strikes.*

Isaiah 66:24

*Then they will go forth and look
On the corpses of the men
Who have transgressed against Me.
For their worm will not die
And their fire will not be quenched;
And they will be an abhorrence to all mankind.*

"Well?" she asks with a perturbed tone, continuing her barrage against me, unwilling to accept my answers as truth.

"One way or the other I will find out who or what you are. You either continue the charade until he comes or allow me the courtesy of the truth and save us both an enormous amount of headache."

My head droops low, and I find myself at a loss for words yet again. It's clear she won't believe anything I say, regardless of my answer. Deception, betrayal, and falsehoods seem to be the currency of this place, and she has become intimately acquainted with them. The air around me feels thin and suffocating as I attempt to draw deep breaths of the emptiness that surrounds me—a sensation that used to bring me solace. But the relentless heat of the flame makes every breath a struggle.

A part of me yearns to surrender to unconscious oblivion, to escape this harrowing reality filled with nameless fears and hidden truths. But I cling to my waning sanity, refusing to succumb to another trance that would plunge me back into eternal darkness.

I double over, my hands clutching my chest, as I struggle to catch my breath. The weight of her words bears down on me, and I can't quite accept that she's right about not needing to breathe in this realm.

"I'm not asking again!" she commands, her patience wearing thin. "I'm tired of playing games with you. You want answers? Well, so do I!"

I press my eyes closed, trying to steady my rapid heart beat (*or just the memory of what a heart beat was?*) and focus on my breathing.

With a determined tone, I reply, "I'm a nobody! I didn't choose to be trapped within tthese flames—I'd give anything to be rid of them once and for all! I hear voices of people beneath me, and all I can imagine is the earth breaking open from inside this flame and swallowing me whole! And there's not a single thing I can do if that were to happen!" I exclaim in frustration.

"I'm defenseless and helpless behind these flames! I'd rather be in your shoes, able to see what's coming for me, instead of being forced to be trapped behind this fire, not knowing when or how something might come for me."

"You wish you were in my place?" she yells back at me, cutting through my rambling. "Let me tell you about when I first arrived here and what I've endured every second since. Maybe then you'll understand why I desperately want to know your secrets and hide within your so-called *prison*."

I watch her silhouette pacing agitatedly in front of the flames, as if gathering herself to continue speaking.

"The day I woke up here," she begins, "I remember lifting my face from the ground, as though it had been mercilessly smashed there. I could still feel the warm blood smeared on the side of my head. I had no idea how I ended up here, but before I could even begin to understand where I was, I heard a low sound, like thunder but it seemed to come from thousands of sources, all harmonizing in eerie unity. All coming at me at once. The unusual rhythm felt alarming, but I couldn't quite understand the significance of what I heard.

"It was, in fact, a signal, a warning of imminent danger. A call to action urging me to flee and hide, but the magnitude of my ignorance was only evident in hindsight."

She coughs between sentences and exclaims, "They came for me!" Her tone drips with audible disdain as she recounts the memory.

She inhales sharply, catching her breath, anxiety amplifying the memory of the moment.

"One bite, just one, from those scaled abominations, and agony seizes your very soul. I first spotted them as a dark, undulating mass, an ominous cloud converging in my direction.

"Paralyzed by fear and bewilderment, I stood helpless as the tide of creatures swelled. Millions of them, their bodies grotesque and relentless, descended upon me like a living storm. They overwhelmed me, devouring my essence and injecting me with their parasitic offspring, which tormented me relentlessly for months.

"Imagine," she pauses, the intensity in her voice increasing to ensure I'm captivated, "millions upon millions of these creatures, a relentless swarm enveloping everyone who stayed behind. Each one a carrier of the same ancient plagues they once unleashed upon humanity on Earth. The marks of their affliction linger within me," she reveals, her voice laden with the gravity of her confession. "I still suffer from the remnants of their poison. The pain flares up unbearably—all because I stood exposed, defenseless against their onslaught.

"There is a heavy toll for your sins here," she speaks in a somber tone. "It wasn't long after the encounter with those abominations that my path crossed with the Reapers. These are vengeful, malevolent beings, hunting relentlessly for souls. Their purpose is to seize us, to drag us away to that dreaded place of judgment," she adds, her voice trembling with the chill of her memories.

"This was different, though," she pauses her story, reflecting on the recent events. "They were searching for someone specific this time—that someone I presume was you. Had you not been shielded, they would have undoubtedly found you. Their calculations and precision are seldom mistaken," she emphasizes, her words imbued with the gravity of a chilling truth.

"Has anyone ever told you the tales of the shadow-born?" she inquires, her voice laden with enigma. "Do you know about the baptismal pools where the ensnared are reborn by the Master of Shadow?"

"No, I am not aware of any such place or stories."

"You don't seem to know anything, do you?" she says pointedly to me. "Forget whatever you thought Hell was. There are powers and principalities here that go well beyond your comprehension or understanding."

"But I thought there was only one principality here," I reply confidently.

"My, how wrong you are," she comments. "Your misguidance will be your undoing if you don't listen and learn. Who did you think I was referring to when I mentioned the Master of Shadow?"

I remain quiet.

"Let me enlighten you about what lies ahead." Her words hang in the air, pregnant with the ominous promise of revelations to come.

"Within these shadow lands, known to many as Hell, Sheol, Purgatory, Hades, Gehenna, Tartarus, and Naraka, the true architect lurks unchallenged—a sinister puppeteer of despair. His dominion is blanketed with snares and traps, much like a spider lying in wait of lost and unsuspecting travelers.

"These traps, unlike any in the mortal world, are insidious and cunning. They don't simply capture the body; they prey upon the very essence of the mind. To this Master of Shadow, we are mere sustenance, each soul seasoned with unique flavors derived from our life's sins and accomplishments, all intricately orchestrated by unseen masters when we were alive and naive to their schemes.

"The traps seduce with whispers that promise solace to those who approach, much like sirens luring sailors to their doom. They take on deceptive forms, shape-shifting into loved ones in need of help, tugging at the heartstrings of wayward souls.

"Unaware of the entrapments that await, the souls are led into the depths of these baptismal pools. Here, the cleansing process commences, washing away any remaining traces of their maker. This meticulous purification ensures that they do not taint the shadowy master when they are finally ripe for harvest."

She pauses for a moment, allowing this image to sink into my mind before continuing.

"Relief is but a cruel tool wielded by his minions, a lure for the weary souls desperate for rest. Those who yield to these seductive temptresses and step into the deceptive waters are swiftly ensnared and pulled into the depths. There, they meet the true Master of Darkness, an entity far removed from any promise of salvation. It is then that the architect himself, Death, rises from the inky black waters, driven by a ravenous hunger. He consumes their essence, seizing the valuable remnants of their lives, before carrying the wayward souls away into oblivion.

"Then, the soul, once buoyant with hope for respite, finds itself eternally ensnared within the icy grasp of Death, doomed to endure his unspeakable torments. Yet, the traps remain strewn across the bleak terrain, visible yet unseen to the untrained eye. Those who dare tread this forsaken land must move with utmost caution, for Death is omnipresent, ever ready to seize the unwary and consign them to a fate unimaginable." Her voice dropped to a sinister whisper, compelling me to lean closer to the flickering flames to catch her words.

"For me," she says, her voice tinged with a hint of sorrow, "my heart was my weakness. Death knew what I was concealing: memories of those I once held dearest. I had safeguarded them within the house of my heart. And when he couldn't unearth them, his fury knew no bounds. So, he reached deep within me and ruthlessly tore out both my heart and my cherished memories." She spoke almost to herself, lost in the painful recollection of that harrowing event.

"This is how I know that the very air in your lungs can be sucked right out of you with a promise of never returning, yet you can still endure this unforgiving reality. This is how I know you can still exist without a pulse or heartbeat."

Her voice returned to full strength, "I don't know if I will ever regain the memories Death stole from me that day, but I can still feel the pain and loss of them deep within me. I find myself longing to recall them, even desperately searching the outer realms for anything that can reawaken them within me and break the curse placed upon me that's causing the amnesia. All I can remember is my pain and the last moments shared with them that continues to haunt me even still. Before then, nothing…"

She trails off, as if attempting to disconnect herself from the pain of the horrors she has already endured and experienced here. It's then that I truly come to realize her desperation to be hidden within this barrier of fire, even at the risk of never escaping. I bite my tongue despite my longing to barrage her with questions.

"I've never been the same since that day," she continues. "I have done things that I know I will regret forever. I have done things I didn't think I could do, and have become someone I never knew I could be. I am in a constant state of suffering paying for these wrongs. You don't know the extent of suffering I have endured!" she cries out, clearly feeling the weight of her own words as she begins to quiet herself so as not to draw attention to herself.

The heaviness of her emotions settles within me as I stand there, watching her words paint a vivid picture upon my flames as I recount her events. I begin to nurture a wish, one not for myself but for her. I wish that she could take my place, even if it means I must confront the terrors she now describes.

"And then," she continues with a change in her composure, "during one of my most unbearable moments of pain and regret, a pillar of fire uniquely different to a trained eye, appeared on the horizon. The mere sight of it was oddly like a beacon of hope for me. It felt as though it was calling out to me, as if it held a secret promise that would help me escape all of my torments and afflictions. I'd turned my back against the oath given to me and had done everything in my power to get here. After all, it was the first natural light I've seen since the night watchers closed up the sky, shutting out the radiance within the small pinholes of the elliptical galaxies. Their actions left us to wander this barren land in sheer and utter darkness, save for the haunting shadows and eerie silhouettes cast by flickering flames," she elaborates.

"The realm is not without light though," she reassures me. "Here it takes on an entirely different meaning and purpose. The concept of natural light was banished, for He no longer graces us with His presence. Instead, the feeble glimmers that pierce the darkness emanate from sinister forces.

"Do you remember the traps I mentioned earlier?" she asks, her pause waiting for my reply before continuing.

"Yes, of course," I respond, my voice tinged with anticipation as I brace myself for what she might reveal next.

"This light, devoid of divine origin, serves as a haunting reminder of our abandonment, forcing us to navigate this realm under the watchful, evil gaze of powers long detached from heavenly benevolence," she chillingly describes.

"Light has been banished?" I mimic, attempting to grasp her meaning. "What do you mean 'light now emanates from sinister forces?'"

"Well, if you dare to tread the paths to the East, you'll catch sight of an ominous glow that breaches the firmament within the lands of Gehenna. But be warned," she advises, "the nature of this light is born from and sustained by the most heinous of evils. Here, you'll find the infamous Valley of Hinnom, where the echoes of ancient horrors have not faded but instead reverberate into the land of the living. Sinister rituals, including the abhorrent practice of child sacrifices and abortions, continue unabated all orchestrated under the malevolent gaze of Death and his chosen acolytes. The very air is tainted with the suffocating stench of decay, and the ground seems to tremble beneath the weight of sins, both ancient and ongoing, that have scarred this forsaken land.

"It's curious," she muses, ensnaring my imagination with horror and a myriad of unanswered questions, yet denying me the chance to pose a single one, "how easily you can adapt to what's been taken away. It's curious how, even in the depths of total darkness, you begin to discern that darkness itself harbors its own shades and contrasts

138

to the extent that you start to forget what light ever meant. You entertain the notion that darkness was the sole existence, even from the dawn of time, erasing any recollection of light until all your senses are attuned to the color of black. Sometimes, the adjustment takes longer than you think, even after you believe you've fully acclimated. Your mind has yet to fully embrace the newfound truth; the truth of becoming a child of the darkness, born from and nurtured by the very essence of shadow." She concludes her reflection, amused somehow by something she's recollected but isn't divulging.

Once again, a million thoughts come over me in the comments she's made but no sooner can I voice a single question when she starts up again, as if a whole new personality just took over.

"You've barely scratched the surface of the darkness that envelops this place," she asserts with a trace of anger in her voice. "And you can't understand the unending restlessness that consumes us. It's a restlessness born of sheer exhaustion because we must keep moving here. If we stand idle, even for a moment, we become vulnerable to the small and unseen pestilence lurking in the shadows, lurking in the dirt. They seize the opportunity to attach themselves to us, burrowing into our flesh and minds to feed on our thoughts, reducing us to nothing more than wriggling worms as we become paralyzed by their condemnation.

"I've witnessed them, you know," she says, pausing for a moment to gauge my belief in her words.

"You witnessed what?" I finally manage to ask, now able to interject without interruption.

"I've seen the madness, the gnashing of teeth, the worms that infest the minds of those who are lost here," she continues, her voice filled with a mix of anguish and conviction.

"Sojourners," she interjects abruptly. "That's what we call them.

"In their past lives, they may have been important, perhaps even royalty. But here, they have no following, no worshippers, no loyalists, or whatever you'd like to call them. No one cares about where they are or who they once were. So . . . they wander, never finding respite and perpetually plagued by the incessant whispers of the little worms. 'Worthless!' 'Meaningless!' 'Forgotten!' These words echo incessantly.

"The Reapers don't want them, and even the flames ignore their existence. It's as if their hell consists of being deemed worthless and abandoned by everything, save for the creatures within this realm that feed on the dead. Those creatures, impartial to everything else, share a singular sentiment—indifference. The only thing these lost souls cared about in life was the perception of others. Here, not even the pests care about their fate," she concludes, her voice heavy with the weight of this grim revelation.

As I listen to her speak, I can't help but wonder about the extensive encounters she must have had with these unfortunate souls in the past, which has led her to speak of them with such harshness. It's almost as if she derives a peculiar satisfaction from recounting their fate, as if she revels in the idea that hell itself seems to have deliberately erased or ignored their existence. For individuals who were once consumed by their public image, perhaps the ultimate punishment lies in the loss of the very thing they held most dear—their identity.

"What's even more amusing," she continues, seemingly unrelenting in her criticism, "is that I've encountered some who are so utterly consumed by their sense of loss that they lie motionless in the dirt. They're no longer capable of movement or coherent thought; their minds are inwardly tormented, devoured by the relentless gnawing of the worms that have fully consumed their once-vibrant thoughts.

"And," she adds with a tone of mockery, "if you listen closely, you can hear them muttering absurdities to themselves, endlessly repeating tales of their own greatness." She chuckles darkly. "As if anyone here cares about them anymore."

She resumes her restless pacing, her silhouette moving back and forth.

"When I finally reached your flame," she continues, her voice imbued with urgency and a hint of dread, "I realized that a voice was emanating from within—within what I had hoped would be my sanctuary. It called upon the forbidden name of the Most High, awakening the dragons lurking in the depths," she murmurs, her expression grave with a heavy sense of foreboding. "The Reapers responded to that call; they came for you."

She suddenly stops and turns towards me, her gaze penetrating as if she can see into the depths of my soul and finds something displeasing.

"It should have been you," she seethes, her voice dripping with anger. "You should have been the one captured. You should have forfeited your claim to the refuge of this flame. You should have faced judgment. Yet here you sit, wallowing in your own suffering, declaring yourself a wretched soul, a prisoner trapped within, when you don't even grasp the darkness we endure out here, the ceaseless terror that haunts us," she says, her words tinged with both accusation and a deep, resonant despair.

Her words linger in the atmosphere, their significance weighing heavily upon me.

"I . . . I'm at a loss for words," I admit, breaking the silence that had enveloped us. "I had no idea. I had no knowledge of what is out there; I only knew what was in here. I would have never thought that what I was experiencing was in any way good."

"What can one say," she murmurs, her voice trembling, "when words have lost their meaning? When the very power they once held to breathe life now carries only the weight of death and deception? What words can be spoken when anything uttered is destined to transform into a curse?" Her words fall softly, as if carrying the gravity of the situation with them.

The flame continues its mesmerizing dance, its flickering undulations casting her silhouette into an uncertain and ethereal performance, and all around us, a profound silence reigns. Her words, like arrows, pierce through the layers of my being, sinking deep into the core of my heart and taking root in the hidden chambers of my soul.

In this moment, it becomes clear that she possesses a deeper understanding than I ever will. She comprehends the profound question of where one might genuinely desire to exist in a realm meticulously crafted to test and overcome the human spirit in every conceivable manner imaginable.

As I watch the flames waver and weave their hypnotic tale, I find myself pondering the profound implications of her words, realizing that the answers to our questions may lie in the very heart of the enigmatic dance of light and shadow before us.

Seated upon the scorching earth, encompassed by the relentless blaze that serves as the confines of my own infernal prison, I find myself deep in contemplation.

Am I, in fact, the fortunate one to be ensnared within this unending flame? I wonder, as the flames dance and flicker around me, casting an eerie glow on the dreary ground.

There's no sense of luck in this surreal realm. Survival, or the illusion of survival, is a twisted dance with the unnatural, a malevolent waltz orchestrated to elicit pleas from those who reject the handiwork of the Creator. The objective seems clear—to warmly embrace those who disdain the uniqueness instilled in us by the Creator. Hell has mastered the art of unraveling the purpose for which we were uniquely crafted. It excels in dismantling the divine image and fingerprints that define our very beings.

Reflecting on the events that led me to this moment and the understanding of the intentionality of my action that night to kill myself, the reality of it all set it. *Suicide, the act of rejecting God.* It's perplexing how everything hinged on a seemingly simple choice when I roamed the realms of the living. My rejection of God equated to rejecting life itself and discarding the inherent characteristics within God that grant us our humanity. The consequence: stripped of all His fruits and the personal qualities He represents, what remains is Hell—a desolate void where the vibrant tapestry of life unravels into nothingness.

As I dwell on these thoughts, I find myself needing answers to the myriad of questions that have surfaced—questions about judgment, the Reapers, the enigmatic lord she keeps mentioning, and so many others that remain unspoken. Despite the mostly distressing or disparaging nature of our exchanges, I'm grateful for the mere presence of someone here with me. I long for more dialogue, a chance to understand the intricacies of this realm.

Her voice reaches out to me once more, this time imbued with a gentleness that seems to suggest a different persona has emerged or that she is finally beginning to open up.

"What is your name?" she whispers, her voice now calm and composed.

I'm strangely taken aback by the question. "What?" I stammer, genuinely surprised by its relevance in a place like this, where names and identities hold little meaning.

"What is your name?" she repeats, gently but insistently.

"My name? It's . . . um, it's Christopher," I manage, still uncertain why she's asking, wondering what significance my name holds in this bleak place.

"Christopher," she says softly. "My son's name . . ." She begins to whisper to herself before abruptly shifting the topic. "All this time, and we haven't had proper introductions. My sincerest apologies. My name is Rochelle," she announces with an unexpectedly cheerful tone.

"Rochelle," I say aloud, "It is a pleasure to meet you, Rochelle. I am glad to make . . ."

But she interrupts me abruptly, her voice filled with an unexpected urgency. "Christopher," she interjects. "I think I know what you are!"

CHAPTER 11

The Ancient Ones

Luke 19:40

"I tell you," he replied, "if they keep quiet, the stones will cry out."

1 Enoch 1:6-7

And all shall be smitten with fear, and the Watchers shall quake, and great fear and trembling shall seize them unto the ends of the earth. And the high mountains shall be shaken, and the high hills shall be made low, and shall melt like wax before the flame. And the earth shall be wholly rent in sunder, and all that is upon the earth shall perish, and there shall be a judgment upon all men.

1 Peter 2:4-5

As you come to him, the living Stone—rejected by humans but chosen by God and precious to him—you also, like living stones, are being built into a spiritual house to be a holy priesthood, offering spiritual sacrifices acceptable to God through Jesus Christ.

Genesis 6:1-4

When human beings began to increase in number on the earth and daughters were born to them, the sons of God saw that the daughters of humans were beautiful, and they married any of them they chose. Then the Lord said, "My Spirit will not contend with humans forever, for they are mortal; their days will be a hundred and twenty years." The Nephilim were on the earth in those days— and also afterward—when the sons of God went to the daughters of humans and had children by them. They were the heroes of old, men of renown."

1 Enoch 6:1-2

And it came to pass when the children of men had multiplied that in those days were born unto them beautiful and comely daughters. And the angels, the children of the heaven, saw and lusted after them, and said to one another: "Come, let us choose us wives from among the children of men and beget us children."

"Christopher," she says again, her voice now carrying an air of newfound confidence and a hint of realization of the profound importance of her inquiry, "I have a question for you. If you answer me with complete honesty, I may be able to reveal valuable insights about your own identity and your current position here. I might even have the ability to unveil the path that lies ahead for you, and offer insights into what eternity has in store. Some of this knowledge may come from your firsthand experiences, while some of it might pose more challenging questions without apparent significance to you.

"Nevertheless, I can assist you in sharpening your senses to piece together this puzzle. After all, it must be quite challenging to be confined behind a fiery barrier since your arrival with no answers or understanding of your whereabouts."

Her offer, while enticing, seems impossible to accept because she refuses to acknowledge the truth of my earlier ignorance.

She continues, her voice laced with a mixture of frustration and resolve.

"I was at the very least able to look out upon the scape of this land when I awoke here. Granted, I was not given much opportunity to explore before being *thrown to the wolves*, so to speak. But, I digress."

As she paces back and forth on the other side of the flame, her anxious steps and restless demeanor make it clear she is unwilling to wait for my response.

"But you—you've had no choice but to play a guessing game since arriving here. You have no idea what this realm looks like and the possibilities that might be waiting for you in it. It may not be as bad as all that, you know. I've heard that some have even moved on from this level, a place the Reapers have claimed this cursed land as their hunting grounds and where Death chooses to remain so that he may still practice his sorcery. Let me be your eyes, not only for right now, but also for the future, so that you may know what to expect."

"What do you mean?" I ask. "Is this some sort of witchcraft that allows me to be open with you?" Until now, Rochelle appeared to be a friend, or at least a helpful soul. But Hell is full of lies and deceits.

"No. You misunderstand me," she assures me. "I'm not requesting you to engage in any rituals or seances. I'm merely asking you to respond to my questions with as much openness and honesty as you can muster. And when you encounter . . . certain revelations, promise me that you'll acknowledge them so that together, we can unravel this mystery."

"You assume I want to know my fate," I reply, questioning her motives in wanting so badly to understand my situation.

"Do you know how long eternity is, my dear boy?" she says with an exaggerated sigh, fully aware that I don't know the answer.

"Eternity is not determined or set on a scale of seasons or time, like that in life. Eternity is set into motion by position. Position and power are all that matter anymore and are determined by the events and decisions you made in life. We all have a position to fill, whether we like it or not, or are aware of it or not; it changes nothing.

"The only thing I offer is a way for you to increase your possible position because of an authority and power you may possess that can help in your ascension, and therefore, mine as well. Do you really want to keep stewing in your flame or are you interested in discovering if there's something you can do about it?" She presents the question to me.

"Here, some are controlled by fear, endlessly fleeing from the Reapers. Then, there are those who learn to control their fear, making themselves exempt from the Reapers' hunt. These individuals, who master this crucial skill, rise above mere torment. Instead of being trapped in constant suffering, they are given a new purpose, one that grants them power.

"However, this power is deeply intertwined with knowledge. I didn't acquire my knowledge easily; it came through great effort and hardship. Yet, I am willing to share this valuable knowledge with you . . . for a price, of course."

"What price?" I say, shaking my head in bewilderment. "Do you think me a fool? You've just shared horror stories from your time here, enough to make anyone want to hide within this flame to escape it all. Then you condemn me for wanting to get out of this flame. Now, you hint at the possibility of having hope, purpose, power, and moving to more acceptable levels? Clearly, whatever you seek from me—especially with your mention of a price—might be more than I'm willing to offer," I retort.

"Christopher," she says, her voice filled with exasperation, "I shared my story with you to make you aware of the genuine horrors that dwell within this place. I have been through far too much to ever have a chance of moving on from the position to which I am enslaved in this realm. I am one of the many who are controlled by the fear that dwells in this place, leaving me always on the run, always in search. But you—all you have seen is fire, and it is this wall of fire that has shielded you from being exposed to the outer realm. You still have a chance to rule over things such as fear, instead of fear ruling over you. My motives, my actions, my words are all controlled by my master," she goes on to say.

"I merely offer my knowledge as recompense for your position, of which you are clearly unaware, in hopes of gaining favor from my lord and master. Will you accept my offer?" she asks.

"After all, I am likely the only one who may be willing or even able to assist you with the means to actually carry it out," she finishes, waiting for me to respond to her offer.

"If I am being completely honest, I don't wish to be here anymore," I reply, my answer laden with anticipation of the possibility of leaving my cell. "I can clearly recognize your desire to be here, although I don't think it will be what you think it is either. However, that is a fair offer, and one that I agree to accept."

"Good!" she quickly responds. "From the moment I approached you and your flame, I knew there was something different about you; something . . . special." She lets her words hang in the air for a moment.

"You could be shielded now because you are not yet ready to enter into your purpose; into your position. But there's power in position! When the Reapers came, it was almost as if they could not touch you or sense you. When you should have been their next victim, another was taken in your place, weren't they? You hold power that you don't yet know." Her words leave me speechless, lost in my own thoughts. It's clear she is withholding information from me.

"Perhaps you could even avoid judgment altogether," she finishes her thought as if wondering what limits such a person like that may actually possess.

"You might be in the place of the damned, my dear boy, but you might be destined for higher levels where torment and pain are not allowed to touch you. Since my arrival, no one has ever commanded such authority."

I gulp, feeling myself tremble with excitement at her words, and for a moment, I allow myself to believe it could be true.

Then, as if she can read my thoughts, she asks, "Shall we find out if there's any truth in this? Shall we find out who you are? No . . . who you could become?" She waits, allowing me proper time to let her words soak in and take root.

There's that question of hers again, I think to myself. Like she doubts everything I already told her of who I am, and yet, I am beginning to wonder if I even know who I am anymore. Maybe this woman from the other side of the flame can tell me; maybe she cannot. Either way, her words are convincing, and her voice rings with promise, and I feel desperate to believe anything again.

"What do you want me to do?" I ask eagerly, my voice crackling with anticipation at the possibility of leaving this wretched flame and escaping my torment with the potential of becoming something— dare I say—great in the eyes of Hell.

"First, listen carefully. There is much I need to share with you before delving into the substance of the story," she says. "Afterward, promise to provide me with your honest answer when I am ready to ask."

"How will a story determine anything?" I inquire.

"It will determine everything," she asserts. "Are you willing?"

I hesitate, then respond, "Yes."

"Very well. Let us begin:

This story was passed down to me by the ancient ones—those who have been here so long that their souls no longer resemble the beings they were before they fell from the heavens. Once celestial and radiant, they have become twisted and hardened, merging with the very rock that surrounds them. Their hearts turned to stone, and soon after, their spirits followed suit, becoming cold and unfeeling.

Even the rocks themselves seem to cry out, emitting anguished wails that resonate throughout the cavernous depths. These mournful sounds emanate from their elevated positions in the guarded and forbidden lands, far beyond Death's forsaken realms to the East. This is a place shrouded in mystery and peril, where few dare to tread. The cries echo through the blood-torn landscape, a haunting symphony of sorrow and despair that reverberates through the air, serving as a chilling reminder of the ancient and tormented souls that inhabit this forbidden territory.

It was these sorrowful cries, echoing endlessly from the rock faces of Dolor, that piqued my curiosity. If there were any here with answers about the time before, perhaps these beings would be willing to share. Or so I hoped when I began my quest to find them. I became determined to uncover the identities and stories of these ancient beings, to understand what could cause such profound transformation and despair. I sought to know the truth about our masters here, if such a thing existed, and to leverage this knowledge for my own gain. After all, their tales are etched into the very fabric of this place, each sorrowful note a testament to the torment and history of those who dwell here. How could they not possess something of extreme importance if they were so well-guarded and locked away, with someone unwilling for their voices to be heard?

"Finding the ancient ones was no small feat," she begins, her eyes distant as if reliving the journey. "I spent months gathering fragments of lore, whispered speculation, and cryptic messages from those who had dared to speak of the forbidden lands. Each piece of information led me deeper into Death's forsaken realms, towards the East, where the air grew thick with despair and the landscape twisted into nightmarish forms."

"Why would you seek them out?" I question her motives. "What would lead you to that realm if few would dare travel there? Surely, it was more than just curiosity. I don't believe you're being . . ."

"IT'S NONE OF YOUR BUSINESS!" she lashes out. "I . . . I had my reasons, and we will leave it at that, or would you rather I stop with my story and leave you to your fate?" she asks with a smug confidence, knowing I will concede.

"I'm sorry, I didn't mean to offend. Please carry on," I express to her satisfaction, knowing she was right that I didn't want her to leave.

She continues, her voice tinged with clear frustration from my outburst:

The journey began with a perilous trek through the Wailing Forest, a place where the trees seemed to whisper and scream, their branches clawing at the sky. The forest was alive with shadows, creatures of darkness that seemed to watch my every move. I armed myself with wards and charms, symbols of protection gleaned from old texts and muttered incantations, and pressed on, relying on my instincts to guide me through the maze of despair.

Beyond the forest lay the Shattered Plains, a desolate expanse of jagged crevasses and treacherous bogs. The earth itself seemed to resist my passage, shifting and cracking beneath my feet. I navigated the terrain with caution, using an old map that had been pieced together from fragments of ancient scrolls. Each step was a calculated risk, and more than once, I found myself teetering on the brink of a chasm, the darkness below promising a swift and brutal end.

As I approached the foothills of the Forbidden Escarpment, the true challenges began. The air crackled with an unseen energy, a supernatural force that seemed to push back against any who dared to ascend. I could feel the power in the very ground beneath me, a throbbing pulse that set my teeth on edge. Undeterred, I pressed forward, relying on every ounce of knowledge and skill I had acquired.

I encountered the first of the guardians at the base of the escarpment. Massive stone golems, animated by ancient magic, stood sentinel, their eyes glowing with an otherworldly light. They moved with a terrifying grace, their stone limbs crashing down with earth-shaking force. I used a combination of agility and spells to evade them, drawing on my understanding of their patterns and weaknesses to slip past their watchful gaze.

Higher up, I faced the spectral sentinels, ghostly apparitions that floated silently through the air. They were drawn to any sign of life, their ethereal forms passing through solid rock as if it were air. I crafted a cloak of shadows, an enchantment that allowed me to blend with the darkness and move unseen. It was a delicate balance, maintaining the spell while navigating the treacherous path, but I managed to slip past the sentinels, my heart pounding in my chest.

Finally, at the summit, I reached the entrance to the ancient ones' sanctuary, a cavern hidden behind a waterfall of liquid light. The water shimmered with a blinding radiance, a barrier that seemed impenetrable. I recited an incantation I had discovered in the depths of an old grimoire, the words resonating with the energy of the waterfall. Slowly, the light parted, revealing a narrow passage beyond.

Inside, the air was thick with the weight of ages. The walls of the cavern glowed with a faint luminescence, casting eerie shadows that danced in the corners of my vision. I followed the winding path, deeper and deeper, until I reached a vast chamber where the ancient ones awaited.

They were unlike anything I had ever seen—figures of stone and shadow, their forms etched with the lines of countless years. Their eyes glowed with an inner light, a mixture of wisdom and sorrow. As I approached, they stirred, their voices echoing in my mind rather than my ears.

"You have come far," they intoned, their voices a chorus of time itself. "Please, sit with us. What is it you seek?"

With a deep breath, I began to speak, laying bare my questions and desires. They listened, their expressions inscrutable, and then, slowly, they began to share their secrets–prophecies of old that hold the power of life and death. The truths they revealed were both wondrous and terrifying, knowledge that had been guarded for eons, now laid bare before me. Knowledge that, if revealed to the wrong principalities, could lead me right back here to share their fate or worse.

It was through their stories that I began to understand the depths of their despair, the reasons for their transformation, and the power that still pulsed within their ancient forms. And as I listened, I knew that this knowledge, hard-won and priceless, would be the key to navigating the treacherous landscape of my own existence.

I will admit, Christopher, fear gripped me with thoughts that if I listened to them, I might be turned into one of them or somehow controlled by their words, as I had seen happen to others. Nonetheless, I stayed. I remember thinking at the time, What kind of prophecy could hold the power of life and death and be so threatening to the dominion of

Hell that these 'ancient ones' would be imprisoned and guarded for their knowledge of it?

My heart longed to know.

Knowledge here is so powerful that it can mean the difference between unlimited pain or unrestricted access. So, despite my fears, I sat and listened on as the ancient ones continued to tell me their story. The ancient ones recounted the event with a gravity that made the air around me heavy.

They told me there was a sudden shift in the celestial cosmos, near the seventh heaven where golden wheels spin.

Casting light through the void of nothingness, the forbidden door of Time slowly began to open. As it creaked ajar, the whole universe trembled, resonating with an unearthly vibration. The darkness, once trapped in Hell and imprisoned within the portal gates of Sheol, was suddenly released. It poured into the physical world with a vengeance, a torrent of shadow and malice seeking to consume everything in its path.

The heavens shook with the force of the breach, celestial beings scrambling to contain the chaos. The golden wheels of the seventh heaven spun rapidly, their light battling against the encroaching darkness. This was no ordinary event; it was a cataclysm that aimed to disrupt the very fabric of creation. The darkness, once confined and subdued since the fall, now roamed free, intent on seizing a dominion it had no rightful authority over.

As the ancient ones spoke, I could feel the weight of their words, the sorrow and regret embedded in their story. It was a tale of betrayal and loss, of a cosmic balance disrupted, and the ceaseless struggle to restore what had been torn asunder.

The ancient ones spoke of the havoc this unleashed force wrought upon the physical world. The forbidden door of Time, once opened, could not be closed, and its dark legacy continued to haunt both the heavens and the Earth.

"From what I could gather," Rochelle paused, her expression grave, "the door to Time was created but never intended to be opened.

Yet, there it was, slowly moving on its ancient hinges for all to see. How or why it was opening would not be understood until much later.

As it creaked open, it exposed a chasm between worlds that had long been sealed. The forgotten fallen within Hell, those ancient spirits of unimaginable wrath, began to unleash their fury upon the physical realm. For generations, this fury spilled over, corrupting and consuming the legacies of men. The lines between the divine and the damned were shattered, as the once angelic hosts now perverted the lines of kings. They fornicated with their women, seeking to corrupt bloodlines and bring about the destruction of an entire species. What was once pure and noble became tainted, as these fallen beings sought to undermine the very fabric of human existence, ensuring their malevolent influence would endure through the ages.

The world was inundated with the lies spoken through counterfeit gods and false prophets, each deceit more insidious than the last. These false deities and prophets, born from the depths of Hell, spread their influence like a plague, twisting truths and sowing discord among the hearts of men.

The once clear line between the divine and the damned blurred. Humanity found itself unable to discern truth from illusion, caught in a relentless storm of chaos and despair. Entire civilizations crumbled under their deceit. The heavens had to intercede on behalf of the few uncorrupted lines of men, purging the earth of the perversions of these abominations that sought to destroy what the Creator had purposed. This intervention was to preserve the story of the One to come.

So, the waters overtook the earth, bringing about a shift not only in the physical realm but also within the heavens. The celestial bodies themselves trembled and realigned as if responding to the profound upheaval below. The constellations shifted and the very fabric of the cosmos seemed to ripple with the consequences of the great deluge.

The separation of celestial bodies, otherwise known as the Veil, marked a significant realignment within the realms. The heavens and the Earth, once in harmonious alignment, now stood apart in every way, *a Veil of divine origin created to separate each with its own purpose and destiny. In the beginning, the Veil was merely a physical separation, a curtain divinely crafted of blue, purple, and scarlet yarn and finely twisted linen, with cherubim woven into it. It represented the separation from the Almighty God and His beloved creation during the fall of the first son and daughter of mankind. But after the Watchers defiled themselves with the daughters of Eve, creating the Nephilim, this separation became necessary to cleanse the spreading stain and purify the bloodlines once again.*

As the realms were divided, the divine hosts took their places in the newly structured heavens, their duties and roles redefined in this new order. The Watchers were further cast down, their influence confined and limited, while the untainted remained in positions of guardianship and guidance over the new world.

"Were they sharing with you the story of Noah and the great flood?" I ask. "Do you know who they were referencing when they mentioned the prophecy?"

"Noah?" she replies, taking a moment to consider my question. "I am sorry, but that name was not referenced in their recount to me. The ancient ones were sharing something of great significance and wouldn't allow my interruptions. I don't recall names unless they were very specific to the story. So, in the same manner they shared with me, I ask that you allow me to recall their stories," she finishes before continuing with her recount of their tale.

This opening of the forbidden door was a catastrophe beyond measure, an event that not only altered the course of history but threatened the very essence of existence itself. The rage and sorrow of the forgotten fallen were palpable, their cries echoing through the ages, a haunting reminder of the price paid for curiosity and defiance.

On Earth, the waters receded, revealing a landscape cleansed and renewed. Humanity, now given a second chance, began to rebuild from the ruins of the past. The survivors carried with them the memories of the great flood and the divine intervention that had saved them. They were acutely aware of the price paid for their previous transgressions and the importance of maintaining the purity of their bloodlines and the integrity of their societies.

The heavens watched over this rebirth with a vigilant eye, their celestial order reflecting the newfound balance. The division between realms ensured that the forces of darkness could no longer easily infiltrate the physical world. The ancient ones, now silent witnesses, continued to guard their secrets. Their tales served as a reminder of the cataclysmic events that reshaped the celestial planes and the truth of those responsible for such destruction.

But as difficult as it had become to corrupt the lines of men directly, Hell found new ways to infiltrate humanity. By their own words and actions, mankind unwittingly opened portals, inviting the powers and principalities of the air to continue their relentless effort to destroy the lines of men. Whispers of deceit and temptation flowed through these self-made gateways, exploiting human weaknesses and turning their own desires against them.

Hell's influence crept in through subtle means, weaving lies into the fabric of society and sowing discord once again. These dark forces used mankind's ambitions, fears, and desires as tools of corruption, manipulating them to further their own agenda. The once-clear distinction between right and wrong blurred again, as people fell prey to the insidious influence that sought to undermine their newfound hope.

The ancient ones watched with sorrow as humanity struggled once more against these unseen enemies. They knew that while the physical barriers had been strengthened, the true battle lay within the hearts and minds of men. The stories they guarded held the key to resisting this new wave of corruption, but it was up to mankind to seek out and embrace this wisdom.

But, a new authority was being awakened within the line of men that would bring salvation against the continued influence of destruction that Hell maintained. There was a prophecy from ancient times that promised the birth of a Savior whose authority would cause a shift in power, not just in the physical realm, but in the spiritual as well.

Something, or someone, had entered into the world and gone unnoticed that would shift the tides and break covenants long established that only a God could break. He, this unassuming Man, had stolen the attention of the entire universe—from the heavens above to the dark underworlds below—through an act of love. An act of sacrifice so great that it would shift the course of humanity for those to come and those once considered lost as well.

The sacrifice He would make would create a deep laceration in time, tearing apart the foundations laid by the sins of man since the fall of Adam. From that pivotal moment, covenants and dominion would be forever transformed.

"Never had the ancient ones witnessed anything like it, nor would creation see anything like it again," Rochelle emphasized, her tone grave, ensuring I understood the magnitude of the moment she described.

This mysterious Man, whose identity was shrouded in both legend and prophecy, seemed to inhabit the physical plane, yet His position was mysteriously suspended between Heaven and Hell. His existence defied the boundaries of the mortal world, embodying a paradox of divinity and humanity intertwined.

A legitimate threat to the kingdom of darkness was forming from this sacrifice on Earth. To restore the old power structure, Hell needed to attack the very thing threatening its sovereignty. Hell, perceiving this enigmatic figure as a dire threat, acted with unprecedented haste and aggression. The dark forces sought to maintain the generational curses they had claimed dominion over since the dawn of mankind. Their desperation to uphold the status quo of suffering and bondage was palpable, driven by the fear of losing their grip on the souls they had enslaved.

The Earth that we once knew as our own turned black with Hell's unleashed sin. Even the sun in the sky refused to give its warmth and light to that dark moment, allowing the cold breath of Death to kiss Earth's soil and fill its waters with a darkness that draped across the land. This Man, through His impending sacrifice, was poised to challenge the very essence of Hell's authority. The spiritual realms trembled in anticipation, knowing that His act would not only disrupt the established order but also offer a path to redemption and liberation from the ancient curses that had long shackled humanity.

As Rochelle's words sank in, the profound implications of this Man's mission became clear. He was more than a savior; He was a harbinger of a new era, one where the power dynamics between good and evil would be irrevocably altered. His sacrifice would resonate through the ages, a beacon of hope and a testament to the ultimate triumph of light over darkness.

Tens of thousands of legions of Hell's armies stood against an opposing army of only one. More curious, though, was that the One they were so afraid of was already nailed in a posture of defenselessness, leading many in the lower ranks to question the Dark Lord's motives to mobilize such a large offensive attack. Why Hell sent everything, every legion and every creature after a single man, no one knew at the time. But now, it is all too clear what the dark one feared.

Hell had made a magnificent show of destruction that day. As the seemingly lifeless body hung, with Death nearby to welcome this Son of Man, no Man was there to meet Death after His last breath was given. The defeat against that army of just One was on stage for all of creation to see—though Hell would not understand this yet, for it seemed a victory in the eyes of the dark forces. All of mankind was watching the powers of the universe at war, whether or not they were aware of the importance of the outcome. For a moment, the Earth seemed to be lost to Hell forever, and all was falling apart.

The prophecy foretold the birth of a king and would be marked by a sign in the heavens. While that sign went unnoticed by all but four, Satan and his armies lay in wait for the birth of the child who would be known as the King of the Jews. As the prophecy stated:

> A great sign appeared in heaven: a woman clothed with the sun, with the moon under her feet and a crown of twelve stars on her head. She was pregnant and cried out in pain as she was about to give birth. Then another sign appeared in heaven: an enormous red dragon with seven heads and ten horns and seven crowns on its heads. Its tail swept a third of the stars out of the sky and flung them to the earth. The dragon stood in front of the woman who was about to give birth, so that it might devour her child the moment he was born. She gave birth to a son, a male child, who "will rule all the nations with an iron scepter." And her child was snatched up to God and to His throne.

They told me that the prophecy was always on Satan's mind. He was ever vigilant, studying the stars, the ancient texts, and the prophecies in an effort to intercept the child and thwart the Almighty's plans. Little did he know, the seemingly insignificant child would be the Son of the Living God.

So on the day of the great battle, the earth shook violently, causing the dark multitudes to fear what was not understood. Death himself, draping his cloak around the now lifeless body on the cross, was left longing. But in the midst of Hell's victory, the same power that was thought to be lost, suddenly was found at the gates of Sheol.

It was then that the ancient ones told me the significance of this Man and the grave mistake Hell made in fulfilling the very prophecies they were so adamant to prevent," Rochelle points out to me to make sure I would not miss it.

As man-made footprints soaked in crimson shades of blood were seen heading towards the Gates of Sheol, it became clear to all that humanity's darkest hour was merely a ruse for humanity's greatest victory. After His final breath in life, an incomprehensible power surged through the realms, breaching Hell with an unstoppable vengeance. The gates of Sheol, towering and formidable now lay defenseless as the Son of Man walked, uncontested, to the base of their immense and intimidating might.

CHAPTER 12

The Prophecy

Psalms 49:15, 86:13, 89:48

*But God will redeem me from the realm of the dead; he will surely
take me to himself. For great is your love toward me; you have
delivered me from the depths, from the realm of the dead.
Who can live and not see Death, or who can
escape the powers of the grave?*

Matthew 12:40

*For as Jonah was three days and three nights in the belly of a huge
fish, so the Son of Man will be three days and three nights in the
heart of the earth.*

Matthew 27:50-52

*And when Jesus had cried out again in a loud voice,
he gave up his spirit.
At that moment the curtain of the temple was torn in
two from top to bottom. The earth shook, the rocks
split and the tombs broke open. The bodies of many
holy people who had died were raised to life.*

John 5:24-25

*Very truly I tell you, whoever hears my word and
believes him who sent me has eternal life and will not
be judged but has crossed over from death to life.*

Very truly I tell you, a time is coming and has
now come when the dead will hear the voice of the
Son of God and those who hear will live.

Acts 2:31

Seeing what was to come, he spoke of the resurrection of the
Messiah, that he was not abandoned to the realm of the dead, nor
did his body see decay.

Colossians 2:13-15

When you were dead in your sins and in the uncircumcision of your
flesh, God made you alive with Christ. He forgave us all our sins,
having canceled the charge of our legal indebtedness, which stood
against us and condemned us; he has taken it away, nailing it to the
cross. And having disarmed the powers and authorities, he made
a public spectacle of them, triumphing over them by the cross.

Ephesians 4:7-10

But to each one of us grace has been given
as Christ apportioned it. This is why it says:
"When he ascended on high, he took many captives
and gave gifts to his people."
What does "he ascended" mean except that he also
descended to the lower, earthly regions? He who
descended is the very one who ascended higher than
all the heavens, in order to fill the whole universe.

1 Peter 3:18-19

For Christ also suffered once for sins, the righteous for the
unrighteous, to bring you to God. He was put to death in the body
but made alive in the Spirit. After being made alive, he went and
made proclamation to the imprisoned spirits—

Hebrews 11:39-40, 12:22-24

These were all commended for their faith, yet none of them received
what had been promised, since God had planned something better
for us so that only together with us would they be made perfect.

You have come to thousands upon thousands of angels
in joyful assembly, to the church of the firstborn, whose
names are written in heaven. You have come to God, the

*Judge of all, to the spirits of the righteous made perfect, to
Jesus the mediator of a new covenant, and to the sprinkled
blood that speaks a better word than the blood of Abel.*

Revelation 1:17-18

*Then he placed his right hand on me and said: "Do not be afraid.
I am the First and the Last. I am the Living One; I was dead, and
now look, I am alive for ever and ever! And I hold the keys of death
and Hades."*

My thoughts are racing with questions pertaining to every spoken word. The truth is almost too much to comprehend. *How did she come by this information?* I wonder to myself. More troubling is the thought of whether or not what she is telling me is even credible or just a ruse to gain trust or something else that I would be unable to repay. Despite my concerns, I dare not question her motives aloud or upset her. Instead, I listen quietly as she continues her story about the ancient ones.

Reaching skyward with an ominous grandeur, the Gates of Sheol have long symbolized the ultimate barrier between life and eternal torment. Their dark, iron-bound structure exuded a menacing power, designed to repel any force attempting to breach them. The impregnable nature of these gates was further ensured by the Great Leviathan, a guardian of unparalleled might and terror, whose very presence struck fear into the hearts of all who dared approach.

However, as if predestined, the once formidable guardian of these gates no longer stood watch. Fourteen hundred years ago, Jehovah Jireh defeated the Leviathan and offered its remains to His chosen people, knowing the day would come when His Son would need entry. In response, the kingdom of darkness offered the once revered celestial beings, the Chalkydri in replacement of the Leviathan.

The Chalkydri, creatures of myth and legend, were not mere guardians but living embodiments of the realm's fierce and unyielding power. Their serpentine bodies coiled with a fluid grace, yet exuded an aura of raw, untamed energy. Each movement was a dance of danger, their scales shimmering with the heat of an eternal fire that coursed through their veins.

Their wings, vast and formidable, were not just appendages for flight but fiery extensions of their very essence. They unfurled like vast canopies of flame, casting an eerie glow that both illuminates and intimidates. When they beat them, the air itself ignited, rippling with waves of scorching heat and light that could sear the soul of any who dared to come too close.

Perched high in their watchtowers, the Chalkydri were ever-vigilant, their blazing eyes scanning the horizon with a relentless intensity. These eyes, like molten orbs, were windows to an ancient wisdom and a boundless fury, ready to incinerate any threat to the realm's sanctity. No mortal or spirit could escape their penetrating gaze; it was said that to look into the eyes of a Chalkydri was to see one's deepest fears reflected back a hundredfold.

Their presence at the gates was more than a mere deterrent; it was a declaration. To have imprisoned and thereby enslaved one of Heaven's most formidable weapons, now repurposed to guard Hell's most vile creations, was a message for all who would dare oppose the sanctity of the realm. This act was a testament to the absolute power and unyielding authority of the realm showcasing the fate that awaited any who defied its decrees. The very essence of these once-mighty beings, now bound to the task of overseeing the damned, served as a grim reminder of the consequences of rebellion. Their eternal vigilance and fiery presence were a constant warning: the realm's justice was inexorable, and its dominion unassailable.

But, as the Son of Man approached the gates, the Chalkydri, instead of launching the expected assault against His claim, postured themselves in reverent submission to the Man. We watched in astonishment as the fiercest guardians of the realm, anticipated to attack, instead welcomed Him as a friend, bowing before His authority. Their deference was *palpable, as if they had long awaited His arrival to liberate them from their bondage and restore them to their heavenly purpose. The Man continued on unopposed, His eyes fixed resolutely on the gates. The silence of the moment underscored the profound shift in the cosmic order, as the Chalkydri recognized and honored His supreme authority.*

As the chains were revealed by the lifting of the Man's hand, the Chalkydri lowered their heads for their shackles to be removed. In a swift and powerful gesture, the Son of Man broke the chains, shattering them with a radiant burst of light. A crescent portal of shimmering brilliance opened behind Him, casting an ethereal glow that illuminated the dark realm. One by one, the Chalkydri passed through the portal, their fiery forms glowing with renewed vigor as they left the realm of Hell behind. The portal closed with a final, resounding hum, leaving nothing standing between the claimant and His prize. The air was thick with a sense of liberation and destiny fulfilled, as the Son of Man stood alone before the gates, His path clear and His purpose unwavering.

Now, bereft of Leviathan and the Chalkydri, the Gates of Sheol, once thought indestructible, were effortlessly torn from their hinges and discarded as if they were nothing more than fragile relics. The very ground trembled as He cast them aside, and the dark aura that once surrounded them dissipated in the presence of His overwhelming light. The very laws that Death had established were now turned against Death himself by the being who had first bestowed his authority eons ago. The Son of Man, once considered weak, frail, and insignificant by Satan and his legions as He hung upon a wooden cross, now stood at their doorsteps, transformed into something entirely different.

The principalities and powers of Hell believed they had an easy victory in their grasp, poised to take over the Earth and enslave mankind following the supposed fall of this unrecognized King. Little did they know, the true battle had only just begun in the depths of their own realm. This unassuming King was not here merely to reclaim the sanctity of what was once lost; He sought an audience with the very lord of the realm, Death himself.

In order to defeat Death, one must journey past the lands of Sheol and step through the portals of Time to change not only the dominion of Hell but also to fulfill the prophecies of old that govern the powers of Time and all those ensnared by it.

But reaching these portals meant one must traverse past the lair of Death for the portals of Time lay beyond the twelve realms; past the dark cliffs that burned with an endless flame and across the infinite darkness only separated by the great chasm. It was in this place, where Death commanded authority and wielded dominion as one would wield a well-placed dagger.

We watched as He traversed deeper within the depths towards His prize. All the while, Death himself was made the fool, gazing at the empty vessel that hung upon a wooden cross. In a swirl of ash, Death vanished through a portal, leaving the forces of Hell in stunned disbelief at the revelation of their grave mistake. Word quickly spread that the gates were breached, the Chalkydri unaccounted for, and a single warrior marched unopposed towards terrae cadentium—the lands of the fallen.

In a frantic mobilization, Hell descended in a chaotic surge to intercept the Man at the edge of the gates that lead to the twelve realms below. The dark forces unleashed a sudden, surprise assault, summoning every dark magic, curse, and pestilence they could conjure. Shadows twisted into monstrous forms, and the air crackled with the sinister energy of ancient spells. The ground itself seemed to writhe with malevolence as infernal beasts and spectral warriors emerged from the depths, all converging in a desperate attempt to bind Him. The very fabric of Hell bent and distorted in their frenzy, determined to halt His inexorable advance.

Eventually, Hell could not halt His slow and intentional descent to the throne of Death. He trod upon these grounds and confronted the very darkness that had enveloped Him. Legions of demons, commanded by their dark lords, waged war on this one Man. The power they saw in Him was greater than all of them combined, and the fact that He came in mortal form mystified and terrified all who laid eyes upon Him.

The battle was fierce and relentless. Demonic forces unleashed their most potent spells and curses, but the Man moved with unwavering determination, His presence a beacon of light cutting through the oppressive gloom. Each step He took left the ground scorched and trembling, His every gesture radiating an authority that the denizens of Hell had never before encountered.

As He advanced, the very elements of Hell began to stir and align themselves with His divine purpose. The fires that once burned with malevolent fury now blazed with a new purpose, their flames coalescing into formidable soldiers of incandescent heat. These fiery warriors marched alongside Him, their presence a testament to the purifying power He wielded.

The winds, which had howled with despair and torment, shifted direction, swirling protectively around Him and solidified into ethereal warriors. Their forms shimmered with a fierce, loyal vigor, each gust a manifestation of the breath of life and hope that He carried within Him.

The earth itself, previously cold and unyielding, trembled and reshaped, rising up as mighty figures of stone and soil. These towering sentinels stood ready to defend their newfound leader, their strength drawn from the ancient foundations of creation that He embodied.

Even the waters, once acidic and poisonous, began to surge with renewed life, transforming into fluid sentinels of pure, flowing strength. They flowed around Him, shimmering like liquid crystal, forming a living barrier that moved with grace and power, cleansing the path before Him.

For a day and a night, the dominion of Hell threw everything it had against Him. Infernal beasts roared and lunged, dark sorceries crackled through the air, and the very earth beneath His feet seemed to rise up in rebellion. Yet, He stood unyielding, His eyes ablaze with divine purpose. The demons' attacks proved futile, their efforts crumbling before His might.

As dawn broke over the land of shadow, the dominion of Hell lay in ruins, its dark forces vanquished. Bloody footprints marked His path, a testament to the battle that had raged and the unyielding spirit that had triumphed. The Man continued on, His gaze fixed on the distant land of shadow where Death and the grave awaited.

With a voice that resonated through the very fabric of the realms, shaking the grounds beneath His feet, the Man called out to Death by name.

"Mawt," He commanded, His words echoing across the chasm, "meet Me at the edge of the great abyss."

Death, lurking nearby, was intrigued by the authority He carried and the ease with which He had destroyed the dominion of Hell. Slowly, from the shadows, Death emerged, drawn to the power and purpose that emanated from the Man who had dared to challenge the very essence of the underworld.

"Very brazen of a mortal demigod to call upon me and seek me out as though I recognize your authority. BECAUSE I DO NOT!" Death called out through the darkness.

Death was the ruler here. Each one of Death's tombs was occupied by a son or daughter of mankind, and fleets of demons were building new tombs by the hour. For whoever carried the stain of sin, carried the seed of Death within them that would one day be ripe for the harvest. The fall of man was Death's greatest achievement and his kingdom expanded deep into the realms of Sheol and beyond the great chasm that no man could cross.

But when Death came to the edge of the great chasm to claim this Man as his own, an unfamiliar emotion invaded Death's being: fear. As he gazed across the void, from which this Man stood, he saw His blood dripping onto the barren soil beneath. The earth reacted to the blood as it flowed, the tombs shaking violently from behind Death.

This Man, who had the embodiment of mystery and power, then raised His hand up and demanded the keys of Death. Death was rarely challenged and clenched tightly to the keys, as he uncovered them from deep within his being, making sure they were safely protected. He displayed no desire to give up what he rightfully owned.

"Who does this Man think He is to enter my domain and demand anything of me?" Death muttered under his breath. "Under whose authority do you call upon me? I know you not. Who are you?"

"I am the Way, the Truth, and the Life," said the Man.

Unrecognizable to Death, this Son of Man was intentionally hidden by the Almighty, preserved by His glory within Himself until the day He would reveal Himself to all of Creation, fulfilling the old covenant. This was something deliberate but inconceivable to all those outside the innermost courtrooms of Heaven.

Opening His outstretched arms, Death saw blood beginning to flow from the palm of the Man's hands. He was intimately familiar with the piercings upon His hands and feet, a form of execution of which Death was most proud. It was then Death realized that this was not just a mortal man; He was not just anyone.

As the blood flowed across the chasm, Death bent down and touched the blood. Rubbing it intently together and tasting of its purity, it had no trace of the stain of sin in it. Purity coursed through His veins. He had come to reclaim that which was once lost and to redeem those who were unjust victims of generational curses and plagues carried out by the sins of others under the command and authority of Death. The pureness of His blood dripped over the sealed and dormant tombs near Death.

As the blood covered the tombs, they began to tremble and shake. The Man knew of things that could not be known: timelines, conversations, and events that never existed in Death's books but yet were recorded nonetheless somewhere unfamiliar to Death. Somehow He was able to hear the cries of the damned that were never given choice in life and were seemingly forgotten ... but not by Him!

"The ancient ones emphasized the importance of this detail," Rochelle says. "Are you still there? You need to know this to appreciate the gravity of your situation."

I remain quiet, my head swimming with the enormity of what she told me. This was the very story of deliverance. I'd heard a version of this my entire life, but never did I truly understand the implications of what had transpired.

Rochelle begins again:

The ancient ones said that nothing in all of creation could separate the love this Man has for those He has called according to His purpose.

As the blood covered the graves, the Man's eyes ignited with fire and a light began to burst outward in high-energy explosions that penetrated the darkness and the depths below.

A powerful mist formed around Death as he conjured an immediate response. The explosion could be felt on Earth above and throughout the twelve realms below. The realm of Death was at war with the intruder, and Death had no intention of surrendering. The mere thought had never before crossed his mind as nothing in all of creation had ever been capable of stripping Death of his authority, granted to him by the laws of Elohim back at the beginning of Time.

However it seemed, Elohim did not create a way to abolish the law but to fulfill it. A fulfillment that none had thought possible when the law was written. He had created within that law a way for mankind to be redeemed through the purest of sacrifices that could only come from the blood of Elohim himself, something no principality or god thought the creator was willing or capable of doing.

A proverbial bridge had been formed that day and as futile as Death's attempt was to salvage his dominion, Death handed over the keys and ordered the Man to go. Yet Death did not get the response he wanted.

The Man simply responded, "Not without taking those who are Mine."

The keys of Death melted within His palms, filling the holes that were once symbols of Death's victory and that were now a forged reminder of Death's greatest defeat. With the keys now under the control of the Man, Death's authority was forever altered. No longer bound by restrictions or the need for consent, He gained access to the portals of Time and the ability to operate freely through universes of unseen and unspoken events that Death had held within himself as a tool for condemnation. The bridge that materialized on that day was not merely a physical connection between realms; it represented a pivotal moment that sent profound ripples through the entirety of mankind's lineage.

Death cried out in rage, but it was already too late. The sons and daughters of mankind were already standing in the midst of the rubble of their broken tombs.

As they stood, the Man reached out His hand and said, "Come to me all who are weary and burdened, and I will give you rest."

The select few that recognized Him and received His words ascended uncontested leaving Death to watch in utter horror.

Rochelle pauses for a moment, signaling a shift in the story.

The ancient ones then reminisced of a time when those long held captive in realms beyond understanding returned to the world of the living. These souls, lost to the ages, awakened in their own times, mere moments after their deaths, as if no time had passed.

"Imagine," one of the ancients commented, "a man who perished in battle, his body left on a distant field. In the blink of an eye, he finds himself back in his village, surrounded by the familiar faces of his loved ones. He speaks of the celestial visions he has seen, of prophecies whispered in the corridors of eternity.

"These returned souls," they continued, "bring with them tales of revelations and fulfilled prophecies. They have walked the paths between worlds and have seen the great tapestry of fate. Their testimonies will shake the foundations of our understanding, for they have glimpsed the secrets of existence.

"And with their return," they said, their voices dropping to a reverent whisper, "the dark thread of sin, that insidious path leading to the gates of Hell, would begin to unravel. Their presence would weaken the very fabric of evil, restoring balance and hope to our world."

The ancient ones nodded altogether in remembrance of the event, their eyes gleaming with a mixture of awe and anticipation. They knew that the fulfillment of this prophecy foretold a moment of profound significance, a time when the boundary between life and death would blur, and the world would stand on the brink of transformation.

Meanwhile, Death was left stunned at what had just transpired. The lands of Sheol were presented no options but to relinquish those whom He had chosen according to His purpose. Death, looking across his lands at the empty tombs, would no longer carry the authority over the grave and would forever be under a new covenant, forged and sealed by the crimson ink written on each tomb. Though many chose to leave, many more chose to stay. Fear and manipulative promises unfulfilled by Death were enough to secure countless souls from this Man of Legend.

For those that remained, the darkness had become so a part of them that they became one with the darkness and they no longer recognized the light, even when He was standing in front of them.

"The story doesn't end there, though," Rochelle proclaims with authority. "While the ancient ones recounted tales of this distant past, they also foretold an impending future. A future that would cast its shadow upon this realm, a realm now ensnared by the Lord of Darkness. This," she continued, her voice tinged with hesitation, "is precisely why the Dark Lord relentlessly hunts for those among us who bear the sacred mark of the Son of Man, as it would grant authority for His return, just as it transpired in ancient times. The ancient ones inscribed this prophecy upon the earthly scrolls, as it reads:

> For I saw a human form, a Son of Man, arriving in a whirl of clouds. He came to The Ancient of Days and was presented to Him. He was given power to rule—all the glory of royalty. Everyone—race, color and creed—had to serve Him. His rule would be forever, never ending. His kingly rule would never be replaced. Then I saw an angel coming down from Heaven, holding in his hand

the key to the bottomless pit and a great chain. And He seized the dragon, that ancient serpent, who is the devil and Satan, and bound him for thousands years and threw him into the pit, and shut it and sealed it over him. But the court will sit, and his power will be taken away and completely destroyed forever. Then the sovereignty, power and greatness of all the kingdoms under Heaven will be handed over to the holy people of the Most High. His kingdom will be an everlasting kingdom, and all rulers will worship and obey Him.

"This was their story," she tells me, "and those who have heard it choose to believe what they want to about it, for some say the story is only a myth, a fable, and nothing ever happened out of believing in such fairy tales. However, there are a few who remember the events and fewer still that know the identity of this Son of Man, as foretold by the ancient ones.

"The Dark Lord has made a concerted effort to eradicate those from long ago, who remember the days of old, from allowing their *lies* to enter back into the minds of the many. I had witnessed one such individual whom our Lord finally found by my hands. The fate of that individual though, I do not know. I was charged to find him and find him I did.

"In his last moments, before I turned him over to the Reapers, he whispered to me, 'Let not your eyes betray what your ears have heard nor believe in the lies of your father whom you now serve. The time is coming when the same choice will be yours. Do not betray the ones within flame.' "

Rochelle pauses and allows her words to hang in the air for a moment as if this was the first time she has ever thought about their full meaning.

"The one within flame!" I echo back to her. "Do you believe that to be me Rochelle? And what of the prophecy? What if it holds truth?" I whisper to her hoping for Rochelle to realize what I believe to be an epiphany about what she had witnessed.

Rochelle sits quietly on the ground without immediately answering me as she is in deep consideration of my questions. She hisses quietly to herself, but I cannot quite make it out. I can tell she is in turmoil about something and is conflicted.

Surely it is the revelation that there is evidence of truth in these stories. Why else would there be such a concerted effort to eradicate or conceal all those who remember the events. I think to myself.

"You know the identity of the Son of Man, don't you?" she asks me. "What do you say that the story is to you? For even though the mouths of men can speak curses of denial, if the heart has been exposed to truth, it will acknowledge what is true." She says this as she lets the severity of her accusations hang in the air with my pause, all but confirming my answer to her.

As I contemplate the repercussions of my decision to answer or remain silent, I find my mind drifting back to a critical moment in my conversation with Rochelle. She had casually mentioned encountering someone else, someone akin to me in some way or another. More importantly though was the revelation that she had willingly handed him over to the Reapers. I can't help but feel a little trepidation at this moment as her words linger in the back of my mind, casting a shadow of doubt and fear over my current dilemma.

I cannot deny Rochelle's perceptiveness; it's a quality that has undoubtedly contributed to her ascent to her current position. Her ability to decipher people and situations is evident, and my hesitation in this pivotal moment may have already sealed my fate.

The realization that my destiny now hangs in the balance, controlled by a woman whose motivations and intentions remain shrouded in mystery, becomes an all-too-real and palpable truth. With each passing moment of uncertainty, I am left to wonder what comes next while the weight of my apprehension presses further into my mind.

CHAPTER 13

The Chosen

The Seals of God

Exodus 13:8-10

I do this because of what the Lord did for me when I came out of Egypt. This observance will be for you like a sign on your hand and a reminder on your forehead that this law of the Lord is to be on your lips. For the Lord brought you out of Egypt with his mighty hand. You must keep this ordinance at the appointed time year after year.

Deuteronomy 6:5-9

Love the Lord your God with all your heart and with all your soul and with all your strength. These commandments that I give you today are to be on your hearts. Impress them on your children. Talk about them when you sit at home and when you walk along the road, when you lie down and when you get up. Tie them as symbols on your hands and bind them on your foreheads. Write them on the doorframes of your houses and on your gates.

Isaiah 49:16

*See, I have engraved you on the palms of my hands;
your walls are ever before me.*

2 Corinthians 1:21-22

Now it is God who makes both us and you stand firm in Christ. He anointed us, set his seal of ownership on us, and put his Spirit in our hearts as a deposit, guaranteeing what is to come.

Ephesians 1:13

And you also were included in Christ when you heard the message of truth, the gospel of your salvation. When you believed, you were marked in him with a seal, the promised Holy Spirit.

Ephesians 4:30

And do not grieve the Holy Spirit of God, with whom you were sealed for the day of redemption.

Ezekiel 9:4-6, 10

And the Lord said to him,

"Pass through the city, through Jerusalem, and put a mark on the foreheads of the men who sigh and groan over all the abominations that are committed in it." And to the others he said in my hearing,

"Pass through the city after him, and strike, Your eye shall not spare, and you shall show no pity. Obliterate the old people, young people, even women and children. Slaughter them all but don't lay a finger on anyone with the mark on his forehead."

"As for me, my eye will not spare, nor will I have pity, I will bring their deeds upon their heads."

2 Timothy 2:19

Nevertheless the solid foundation of God stands, having this seal: "The Lord knows those who are His," and, "Let everyone who names the name of Christ depart from iniquity."

Revelation 7:2-3

Then I saw another angel coming up from the east, having the seal of the living God. He called out in a loud voice to the four angels who had been given power to harm the land and the sea: "Do not harm the land or the sea or the trees until we put a seal on the foreheads of the servants of our God."

Revelation 9:4

They were told not to harm the grass of the earth or any plant or tree, but only those people who did not have the seal of God on their foreheads.

Revelation 14:1

Then I looked, and there before me was the Lamb, standing on Mount Zion, and with him 144,000 who had his name and his Father's name written on their foreheads.

Revelation 22:3-5

No longer will there be any curse. The throne of God and of the Lamb will be in the city, and his servants will serve him. They will see his face, and his name will be on their foreheads. There will be no more night. They will not need the light of a lamp or the light of the sun, for the Lord God will give them light. And they will reign for ever and ever.

The Marks of the Beast

Revelation 9:7-11

The locusts looked like horses prepared for battle. On their heads they wore something like crowns of gold, and their faces resembled human faces. Their hair was like women's hair, and their teeth were like lions' teeth. They had breastplates like breastplates of iron, and the sound of their wings was like the thundering of many horses and chariots rushing into battle. They had tails with stingers, like scorpions, and in their tails they had power to torment people for five months. They had as king over them the angel of the Abyss, whose name in Hebrew is Abaddon and in Greek is Apollyon (that is, Destroyer).

Revelation 13:15-17

The second beast was given power to give breath to the image of the first beast, so that the image could speak and cause all who refused to worship the image to be killed. It also forced all people, great and small, rich and poor, free and slave, to receive a mark on their right hands or on their foreheads, so that they could not buy or sell unless they had the mark, which is the name of the beast or the number of its name.

Revelation 14:9-11

A third angel followed them and said in a loud voice: "If anyone worships the beast and its image and receives its mark on their forehead or on their hand, they too will drink the wine of God's fury, which has been poured full strength into the cup of his wrath.

They will be tormented with burning sulfur in the presence of the holy angels and of the Lamb. And the smoke of their torment will rise for ever and ever. There will be no rest day or night for those who worship the beast and its image, or for anyone who receives the mark of its name."

Revelation 16:1-2

Then I heard a loud voice from the temple saying to the seven angels, "Go, pour out the seven bowls of God's wrath on the earth."

The first angel went and poured out his bowl on the land, and ugly, festering sores broke out on the people who had the mark of the beast and worshiped its image.

Revelation 19:19-21

Then I saw the beast and the kings of the earth and their armies gathered together to wage war against the rider on the horse and his army. But the beast was captured, and with it the false prophet who had performed the signs on its behalf. With these signs he had deluded those who had received the mark of the beast and worshiped its image. The two of them were thrown alive into the fiery lake of burning sulfur. The rest were killed with the sword coming out of the mouth of the rider on the horse, and all the birds gorged themselves on their flesh.

Revelation 20:4-6

I saw thrones on which were seated those who had been given authority to judge. And I saw the souls of those who had been beheaded because of their testimony about Jesus and because of the word of God. They had not worshiped the beast or its image and had not received its mark on their foreheads or their hands. They came to life and reigned with Christ a thousand years. (The rest of the dead did not come to life until the thousand years were ended.) This is the first resurrection. Blessed and holy are those who share in the first resurrection. The second death has no power over them, but they will be priests of God and of Christ and will reign with him for a thousand years.

The flame flickers and dances within the shadows that separate us, casting a weighty darkness that envelops the empty spaces around. There's an unmistakable desperation in her voice as she poses her question, almost as if she hopes for a particular response. It's a kind of desperation that resonates like a muffled cry for assistance, but assistance from what, I ponder to myself.

Surely she isn't oblivious to my evident hesitation in answering her inquiries. It must have been glaringly obvious that I knew who she was talking about, I internalize, grappling with how to navigate our conversation from this point onward after such an unmistakable revelation.

"Why does it matter to you what this story is to me?" I ask, hoping that Rochelle doesn't realize the error of my pause. "If I answer that I know of the person in whom you speak, knowing you already betrayed the trust of another, what then will you do with me?"

"Please," she implores, her voice resolute, "you made a promise. You gave me your word that you would respond honestly to my question."

"Why do I suddenly feel like your question is a trap, Rochelle?" I retort, alluding to my earlier inquiry.

In the backdrop, her disquiet manifests audibly as she paces back and forth, the cadence of her footsteps echoing the restless currents of her mind. Suddenly, a crescendo of anger explodes against the flames that surround me as if an object was hurled in frustration, punctuating the charged atmosphere with a thunderous burst of emotion.

"Well, why would he trust me? STUPID . . . Stupid . . . stupid . . . why would he trust me not to do the same as thing I did to . . ." Rochelle mutters to herself, her words audible enough for me to catch most of what she was saying.

Hearing her frustration and recognizing the authenticity in her self reflection, I decide to interrupt her outburst and answer her. *What would I do otherwise? How long until anyone else finds me . . . if ever.*

"I know of the *Man* in whom you speak." I respond, my voice breaking the palpable tension in the air forming between us.

Without delay, Rochelle's response to my willingness to answer her question is marked by a sudden surge of excitement. I can almost visualize her hastening toward the edge of the flames, eager to draw as near as possible, as if afraid of missing even the slightest nuance in my response. The flickering flames seem to reflect her anticipation, dancing with newfound intensity as though mirroring her heightened curiosity.

"His name?" she asks with enthusiasm.

"Do you know his name?"

Pausing one last time in reflection of my options, I know there is no going back at this point.

"Yes, Rochelle, I know his name," I say with an almost defeated tone in my voice. "His name is J.e..s…u…"

"STOP!" she screams at me in a desperate plea not to mention the name aloud. "Few in this place are unfortunate enough to even know that name. Far fewer would dare to utter it, and here you are, on the verge of speaking it loudly enough for all to hear. Have you learned nothing about your surroundings?"

She seethes with contempt, her words heavy with disapproval. "I asked for an honest answer, but I didn't think you would be foolish enough to actually speak the name."

"But it's just you and I," I reply. "How else would I have answered you without saying the name aloud?" Her outburst frustrates me.

"Who would have heard me when we are barely speaking loud enough to hear each other, let alone loud enough to be heard by something else?" I try to rebut. "Besides, you specifically asked for

His name. Did you not?" I inquire, my confusion deepening at her reaction to my compliance with her own instructions.

"The power of Life and Death are in our words, Christopher," Rochelle says to me in a hushed tone, just audible enough for me to hear. "I apologize for my outburst. You remind me of someone dear to me, and for a moment, I could almost hear. . ." Rochelle's sentence trails off into silence, leaving me waiting for the conclusion that she chose not to provide. I decide not to press for a further explanation, sensing the sensitivity of the subject.

"All that matters," she continues after collecting her thoughts again, "is that you understand there are very powerful words created that carry with them the power of Life and Death. In this realm, words that once offered Life now bring Death. Terrible forces exist here, Christopher, that you know not of, purposeful in their mission to deter all from uttering such words."

A couple of minutes pass in complete silence. I, for my part, am deep in thought, contemplating the forces she alluded to that were evidently beyond my knowledge as well as the mountain of information she just dumped on me about the ancient ones and prophecies that led to an apparent shift I had never even considered until now. As for Rochelle, her silence carries a different weight; it's as if she has chosen stillness to keenly listen and ensure that nothing approaches our vicinity.

"I apologize," Rochelle says softly. "I should have been more cautious, asking for a description or simple acknowledgement. I don't know what came over me when I asked you to speak it aloud, as I did. When the ancient ones posed the same question to me, they were far more deliberate in their phrasing than I was. Unlike you, at that time, I didn't know *Him*. However, it drove me to seek answers that are exceedingly hard to obtain in this place. My hesitation in answering their question clearly indicated that I was unaware of the identity they were alluding to. In my reluctance to respond, they shared this limerick with me, which might mean something to you since you were already aware of His identity:

> In judgment's realm, two men we see,
> Foreheads marked, their destiny decree.
> One finds salvation, the other in despair,
> Serving two masters, they both must bear,
> The Son of Man's seal, their hearts set free,
> Unscathed by death's kiss, their fate decree.
>
> A permanent seal, inheritance divine,
> For those who embraced the Son's design,
> Unyielding, unbroken, in spirit they stand,
> But deniers bear death's mark, as planned.
>
> Second death approaches, no escape in sight,
> For dominions, gods, none evade its bite,
> Captives freed, the dragon confined,
> In fire, the fallen shall be defined.
>
> Prodigal daughters and prodigal sons,
> Carrying the seal, but darkness shuns,
> A choice awaits in the shadow's embrace,
> The second kiss, deciding their place.

Rochelle fell silent after her recitation.

"I don't understand," I reply, still trying to grapple with all the hidden meanings within her words.

"The seal," she says, her shadow turning towards me. "That's what's most significant about their limerick. It is a mark upon the forehead of those who once accepted or denied the truth of the Son of Man.

"It is said that mere knowledge is not enough for a covenant to be made. It's not just a matter of knowing it in one's mind, but it's about accepting that truth deep within that central, life-giving organ of the body—the heart. They say that once the heart has accepted this kind of truth, its rhythm of beating is forever changed. Even through the ashes of death, it still beats to the rhythm of He who gave them life.

"That's when the seed of truth plants itself deep within the soiling grounds of the heart. Roots begin to shoot out, first reaching into the mind and forming a peculiar mark across the head, known as the seal of the Son of Man. Though the seal is not noticeable in the physical realm, it is very noticeable here. Those who carry it try to conceal it, for where it was once a symbol of protection on earth, here it is a signet of damnation."

"A signet of damnation? How could such a seal, from the Son of Man, exist in a place like this?" I ask.

"Because not all who say '*Lord, Lord*' will enter the kingdom of heaven, but only those who walked with He who sits upon the eternal throne in their last hours and shared in His suffering," she conveys with conviction.

"Those who are marked by the Son of Man carry a heavy bounty upon their head," she continues. "The one known as the deceiver, the master of the principalities of the air, pays a high price for taking even a single soul marked with the seal of the Son of Man.

"Much time has been invested in the course of a single human's life. Even those who have claimed they are saved still have a will to exercise, and it is those on earth—those who have accepted the gift of salvation—that the prince is after relentlessly in hopes that one day he may find their will worn out and tattered, lying in the dust of hell. It is his way of taking revenge against the Son of Man by deceiving those who were once His into having them fall away from the relationship with the One Who Saves, just as the Dark Prince once fell away from his place in another life, eons ago."

"That's so twisted," I say aloud, confused by both the ancient ones' warning of the seals as well as Rochelle's extended interpretation of them.

"It is indeed. The many will endure the wrath, serving as punishment for the choices from which the few who have truly accepted the Truth are freed. But for those who knew the truth and chose to turn a cold shoulder, a different fate awaits them.

"Many questions have answers that are above what I dare try and understand," Rochelle continues on, "nor do I dare risk trying to find their meaning in a place like this. What I do understand, though, is that those who are marked, who have been led here through the deceptions of giving into their worldly appetites, are not fully banished into eternal damnation until they are captured and brought before the Dark Prince for their judgment."

Speaking with an eerie confidence, Rochelle says, "The prophecy speaks of a second coming and a second death. There is a rumor that the Son of Man will never be separated from those He has called. It is said that He will once again break open the tombs of the condemned, who have been remade, and forever seal the land of Sheol.

In His wake, He will cast their masters into the lake of endless torment. It has been long believed that those He's claimed bear the seal. That's why the Dark Prince has been searching for you since learning of your arrival. Battalions of Reapers, soul collectors, seekers, bloodhounds and enslavers have been sent to capture you. There is one thing the Dark Prince of the underworld is afraid of, and that is giving the Man of Legend any reason to come back to Hell as the prophecy foretold. The Dark Prince knows that nothing can separate the Son of Man from those He loves. For it is whispered that He has a jealousy more fierce than a mother lion protecting her cubs. But perhaps that's all rumor," Rochelle finishes with a chuckle.

"This is Hell after all, where fear rules and deception is our daily appetite. Nevertheless, one cannot help but notice the shift in the air. There's been an obvious re-distribution of power here to find something very specific, and it doesn't take a fool to see that it's of great importance." Rochelle finishes her thought with a pause and sighs as if remembering specific key moments over the past many days or hours or *whatever metric of time is used here,* I think to myself.

"The Dark Prince's loyal subjects are vital in capturing such souls, but over time they have become complacent, and that, Christopher, is why I am here," Rochelle speaks again.

"Exactly why are you here?" I ask, as if a trap door is now shutting in on me.

"I am here, Christopher, to bring you to the Dark Prince. I am here to bring you to judgment!" she says with conviction as a trepidatious feeling immediately overtakes me.

"Granted, you've had this feeling since meeting her," I say aloud to myself, "but I honestly thought it was more related to where I am and how little I can control my situation than it was her." I stop talking, embarrassed that she may have heard me.

In all honesty, I found more solace in her being around than fear of her betrayal. Even now, I don't feel angered at what she said because there is nothing I can do either way. Whether she leaves me again or betrays me matters very little to me in this moment.

"I know how you feel Christopher," she says softly with reassurance. "If there is any comfort knowing, I too have been judged. There are not many who have been judged by him and seen again in this realm. He showed mercy upon my soul because of the answer I gave to the ancient ones upon hearing their story. After all, our Lord is wise in his knowledge of his kingdom's affairs and in knowing these particular things about the souls who occupy his regions beyond his sanctuary."

"What was your answer?" I ask Rochelle.

"I discredited their story," she replies. "Knowing the power of Death and of the dark forces of the air by his side, I couldn't possibly comprehend who could carry authority over Death and the great dragon. I denied this *Son of Man* at the seat of judgment and scoffed at the allegations that this *Man* would return to defeat Death within his own realm.

"The Dark Lord told me that he had known me by name, even in my former life on Earth, from the very moment I was born into existence. He whispered to me of my importance to his kingdom and that should I prove my loyalty to him, I would have a position as servant within his counsel. Our Lord is training and testing my allegiance to himself, Christopher, and after delivering to him seven hundred marked souls without wavering or hesitating, only then will my training be complete in order for me to rise to higher positions."

"Rochelle," I plead softly, exposing my vulnerability, "you do not have to do this. Do not cast this shadow over me. Do not bring me to him."

There is a pause, a silence that makes me feel as if the time spent with Rochelle may possibly have swayed her. Perhaps there is something about me that does in fact remind her of someone long past but not completely forgotten.

"I have told the story of the Son of Man, just as the ancient ones told it to me and also to one thousand six hundred and eighty-five souls. Out of them, I have delivered six hundred and seventy-five souls into the hands of our Lord. You shall be my six hundred and seventy-sixth," she says boastfully.

"My training is almost complete, and I won't jeopardize all that I have accomplished for anyone, not even you. I'm sorry, but perhaps you too may gain favor with our lord. That is the most that I can offer in recompense."

"What do you mean to do with me, Rochelle?" I ask in a quiet voice now seeing there is no escaping what lies ahead of me.

"What I have no choice in doing," Rochelle answers. "Your lips have proclaimed the knowledge of Him who shall not be named—the answer that I was actually hoping not to hear this time. You are one of the marked. I have an obligation that is measured by a fine line of complete and utter obedience on my part in order to keep my position within this realm.

"It may appear to be Hell, but it is not the Hell you think you know. This is but a holding area, a place in-between where the dead arrive awaiting judgment before being placed into the lower realms from which the principalities that govern them have risen to power through unspeakable evil."

As I gather my thoughts, a million questions flood my mind, but she interrupts once again: "They will be here soon, Christopher. There is nothing that can be done now."

"Why are you doing this?" I declare, my fear rising in suddenly not wanting to leave the familiarity of my flame.

"Just walk away!" I plea. "Just pretend you never came across me!"

"Do you hear them?" she eerily says as if not even acknowledging my cry. "I can hear the wails of the damned in their wake even now . . . I have no choice, Christopher."

"Please, Rochelle!" I say out of desperation, "please don't . . ."

"Don't beg me, Christopher," she snaps, cutting me off.

"You're only exposing your humanity that reeks of weakness. If there is anything you must learn from me, learn this: if you beg, if you plead, if you show any weakness, you will be consumed by them. They feed on the weaknesses of men and will devour you. You must present yourself strong and worthy of consideration. Only then will you have a possibility of being bought for service. Show them your greatest strengths and just maybe you will avoid an eternity in some of the lower realms where sorrow can be heard even here if you have a discerning ear."

How did I get here? I think to myself as I watch Rochelle's movements in the corner of my eye, the flame matching her in its smoldering colors as if reacting to her attempts to gain access to me.

"You've made your bed, Christopher. We all have, and now we must lie in it. I was hoping for a better outcome for you, I really was.

I wanted your answer to be different, like mine, in response to the story of the ancient ones. I wanted to be able to ask permission from my master to redeem you, so that you and I together could join forces in making way for the Dark Lord's kingdom to come on Earth as it is in Hell. I wasn't lying about the possibility of rising to higher levels here, and I wanted you to ascend with me. You're different from the others, Christopher. You're special. I've never seen anyone graced with a covering of flame before.

"When I first approached you, I really was seeking a means of escape; a means of shelter to run away and hide from the calling the Dark Prince has put upon me. I truly thought you to be a sorcerer, someone capable of hiding within the elements and escaping their judgment. I was momentarily weak, and in my weakness, I almost lost everything when the Reapers appeared. Had they noticed me, they would have consumed me and brought me back before my master, all of my work up to this point lost. And for what?" she yells. "For just another stupid boy lost in a world he knows nothing of? NO! I won't be persuaded to abandon everything I have built. I must remain strong and remain I shall.

"There's no way of escape once you're here. Oh how great it would have been to command the flame," Rochelle utters to herself as if reminiscing the thought of such power.

"The possibility of escaping the gaze of my master just long enough to get to . . ." She pauses for a moment.

"I've said too much. Either way, it makes no difference now. Our Lord knows of your position, and I mean to carry out my duties. The Dark Lord has shown me mercy by allowing me the honor of my position here, and perhaps you too can hope for mercy. But this is the only way for me, Christopher. I am sorry for ever having run into you.

"Besides, at least you had some savior to turn to when you were alive!" she spits her angry words towards me.

"Unlike you, I knew of nothing of such a man nor did any such person come to my aid. No one ever rescued me in all my time of need back on Earth! I had to fend for myself! I did what I had to, fighting in the name of love in order to *save* those I loved! And look where I am now, Christopher. I lost everything—everyone I loved. My sole purpose, tasked by the Dark Lord, is to do the exact thing over and over again that unintentionally led to the death of everyone I loved when I was once alive!"

Taken back by what I just heard, I, on some small level, am starting to unravel the mystery of this *friend*.

"What happened?" I ask Rochelle. "What happened in life that led to the death of your loved ones?"

I hear Rochelle's breathing change as if she stopped breathing altogether. Moments pass without so much as a whisper and I can't help but wonder if she is still there.

"Rochelle? " I inquire, not to push her but just to know she hasn't left.

"I'm here," she softly answers.

"It's been ages since I last thought about it. This place twists you, reshaping you into the very essence of what you once loathed. In my case, it has molded me into the monster I vowed to annihilate—the one who shattered my world, leaving nothing but ruins of everything and everyone I ever loved."

CHAPTER 14

The Repercussion

Proverbs 4:16-17

For they cannot rest until they do evil;
they are robbed of sleep till they make someone stumble.
They eat the bread of wickedness and drink the wine of violence.

Ecclesiastes 3:16

And I saw something else under the sun:
In the place of judgment—wickedness was there,
in the place of justice—wickedness was there.

2 Peter 2:20-22

Those who have been pulled out of the cesspool of worldly desires
through the knowledge of our Lord and Savior Jesus, the Anointed
One, yet have found themselves mired in it again are worse off than
they were before.
They would have been better off never knowing the way of
righteousness than to have known it and then abandoned the sacred
commandment they had previously received and dived back into the
muck! In their case, the words from Proverbs hold true:

"The dog goes back to his own vomit,"
and as the greeks say,
"the sow is washed to wallow in the mud."

Rochelle pauses, debating whether or not she should tell me her story. Then, as if realizing she loses nothing for sharing, she begins:

The world was at war, and my family and I were caught in the middle of it. It was brought to our doorstep in late June. A darkness swept over our nation, and a lie consumed our leadership, convincing them that there were those among us—our own countrymen—who were so unwanted that they were condemned to death. People we knew, families we grew up with now considered less than human and executed or taken away to unknown places.

My family and I could not stand by while these atrocities continued in our community. It was inhuman and immoral, yet there was no escaping it. A family that lived nearby, with whom I grew up and loved very much, was one such family that would be led to the grave by our leaders' hands. I could not stand by and watch this without trying to do something about it.

My husband and I, with the help of our kids, hid the family under the floors and in small spaces of our house where we would store dried foods. When the soldiers came, and the family was gone, they knew someone was to blame. Several people in our small village had already been hung or shot, murdered for information. Many more earlier in the week had been brought into a public square and beaten to death for all to watch.

Shortly after the first inquiry, a prominent member of rank came to our home. He carried the mark of death on his head as a badge of honor and was revered within his party for his ruthlessness. My husband was questioned, likely due to his occupation, then beaten. They strung him up behind our home in the same tree where he had proposed to me long ago. I remember holding the kids back as they screamed for the men to let their daddy go.

Unable to watch any longer or hold back the cries of our children, I screamed out to cut him free, and I would tell them what they wanted to know.

196

Rochelle begins to weep. For the first time since meeting her, there is a genuine vulnerability about her that I think she had forgotten about or had been made to forget.

"Please continue, Rochelle. I know it must be hard recalling that day," I remark with a sincere compassion that could be felt in the thick air around us.

The soldiers cut my husband free upon my outcry. A deal was made with this infamous leader known as Death Dealer.

"My husband and my four children's lives for the lives of the family who we shelter," I bargained with the commanding officer.

"You have my word!" the officer assured me.

"Show us where the family is and no harm will come to yours."

"The stove in the kitchen," I cried out as my husband yelled for me to stop and not say anything else. "Move the stove. There is an access cut into the floor where the family hides."

The man had very little expression but gave me assurance that our deal was good and would be honored.

"Bring them to me!" the officer yelled at his constituents.

They tore through our home, and one by one they pulled the family out from underneath the floor. I can still remember their screams, their horror, their fear.

As she speaks, I can tell that she is reliving the moment with such vivid clarity that it feels as if the scene is unfolding before her eyes. The imagery in her mind is so intense, it mirrors the way I've experienced my own memories since arriving here, as though they are happening. Every detail, every emotion, comes to life with startling realism, bridging the gap between past and present. Memories here come alive with smells and sounds I never remembered in life. I'm certain she can even recall the conversations of those nearby, just as I've been able to do.

She continues:

The betrayal in their faces haunt me to this day. Each one helplessly dragged from my home. A father, a mother and their five children. We were ignorant to their intentions, I swear to you.

Had I known . . . had I . . .

The soldiers lined them all up according to their age from youngest to oldest. In one single motion the officer, while looking back at me, his eyes fixed on mine, raised his hand fully outstretched high into the air and quickly flung his hand down toward his hip. As soon as his hand fell to his side, his soldiers, instructed by their commanding officer, brutally beat the entire family to death one by one.

We screamed in horror at what we just witnessed. My youngest daughter ran towards them crying as her best friend fell to the earth, lifeless. More sickening than this was the fact that the men were all clapping and cheering as each body fell inert. Never had I witnessed such barbarism. They were monsters, not men.

She finishes.

Trying to gather my thoughts and form some sort of response to what she just told me, Rochelle interrupts as she bursts out in anger.

"I . . . I am responsible . . . I am responsible . . . It was my fault," Rochelle repeats to herself.

"I truly have no words, Rochelle. Surely you can't blame yourself though. How could you have known that they were going to do that?" I try to comfort her with my words.

"You think I care what happened to that family?" she screams back at me. "I didn't care! I only wanted to save mine." She begins weeping again.

"I don't understand," I comment quietly to myself.

"I thought you did save your family, Rochelle," I say to her hoping for a reasonable explanation.

She continues on, ignoring my question, as if the answer lies in what is about to unfold.

He walked back over to me to speak to me as his men finished celebrating the murder of our friends. My husband and I did all we could just to contain our rage and secure our children. As distraught as I was over the event, I glanced over to my children and my husband, and I was just thankful it wasn't my family lying on the ground lifeless.

Now standing directly in front of me, he wasn't expressionless this time. No, there was a grin on his smug arrogant face.

"I am sorry," he said to me with a chuckle as if it were a punch line to a sick joke, "but I am going to have to rescind my promise I made to you."

"What?" I screamed out in horror. "You promised! You can't do this! Please, STOP!" I begged.

"Restrain her!" He commanded his right hand man as he threw me to the ground violently and pinned my face to the dirt. Holding my head upward in their direction with his fingers stretching my eyes open so I wouldn't miss anything, the Death Dealer walked right up to my husband, a lead pipe in his hands, blood still dripping off of it from moments earlier."

"You forced my hand," the officer said to me as his men held my husband and four children in front of me. "Your family will be made an example to anyone who dares defy our authority again," he chuckled. "Fortunately for our campaign, the past few days have been rather successful. It is unlikely we will need further demonstrations of our resolve in this region. For that I thank you."

She breaks her retelling momentarily. "I THANK YOU! He said to me as I watched my sweet husband fall lifeless to the earth after being ruthlessly beaten in the same fashion witnessed moments earlier." I hear a sharp intake of breath as she begins to speak again.

"Without your betrayal," he explained to me while my face was still being forced to watch as my children screamed and tugged at their dad's extremities to wake up, "we would not have ever learned about them. We actually had no knowledge they were still in the area and were investigating a different matter altogether. Our tactics were only harsh to invoke fear in the community so that no one would ever try and conceal anyone in the future. But you, you handed them right over. We were only going to hang your husband, nothing more."

"I can still hear their laughter as they mocked me. It was in that moment of reflection that I realized I had caused all of this. My fear caused all of this. I was so eager to save my family that I selfishly offered up another in sacrifice," she says.

"But your kids," I say to Rochelle, "your kids were at least saved. Surely you can find solace in that?" I comment hoping to encourage her.

"My babies . . . my babies . . . my sweet beautiful babies," she repeats over and over. "My children were all lined up and executed, Christopher," she says without disclosing further details.

I gasp in shock at what she just revealed and want to ask more but know to hold my tongue.

I laid there lifeless as the love of my life and my four beautiful children were just taken from me. The soldier removed his hands from my face and placed a gun on the ground beside me.

"Kill me if you like," the officer said to me as I snapped to my feet holding the pistol outstretched towards him.

"But know this," he said arrogantly, "there is only one shot in that pistol. Kill me and you will live a long life knowing that you killed your entire family and everyone you loved. Or, use that one bullet for the only good thing you can do left in your life and put an end to your suffering. Go be with your family in death."

Rochelle doesn't tell me how it ended, though it requires little speculation. The silence between us seems to stretch into eternity. I am left to imagine the conclusion while Rochelle collects her thoughts and emotions before continuing.

"Now I am a slave to my Master," she whispers to me after a long pause, "and I can never turn back. I am tasked with the very thing that led to my family's death: betrayal. I am to deceive those desperate enough to believe that I can somehow save them, when in fact, I am doing the exact opposite." Her words hang heavy in the air, leaving me to bear the full weight of their meaning.

"I've told you why I'm here, Christopher, but do you know why you're here?" she asks rhetorically, clearly angered that she had divulged so much about her own past.

"You're here now because you allowed your salvation to slip away from you, and it was replaced with darkness. Walking a fine line in the living is as good as tightening your own noose. I've seen it over and over in many people just like you. You at least knew the truth and chose to walk away from it. DIDN'T YOU?" she yells out, as if taking her anger out on me for the things she's done.

"Ha, you probably didn't even realize in your last moments that you still had a choice. Did you?" she questioned, laughing at the thought of my own death.

"The darkness concealed the truth from your eyes," she again answers without giving me a moment to give my thoughts, "making you think your only choice was the darkness. Your complacent soul was an easy target to deceive in order to lead you down the path of darkness, for why else would you be here?

"Truly I tell you, it would have been better to have never known of the Son of Man, then to be here having rejected Him. The Man of Legend should have no reason to come back for the likes of you. You would only shame Him for having rejected His sacrifice.

"Yet," she pauses for a moment while almost questioning herself, "the Dark Lord still must worry about your *influence* here. Why else would he want for you, and all those like you, to be brought before his council? Such a rare and special privilege to have our lord present for judgment. There are so many more important matters that occupy his attention. So clearly, there is great value to him by either what you know, or what you have within you still that forces a personal visitation."

She pauses for a moment to absorb her comments while I too ponder what she says. I remember the sounds I heard from beyond my flame prior to meeting Rochelle. I can only imagine the fate of those who were found and collected. I can see that the deal she struck with the Devil must have been very significant to drive her to betray one soul after another.

Yet, the underlying question lingers within me: *why does she serve him? What grip does he maintain over her, compelling her to persist in this dark path?*

Is it solely fear, or is there something deeper at play? I ponder to myself.

With no answers to the questions swirling in my mind, and seizing the opportunity during her pause, I break the silence and ask, "Why do you serve him? Was it not fear that I heard in you when we first met that made you desperate to escape this place? You came to me seeking shelter. Did I mistake your desperation as an act to win my favor?"

"This shelter is not yours to give!" she spits towards me.

"There is nothing more that I want than to escape the hell that I am in. But no matter how far I run, no matter how far I go, I can never escape the hold that the Devil has on me and those whom I long to see again."

"Those you long to see again?" I question her. "Do you believe your family is here? Is that what Satan holds over you and why you continue to do his bidding?" I ask.

"Satan has been the closest thing I have come to know as a savior," she begins to remark.

"He saved me from the others," Rochelle says softly. "Even though the council of elders had passed judgment on me, he pulled me away during my judgment to give me a second chance. What he saw in my final moments on earth gave him inspiration for my *appointment* here in this realm. But being saved by the Devil comes at a high cost, and now I must pay for my redemption; I must pay for their salvation."

Their salvation? I think to myself. *Who is she talking about when she refers to "their salvation?"*

Maybe I have Rochelle all wrong. There has been a lot to absorb in such a short period of time, but I must hurry in my effort to gather information. If what she says is correct, those whom she serves are coming to claim me. I must try and quickly gather any information there is to gain before my final judgment.

"There is no permanent place of security here, Christopher," Rochelle says, interrupting my thoughts.

"Any mercy shown must be taken advantage of and not discarded. I have seen those who go before his majesty prideful, arrogant, and demanding of him to recognize who they once were on Earth as some badge of honor before our lord. He is not understanding, not kind, or compassionate! His agenda is far more valuable than the worthless claims of recognition from the once beloved *shades of dirt* that stand before him. He cares very little of your ability to sway the ignorant or gain favor with the blind. They are all powerless now in the land of the dead where there is no more *audience* left to admire their fame, no more influence to be gained in the land of the living.

"I, after witnessing much, took my judgment as a form of salvation from where those that came before me had been sent. As crooked and as vile my judgment was to swallow, I hoped that what was privately held between Lucifer and I may actually be honored one day upon the fulfillment of my vow."

I see Rochelle's collapsed silhouette on the ground and rise a little as if she has renewed her resolve to once again continue the effort to find redemption for her sins. Her cry for help is now made evident to me.

She's not running from the Devil, she's running from the guilt of her past. That, plus some promise that he can reunite them or somehow "save" them must be the hold the Devil has over her, I think to myself after pondering all that she disclosed.

An audience with the Devil must be rare, as she mentioned. In life I just assumed that everyone passed through some form of judgment but the more I think about it, the more ridiculous that sounds. If the Devil is focused on a continual war on Earth and isn't omnipresent, then it would be ridiculous to think that all would go before him to be judged.

At this moment, though, I find myself distracted by her pain. Strangely, I am more concerned about my betrayer's well-being than my own. How can that be? We are both in Hell, and my fate seems sealed. Through my own admittance and acknowledgment of the Son of Man, I am one of the marked; one of the highly sought after, one of the highly valued to the Devil which gets her one soul closer to accomplishing whatever deal she made with him. Perhaps my fears will be laid to rest when I finally come face to face with the one who has chased after me my whole life. In the meantime, I feel slightly shocked as I hear myself utter these words aloud:

"If my capture helps pay even a fraction of your debt, then I will go willingly, Rochelle. But on one condition."

"What?" she says in bewilderment.

"I too need any advantage within the realm of judgment to escape whatever fate lies ahead. Tell me of your judgment and whatever secrets you may be able to recall that could be advantageous for my time before *him*. Then, I promise that I will not fight them when they come to claim me."

Taken by surprise at what I have offered to her, Rochelle agrees.

"Tell me, Rochelle, what awaits me at judgment?"

CHAPTER 15

The Morning Star

Ezekiel 28:12-19

Thus says the Lord GOD:
"You were the signet of perfection, full of wisdom and perfect in
beauty.
You were in Eden, the garden of God; every precious stone
was your covering, sardius, topaz, and diamond, beryl,
onyx, and jasper, sapphire, emerald, and carbuncle; and
crafted in gold were your settings and your engravings.

On the day that you were created they were prepared. You were
an anointed guardian cherub. I placed you; you were on the holy
mountain of God; in the midst of the stones of fire you walked.

You were blameless in your ways from the day you were
created, till unrighteousness was found in you.

In the abundance of your trade you were filled with
violence in your midst, and you sinned; so I cast you
as a profane thing from the mountain of God,

and I destroyed you, O guardian cherub,
from the midst of the stones of fire."

1 Enoch 14:9-14

And I went until I drew near to a wall which is built of crystals
and surrounded by tongues of fire: and it began to frighten me.
And I went into the tongues of fire and drew near to a large house
which was built of crystals: and the walls of the house were like
a tessellated floor [made] of crystals, and its groundwork was of
crystal. Its ceiling was like the path of the stars and the lightnings,

*and between them were fiery cherubim, and their heaven was [as
clear as] water. A flaming fire surrounded the walls, and its portals
blazed with fire. And I entered into that house, and it was hot as fire
and cold as ice: there were no delights of life therein; fear covered
me, and trembling took hold of me. And as I quaked and trembled,
I fell on my face.*

Isaiah 14:12

*How you have fallen from heaven,
Morning Star, son of the dawn!*

After pondering the question that lingered in the air about what awaited me in judgment, Rochelle finally agreed to help me. She is still bewildered by my response—that I was willing to help her pay her debt by offering myself and not fleeing—should she help me gain a greater understanding of the things I still did not know. Breaking the silence that stood between us—her with her initial doubt and confusion, and me with my fears of the unknown—she begins to recount her journey of judgment:

*The ancient covenants that have secretly been taking place throughout
the ages of time have all manifested behind the inner courts of Sheol.
Kings and kingdoms have been forged in the promises and betrayals of
the fallen lords that go before them, during a time not recorded by the
living. Each one of the fallen kings, in an effort to save themselves, set into
motion claims to purify the world of the stain within man so that a new
order and power could one day rise out of the ashes. Promises are made
here; unbreakable covenants forged for the bloodlines of the unborn to
align themselves with the will of our lord that they may bring about the
fruition and seed of iniquity upon the earth. Though man is unaware of
these covenants, they are undoubtedly affected by them. Each contract
made is held before the Almighty in the courtrooms of Heaven against
the innocent, generational curses and agreements negotiated with the
dead for the future of the unborn.*

"This is judgment!" she exclaims.

This sacred trial took place in the mountains of the giants, where jagged peaks, like ancient teeth from a fallen god, protrude from the bowels of the abyss, suspended in nothingness. There, in the valley of the cliffs, where endless fire draped the mountain's edge, a pendulous keep held the chambers of the seven-seated throne room: the temple of the great dragon. Its splendor and magnificence were incomprehensible to the eye but terrifying in the same breath.

Protected by fire, the likes of which I had never seen, the outside of the walls was ever shifting and moving, yet the inside reflected differently, as if I was entirely in another place altogether. Walking across a suspension of flame, as I was ushered past the gates, a great door stood before me. It reminded me of opal in the way it shimmered in the light of the flame, its soft and elegant hues playing tricks on my mind as to what true color I saw.

As the doors opened wide in anticipation of my arrival, the corridor I was led through was magnificent. The crystal floors on which I walked refracted the light of the pillars of fire that illuminated the room. So too the walls were solid crystal and were ornately fashioned with intricate carvings unlike anything I had ever seen on Earth. Its ceiling was illuminated as if it were alive with the cosmos where infinite stars showed down. The lighting played tricks on my mind as I was led to the great hall. As magnificent as the contrast between the soft hues of the stars above with the harsh pillars of fire are to behold, they illustrated to me that there was great conflict here.

I was ushered into a great throne room brought before the thrones of the gods, fiery Cherubim standing guard. Fear instantly enveloped every part of me. The room was completely devoid of peace and the weight of the air pressed firmly against my chest as though thousands of pounds of stone were crushing me. Great evil had been done in this room.

Seven thrones could be seen, the individual craftsmanship and materials used for each personally reflected the specifications of the lord that sat upon it. Equally spaced, six encircled a terrible and deep chasm of fire from which the lords ascended. The principalities and powers of the deep already awaited my arrival, or the arrival of another, yet to be seen.

The seventh throne, made out of onyx and opal, stood to the North, in a place of power over the six smaller thrones below. This was where the morning star rose and looked to the south, where the evening star set. The seventh throne was the only place where one could still catch glimpses of the morning star's radiance as it shone down into the throne room and on to he who sat upon it. This throne belonged to Satan, who converted back to his former self, Lucifer, the all revered Morning Star and Bearer of Light in Darkness, during these proceedings.

"What do you mean?" I ask Rochelle. "Is Satan not the same as Lucifer?

"No, and at the same time, yes," she says. "It will become more clear once you understand the order of things.

With each principality standing before their thrones, the room fell suddenly dark. An emptiness suffocated me and blackness fell from the outer walls above and draped itself over me. It penetrated every part of me, unwillingly, as it pierced through my being and pulled from me every memory, every hope, and every fear before settling to the crystal floors below. A large black figure rose from the empty spaces cloaked in darkness and formed out of that very blackness that just violated my being.

Making his way to the seventh throne, the darkness melted off of him like hot wax as the radiance from the morning star above fell upon his countenance. No longer did he resemble the dark and sinister figure that had momentarily stood in the room; instead, he now shone with an almost ethereal beauty, his features illuminated by the celestial light. The oppressive gloom that had once clung to him was utterly vanquished, revealing a visage that was both majestic and awe-inspiring, as if reborn in the light of the dawn.

He was suddenly beautiful to behold, adorned with gems of such extraordinary brilliance and variety that I could scarcely comprehend them, let alone name them. The jewels shimmered with an array of colors, each more dazzling than the last, casting prismatic reflections that danced around him. It was as if he had been transformed into a living constellation, each gemstone a star in its own right, illuminating his presence with an almost otherworldly splendor. While his appearance was magnificent, his countenance was ferocious. The six principalities below honored him, standing before their thrones, waiting for him to be seated.

Lucifer glared down at his "elders," the six principalities of the highest order, as they awaited his instruction. Finally, he took his seat, with Satan looming in the shadows cast on the walls behind him. As if rehearsed, each principal demon sat and, with books opened wide, took turns sharing accounts of my life as I knelt before all seven. I had been counseled early on by the two large demonic entities behind me not to speak or risk immediate and irreversible judgment. So, I knelt in absolute silence, listening to each of the six recount my life from perspectives unknown to me. I was shocked by the detailed accounts they gave. Each demon, with differing opinions and vantage points of similar events, was bidding on my future to the lord of light, Lucifer, as though they were offering to buy me for a price I didn't understand. Their currency wasn't paper or precious metals; it was knowledge and positions of authority. They were offering territory to Lucifer in exchange for me.

"They were bidding on you?" I interject, my thoughts racing with the vivid images of such an experience.

"Yes," Rochelle replies, unprovoked by my interruption this time. "Like ravenous wolves, each fought over what was to become of me. They knew my thoughts, my feelings, and even the outcomes of some of my choices that led to pain and suffering for others—

outcomes I wasn't even aware my actions or words had caused. To them, these were accomplishments, not judgments. They saw the harm I had caused as tokens of achievement to exploit for their gain." Her voice crackles with shame as she recalls the moment.

"But you said earlier that Satan saved you, right?" I ask, remembering her earlier comments. "How did he save you?"

"Save me?" Rochelle pauses to contemplate the words more closely. "A savior looks very different here, Christopher. It will make more sense shortly.

In the midst of my judgment, two of the lords had come to an agreement, while the others had already settled their claims over me. I was lifted by the two large demonic entities standing guard and ushered to the throne of the principal demon with the greatest claim over me. Lucifer, still seated on his throne, held out his hand to accept the offer from the winning elder. I lay at the base of his throne, terrified at the sight of the being before me, knowing there was nothing I could do to stop his advance.

After bowing before Lucifer and the payment being accepted, his gaze met mine. A whip slowly unfurled from the sleeve of his robe, and with hatred in his eyes, he flicked his wrist, sending the whip backward across the floor in one fluid motion. Our gazes locked, and I braced myself for the inevitable impact when Satan interjected. His dark mass enveloped the courtroom, showing his opposition to the judgment.

"*Lucifer rose to his feet, visibly annoyed by the interruption but willing to hear out his brother. Such an interruption from Satan must have been a rare event, compelling Lucifer to listen. The power dynamics in the room were clear,*" Rochelle says pointedly.

"*The elders below offered no rebuke, lowering their heads to Satan as he swiftly encircled the thrones. His shadow coiled around each of them, daring any opposition. Each of the six principal elders lowered their eyes, their faces showing anger but unwilling to oppose his outburst. With no opposition, Satan presented his argument to Lucifer. I couldn't hear what was said, but the deliberation took only moments before Satan returned to the shadows behind Lucifer's throne.*

"Sitting back down, Lucifer beckoned me forward to hear his judgment. Salvation, as I stated earlier, doesn't look the same as what you may have imagined, Christopher," Rochelle says to me, knowing my mind is still grappling with understanding what had transpired.

"I was given a new master, not among any in the room, to whom I would be held accountable. Though it doesn't seem like I was saved, you cannot imagine the vile things spoken by the six principalities that pleaded cases against me. An eternity under any of their dominions would have been a level of hell I never wish to experience.

"This was judgment," she says, her voice crackling with fear as she recalls the events.

"So Lucifer held the proceedings, but Satan was the ultimate judge?" I ask, still trying to understand the relationship between Satan and Lucifer.

"To answer your question more thoroughly, think of it this way: Lucifer embodies the corporeal form, while Satan represents the spiritual essence. Together, they operate in body and spirit with an authority that brings fear to any who oppose them."

"An authority? Whose authority?" I question. "Is it Satan's authority?"

"No, Satan is an entity that wields the authority of the vessel of power given to them during their union," Rochelle explains, leaving me with more questions than answers.

"The vessel of power?" I whisper to myself, trying not to get too caught up in my thoughts so I can hear what she has to say.

"Satan wasn't always a part of Lucifer, Christopher. You see, the Creator exiled Lucifer from the heavens when war rumbled in the wake of creation. This 'Angel of Light' was cast into the sea of shadows upon the Earth. Darkness clung to him there, pulling him down to the depths of a formless world.

"It was there, in the midst of darkness, after being rejected by the Creator, that a new purpose and revelation were birthed; his eyes opened to a new order and authority that had lain in the shadows for centuries. It was in darkness that he became 'purified' from the Creator's light. It was in darkness that he was introduced to a new side of himself—a part of himself that became more alive in the midst of darkness than he had ever found within himself in the midst of light.

"There," Rochelle emphasizes, "the prince of evil spirits, Satan, was revealed to Lucifer's consciousness, tending to his scars left by his own betrayal and revealing to him the powers he now possessed. This was the beginning of a union that would change the course of humanity and the world.

"Though the judgment of the Almighty still resonated within him," Rochelle carries on with her tale, "darkness consumed him, filling him with a ferocious hatred for the sons of Adam and especially the daughters of Eve."

"Who is Adam?" I interrupt once more. " And who is Eve?"

"You've not heard of Adam and Eve?" Rochelle replies, confused by my ignorance. "They are the firstborn son and daughter of creation. I will explain more about them and how they enter the picture shortly. It's important not to jump too far ahead. You must first understand how Satan came into the picture and who fashioned the vessel of power, I mentioned earlier, that would give them authority in the upper realms.

"Shall I continue?" she asks.

"Yes, of course," I reply, anxiously awaiting what she has to say while feeling a bit foolish for not immediately realizing she was referring to Adam and Eve from the Bible.

"He was acutely aware of his fate," Rochelle continues, *"—an eventual fall into the endless lake of fire, as prophesied during his*

judgment before the Almighty. But he resolved to exact retribution on those who caused such division. With a malevolent determination, he orchestrated a multi-generational campaign against the bloodlines of Adam, determined to thwart the fulfillment of the ancient prophecies of the Son of Man. His vengeance would be relentless, his every action driven by an unyielding desire to change the prophecies of old: to see the Almighty defeated, or at the very least, His beloved "children" turned against Him.

The day Lucifer was baptized by the Lord of Darkness, he and Satan crafted their own set of laws, even their own throne of judgment—a dark counterpart to the divine order. Their pact was a defiant challenge to the plans of the Almighty, establishing a system of justice that stood in direct opposition to the righteousness of the Creator.

Baptized by the Lord of Darkness? I wonder. *Does she mean Death?*

"This sinister agreement was designed to enslave and corrupt all who followed their path, embodying the antithesis of divine judgment and eternal justice. Their throne of judgment mirrored the Creator's in form, but was fueled by malevolence and deceit, seeking to rival and undermine the purity of God's will."

"How do you know about all of this?" I inquire.

"You asked about judgment, did you not?"

"Yes, I . . ." I start to respond, but she interrupts. It's becoming an ever-growing theme in our conversations.

"Then allow me the courtesy of your silence as I share," she rebukes my inquiry.

"A cleansing ritual must take place before you can enter into his presence," she tells me. I flinch at her words, fear gripping me. The thought of her leaving and never returning fills me with dread. So I quiet my mind, suppressing my thoughts to avoid angering her and to absorb whatever I may need to know before the time comes for me to stand before his throne, just as she had.

Every soul undergoes a baptism in the pool of shadows where Death first immersed Lucifer. This dark transformation reshapes you completely, preparing you for the isolation that follows. In this isolation, you relive the fall of our lord, experiencing his thoughts, his emotions, and the harrowing baptism by Death that bestowed upon him his dreadful authority in this realm and on Earth. It is a journey through his torment and power, a forced empathy with his suffering and dominion, that marks the beginning of your own transformation.

You see, dear boy, I have seen his story; we all have. We are made to see through his eyes the "weakness" within the Creator so that we too may cast judgment upon any who have ever known Him, as you have.

You must understand, there were compelling reasons for Heaven's first war and the descent of one-third of the hosts. The origins of judgment are intertwined with these events, and without understanding them, you cannot truly comprehend why judgment exists at all.

It all begins with the tale of Lucifer, the Morning Star, whose pride and rebellion ignited a celestial war, setting off a chain of events that shaped the very fabric of our existence. Through his fall, we uncover the truths of creation, the first judgment, and the eternal enmity between the serpent and the sons and daughters of Eve.

"To truly grasp the concept of judgment, as you've requested, we must start at the beginning," Rochelle continues. "This is his story. Though he was first created in light, his journey truly began in darkness."

Intrigued by Rochelle's words, I lean back, my hands outstretched against the soil as I look up slightly, watching as her descriptive words cast images before me as if she is able to project them through some magic unknown to me.

As I watch, the cascading colors take shape, swirling and melding into vibrant patterns that become increasingly distinct and vivid. The dim light, cast solely by the surrounding flames, gradually transforms into a strange comfort, casting dancing shadows that seem to tell their own tales. The fears that consumed me just moments earlier begin to fade, replaced by an almost hypnotic fascination. The warmth of the fire and the vividness of Rochelle's story transport me to another world, one where the boundaries between reality and imagination blur, and the flames themselves seem to whisper the ancient truths of creation and judgment.

Who can say they were a witness to the Earth when its foundations were laid? Who can attest to the majesty of the heavens when they were formed? With which of the angelic hosts did the Creator share His very thoughts and opinions with when the Earth lay bare and formless? Who did the Creator allow in His midst during the wonder of the creation of the heavens and the Earth, as if to share with him the secrets locked within them? Who among creation could walk in the midst of the stones of fire unscathed by their fury, or be welcomed into existence adorned in splendor, on the day of His creation? Who among the angels was created as a symbol of perfection and walked within Eden, the garden of God, when He revealed its beginning to the heavens? Who held the envy of the angels as one among a countless congregation and was allowed to ascend to the mountains of the Most High and enter into the throne room of the Eternal One? Was it one from the race of man, made from lower particles of the dust of the earth? Surely not, for their existence had not even taken its place in time. It was he, the one they called Lucifer, the Light Bearer, the Anointed Guardian Cherub, the one created to be the utmost standard of perfection.

The angels had to consult with Lucifer before they could seek an audience with the Creator, and it was left to Lucifer to authorize those whom he deemed worthy enough, outside of himself, to enter into the gates of the Creator's presence during the majesty of His creation. Lucifer was revered and respected for his appointed position he held, for the

Creator gave to him the gift of wisdom in order to handle all of Heaven's affairs.

The angels were captivated by Lucifer's other abilities as well. It was said that Lucifer had a mysterious affinity for music, something that few possessed and none ever compared to that of Lucifer. When he played, something would come alive in him, creating light that would radiate from his entire being, as if the music came bursting forth from within him. It was as though he and the light had become one through singing— dancing in an endless display of harmonious brilliance and rhythm. Heaven was captivated by his performances, the angels mesmerized by his beauty and abilities.

His broad knowledge of words, and the power they carried were whimsical in nature and mystical in speech which Lucifer used to gain the attention and favor of the heavenly hosts. He was a master at captivating any audience and he especially loved to capture that of the Eternal's attention through his words that flowed through his expression of melody when playing for the Eternal in His heavenly courts.

It was Lucifer's utmost delight to spend time in the presence of the Eternal One. He relished the days he would commune with the Eternal in deep conversations over the philosophies of eternity, and the mysteries of the Eternal's perfect works, especially when it pertained to Lucifer himself. The Eternal was delighted with Lucifer, this Angel of Light, this creature of perfection with unmatched beauty. Lucifer considered himself honored that the Eternal One had created such majestic examples of perfection as he had seen within himself and the heavens which surrounded them.

Heaven was perfect.

The angels were perfect.

It was in this perfection that Lucifer imagined his place beside the Eternal One forever.

But Lucifer's story took a twisted turn that no one amongst the host saw coming, and it started with a rumor that spread like wildfire throughout the realms of Heaven of a new plan about to unfold in the cosmos. A new realm was about to be born, a new order about to be put into place. A new creation was at hand, another story was about to be written in the Eternal's book, but this one was said to be something quite unique and unlike anything the Creator had ever done before.

Each phase of creation was meant to tell a unique story about the character of God and a new chapter was about to be revealed. Excitement buzzed in the heavenly realms of what was to come, because this time, the Eternal was going to be writing a new side of Himself and imprinting upon His creation His very image. Something never thought possible.

The realm to come would contain this new creation as well as many new creatures the Almighty was excited to share. There would be a new race and these beings would be made like vessels to hold within them something very sacred and powerful to the Eternal—His love.

The knowledge of love was deeply discussed and understood in Heaven, but the emotion of love was something unwitnessed and held dormant within the Creator until His new creation could be revealed. True love shines brightest in the midst of adversity, weakness, and frailty. Angels, in their perfection, design, and nature, were the opposite; they could never fully comprehend or be made to understand the true nature of love without sacrifice. True love requires the ultimate sacrifice: to lay down one's life for another. The Eternal One had much to reveal to all, and much needed to be written in what would forever be known as His Living Word. He had told the story of perfection through His hosts, but now it was through the creation of man that He was writing the story of love. Each piece of this new creation would be a piece of the Creator which, through His divinity, would be set apart from any other so that the whole story of love could be told.

Lucifer could not escape from the growing rumors and found himself deeply disturbed by them, for if they were true, why did the Eternal not consult with him about such matters as He had done so many times in the past? Why did the Eternal One not share His thoughts and allow Lucifer access to His plans as He had done so many times before?

Was he not worthy enough to share in this exciting new phase of creation and experience for himself the intricacies of love? Did the

Almighty not love his angels anymore or believe them incapable of love? Did He not love Lucifer? Why was the Eternal holding back from Lucifer the secrets of this creation when Lucifer was given special audience to the heavens and earth when they were formed? Had the Eternal One become unsatisfied with his heavenly angels—or his favored son the Morning Star?

Confusion swept over Lucifer's mind like a tempest stirring a calm sea. Lucifer had never felt confused about anything, for how could a being, created to be perfect, be consumed with jealousy and envy as though challenging his own perfection and position within Heaven? He was held in charge of Heaven's affairs because of his sound and perfect wisdom granted to him by one of the Spirits of God. But why was his wisdom betraying him now when he needed it the most?

Troubled by these unfamiliar emotions, Lucifer decided to consult with the Eternal One and lay these rumors and fears to rest once and for all. However, when Lucifer approached the throne room of the Almighty to consult with Him about these concerns, in hopes to be comforted by the Almighty's explanations of what was to come, he found that the gates to the Eternal's throne room were closed. Two archangels stood in front of the gates, demanding Lucifer to turn around and leave, explaining to Lucifer that the Eternal had shut the gates to the throne room so that He could consult with Himself.

Lucifer's fear transformed into an abrupt outburst of rage, his voice roaring with curses directed at the archangels—a behavior he had never exhibited before. His anger surprised even himself, but he swiftly sought to rationalize it.

"How dare these archangels assume that the Eternal wouldn't consult and discuss such profound matters with the leader of His heavenly host, the very beacon of Heaven's light!" he exclaimed, his thoughts consumed by an unfamiliar and escalating emotion.

Profound issues demanded discussion with the Eternal, yet the archangels remained steadfast, reminding Lucifer that their obedience was unwavering, prioritizing the commands of the Eternal God above all else.

Lucifer, consumed by seething anger, departed abruptly, his resplendent golden cloak billowing behind him like a banner of his fury. As he left, a rising tide of fears and insecurities gripped him, planting insidious doubts within his once-unshakable confidence.

He began to entertain the troubling notion that perhaps the Eternal, the very source of perfection instilled within the angels, had grown weary of celestial perfection.

"Could it be that the angels were no longer sufficient to satisfy His divine desires?" he seethed in his inner turmoil.

Lucifer's pride further fueled his anxieties, prompting him to question whether the Creator had also grown disenchanted with his own wisdom and insight that could be useful to Him during these proceedings. The Creator's prolonged silence, in Lucifer's eyes, seemed to confirm these unsettling suspicions, stoking the fires of his contempt as he interpreted these events through the lens of his own wounded ego.

Deprived of access to the Creator's presence, Lucifer's mind became an arena of relentless turmoil. His thoughts, once sources of divine insight, transformed into treacherous adversaries that sowed the seeds of deception within his very soul. For the first time, Lucifer found himself in a state of profound unrest, a sensation he had believed impossible.

As his thoughts spiraled, they conjured nightmarish visions of the new creation and how it might disrupt his lofty position. He envisioned this new order replacing him, supplanting his role within the Eternal's innermost chambers. In his inner turmoil, Lucifer grappled with profound questions. How could the Creator fail to grasp the havoc this new creation might wreak upon the perfection and sanctity of Heaven and Earth? Why had the Eternal kept this revelation from him, excluding him from the divine plan?

At the core of Lucifer's thoughts lay a profound sense of betrayal, a foundational emotion that fanned the flames of his discontent and set him on a dangerous path.

When the Eternal finally broke His prolonged silence to unveil His divine plan to the angels, Lucifer retreated to his secluded sanctuary, already harboring convictions he had woven into a narrative he deemed irrefutable. From a distance, he observed the Mountain of the Most High, where the Creator addressed all of creation. At this moment, Lucifer cared little about not being placed front and center to witness the unfolding revelation. The venom of jealousy had surreptitiously crept into the recesses of his mind, and his consciousness had already embraced a distorted vision of what lay ahead, even before the Creator had uttered a word.

As the Almighty's words resounded, Lucifer chose to listen from a distance, his gaze averted from the majesty of the Creator's warm and tranquil presence. This pivotal moment marked the inception of his downward spiral into darkness, as the poison of envy clouded his perception and separated him from the radiant grace of the Divine.

The Creator's long-anticipated revelation echoed through the gathering of the heavenly host.

"From the very dust of the Earth, a new creation shall emerge," declared the Creator, His divine proclamation echoing through the celestial realms. "You, my beloved messengers and ambassadors, shall be entrusted with the sacred duty of serving and guiding this nascent creation I shall name Man. Through them, I shall impart my own image and unveil the wonders of my boundless grace as I intricately weave the tapestry of love into existence."

Within the confines of his own sanctuary, Lucifer's thoughts churned with indignation.

"How dare the Creator choose to bestow His essence upon such frail vessels!" He fumed internally while voicing his concerns among a few of his angelic brethren who followed him. "I, the paragon of perfection, brimming with wisdom and adorned in flawless beauty, shall never bow to the will of such inferior beings."

Lucifer's pride recoiled at the idea that the Creator had not even considered entrusting something as powerful as this divine imprint to him or his fellow angels. He viewed it as an affront to the Creator's own divinity, a grave offense, and a personal insult to Lucifer and the six commanders who served beneath his leadership. But, he did not contain his emotions within himself; rather he spread his lies within his ranks causing others to question the Almighty's intentions.

What began as a small seed of confusion led to a mighty oak tree of fear and doubt. In fact, had he been allowed to stand in the presence of the Most High, with his heart being corrupted by the seed of anger, the Eternal's righteousness would have consumed him. The Eternal's righteousness would have consumed Lucifer had he been allowed to go in the inner courts and stand in His presence. The Most High was protecting Lucifer from His glory, but Lucifer did not see it that way. Lucifer's light was cast away from him in anger that day. He harbored an anger so unfamiliar to him that others within his charge also began to fall victim to the lies he was spreading. An arrogance arose within Lucifer that led him to believe the Creator to be flawed, impetuous, and imperfect.

How could the Eternal One create flawed and imperfect creatures unless He too was flawed and imperfect, *he thought.*

Not willing to sit by and watch his position slip from his grasp, Lucifer convinced all those within his inner courts to demand of the Creator an audience to adjust the Creator's plans and remain a single unified heavenly order under his command. Believing his numbers to be a symbol of his new found authority within the heavenly ranks, Lucifer ascended the mountain of the Most High with his army of heavenly hosts behind him. But he was not met by a god willing to alter the plans of creation with those whom He had created. Instead, Lucifer was met by the King of Kings, the Lord of Lords, hallowed be His name. Descending from the throne of the Most High was the remainder of His untainted host bearing arms against the ascending power that would dare challenge the authority of the Most High God.

In the celestial expanse, the symphony of war reverberated, stars cascading like meteors from the heavens, while division shook the very foundation of the inner courts. In the ethereal realm of Heaven, where *once there had been only harmony and serenity, now erupted the first cataclysmic battle among the celestial beings. Angels, beings of pure light and divine purpose, now clashed with one another, their celestial armor and weapons gleaming with a radiance that had never known the horrors of war. The heavens themselves seemed to convulse as the very essence of creation recoiled at the violence unfolding within its sacred confines.*

As the angelic legions collided, their wings of iridescent feathers and eyes ablaze with determination, they met their celestial kin in a tumultuous clash of wills. Swords forged by the Creator's hand clashed with dazzling spears of light, and shields adorned with ethereal gems met blows of unimaginable force. With each clash, stars fell from the skies like tears shed for the celestial conflict, their luminous trails marking the descent of celestial warriors locked in combat.

Galaxies were ripped apart by the rift torn in the wake of this celestial strife, and the very fabric of the universe quivered in response to the unprecedented battle unfolding among the angels. The echoes of their conflict reverberated through the cosmos, leaving behind scars in the tapestry of creation, and the destiny of realms hung precariously in the balance as celestial beings fought with a fervor and intensity never before witnessed in the heavenly abode.

As the third sun descended behind the majestic imperial mountains, the cosmic battle in the realms of Heaven approached its culmination. Lucifer, witnessing the fall of his angelic brethren one by one, stealthily slipped away.

Each step he took towards the outer gate of the divine throne room fueled his confidence, bolstered by the broken and battered remains of his misguided followers who had paved his treacherous path. Rising from the distant rocky terrain, a magnificent gate marked the entrance to the Almighty's sanctum. Its ethereal radiance, adorned with pearls and pure gold, cast its luminance far into the cosmos, with stars and galaxies above reflecting off every column, baluster, and spike.

Lucifer believed he had triumphed and that he would ascend to the heavens and establish his throne above God's stars. He envisioned ruling from the distant mountain of gods in the northern realms, ascending to the loftiest heights to become akin to the Most High.

In the distance, Lucifer could discern the presence of one of the archangels, Michael, as though he had anticipated his arrival. Recalling their previous exchange, where Lucifer had spewed curses at Michael, he felt an unwavering confidence in his ability to overthrow him. As Lucifer approached Michael, the archangel and defender of Heaven, leader of God's celestial army and the mightiest of the ninefold hierarchy, he too exuded assurance in the authority bestowed upon him by the Creator.

For Michael, this long-awaited moment was an opportunity to unveil a power that no one had witnessed before. He, along with others of his kind known as the Seraphim, had never employed the tremendous authority vested within them. There had been no prior wars or threats to the heavenly realms that necessitated their utilization. Nevertheless, they had always existed, their unseen power concealed despite their immense size and magnificence. Among the angelic hosts, particularly those under Lucifer's command, the Seraphim were considered lesser beings in the heavenly hierarchy due to their untapped and unknown authority.

Michael stood before Lucifer, a towering figure adorned in resplendent garments and scaled armor. His majestic wings stretched fully to either side, obstructing any path Lucifer might have contemplated. This unspoken declaration made it clear that Michael had no intention of permitting Lucifer to draw any closer. Michael's very presence emanated an unprecedented glory and power, never before witnessed by anyone.

Despite the evident transformation within Michael, Lucifer, resolute in his self-proclaimed authority, refused to yield to Michael. While the changes in Michael's appearance were unmistakable, Lucifer clung to his belief in his own superiority.

Their battle could be heard throughout the heavens. Lucifer, although untrained against such an opponent as Michael, manipulated his body around the battlefield like a serpent. Like a skilled swordsman, he parried one attack after another against Michael. Slithering in and out of Michael's hands, Lucifer manipulated the light around him to disorient his opponent.

Lucifer began to believe he was gaining the upper hand. His power had grown immensely, and his influence spread like wildfire among the angelic hosts. Yet, in his rising arrogance, he underestimated Michael. After all, they had known each other for millennia, since their creation long ago, and their bond was as close as that of brothers.

Lucifer, blinded by his own pride, failed to see the true depth of Michael's strength. Michael was humble but fierce, quiet but commanding. His unwavering faith and dedication to the authority of Heaven made him a formidable opponent. The power Michael wielded was unlike anything Lucifer had ever witnessed, save for that of God Himself. In the end, it was Michael's steadfast resolve and the divine authority he embodied that proved to be Lucifer's greatest challenge.

In an effort to strike at the heart of Michael, Lucifer's confidence betrayed him. The battlefield crackled with tension as the two celestial beings clashed, their auras illuminating the heavens with an otherworldly light. Lucifer, fueled by pride and ambition, lunged with all his might. But Michael, his resolve unshaken and his loyalty to Heaven unyielding, anticipated Lucifer's next move with an almost preternatural insight.

In a swift, decisive motion, Michael met Lucifer's attack with a blade to the chest. The impact resonated through the ethereal plane, a testament to Michael's strength and precision. Lucifer staggered, his once formidable power now dwindling. The realization of his defeat washed over him as he fell to his knees, the weight of his hubris dragging him down.

Laying face down after Michael's last blow, Lucifer's wings lay tattered and his spirit broken. He was powerless to stop what was to come. Michael stood over him, his expression a mix of sorrow and resolute determination. The authority of Heaven surged through Michael, a palpable force that Lucifer could no longer defy. The finality of his defeat was inescapable, and as the heavens watched, Lucifer's reign of rebellion came to an end.

Seven stars stood before the Lord of Hosts, splendid in every way, fashioned by the Almighty Himself. Like burning mountains, their presence radiated into the heavens above for all to see. Each commanded the legions of Heaven with authority over the gates of the ancient beasts beneath. The Eternal's gaze, both sorrowful and resolute, bore into their beings as He pronounced His divine verdict. It was a moment that would echo through the annals of eternity, a sentence that would forever alter the course of history. There would be no reconciliation for their actions against the Almighty God. No mercy for their betrayal against Heaven and against the Almighty's angelic host who, betrayed and manipulated by each of them, would share in their fate. Damnation could be the only recompense for their actions. And so, seeing unrighteousness within the stars, the Lord said to Raphael, "Bind them and cast them into the darkness."

Raphael, fashioning chains made of the purest light, bound each of the seven, as well as their legions, and opened a portal of Heaven beneath the inner courts, revealing the realm of Dudael beneath the Great Throne Room of the Most High. For the first time, the stars bore witness to the empty, jagged lands where fire burned endlessly, relentless in its pursuit to persecute all the luminaries of Heaven whose hearts revealed the very blackness that befitted their damnation.

With one hand holding the great chain binding the seven stars and the legions under their command, Raphael slung the chain downward like a great serpent's tail whipping its foe, casting the unrighteous stars of Heaven like lightning from the sky into the exposed forbidden lands beneath the earth.

In a climactic moment, felt throughout the realm, Lucifer, the once revered Morning Star and a third of all of the hosts were banished from the heavens, their luminous forms plummeting from the heavenly heights like bolts of lightning streaking across the starlit firmament.

The other angels, witnesses to this unprecedented event, gazed in awe and sorrow as their once-beloved brothers and sisters fell into the abyss below. As they descended, the heavens wept tears of radiant light, mourning the loss of those they had loved. The cries of the fallen echoed through the void, a haunting lament that resonated with the tragic gravity of their rebellion. Darkness draped over them like cascading water, penetrating their beings. Their screams were drowned out as the inky blackness forced its way into their mouths, drawing out any last cries for redemption, washing away the purity once refined by the Almighty. Darkness enveloped them, each according to their transgressions. As the pain of betrayal became more pronounced, a corresponding transformation took place, rendering each unrecognizable to the other. They fled further into the darkness, seeking solace within the realms of the forgotten.

But Lucifer did not hide away in shame as the others. He descended further, the darkness enveloping him like a suffocating shroud. It was a darkness so profound that even the divine radiance of the Eternal's light from above could not penetrate it. Lucifer found himself in a forsaken abyss, far removed from the celestial splendor he had once known.

He knew what lurked within the shadows here; within the chasm of the abyss. He knew of the beasts that lay within the darkness of creation awaiting the prophecies of old to be fulfilled. Never had he imagined that he would be part of the prophecies he had read, but the time was upon him now.

One such creature of darkness, Folly welcomed and embraced Lucifer as one would welcome a longtime friend. But he was disgusted by the presence of her, and what he knew she represented. He sank deeper into darkness not yet ready for any acknowledgment of her presence nor any recognition of what lay within this realm.

Upon banishment, Lucifer had been stripped of the heavenly treasures he'd proudly worn to reflect his rank and status. One such article he missed most was the Cloak of Wisdom given to him by the Lady Wisdom herself. Without this and the other items, Lucifer was left bare and tormented with his thoughts. He felt powerless and lost, unable to gain insight as to where he was to go or what he was to do next. He sank deeper into the uncharted territories of darkness until he came to the end of himself. Shadows of regret and sorrow enveloped him, tearing at the fabric of his identity until he was but a shattered remnant of his former self, lost in the abyss of his own making.

The Angel of Light found himself cloaked in the very thing he was taught to detest and forced to embrace the haunted cries of brokenness and phantom screams of despair heard far and wide from the once magnificent hosts who would no longer walk in the presence of the Almighty nor dwell in the realm of light again.

Cast into darkness, the door of Heaven barred against him for all eternity, Lucifer toiled and writhed for many moons, struggling to discover his new identity in these lower realms of creation. He had never witnessed the power of the Eternal rise in anger and was deeply ashamed of his arrogance in thinking that any creation, regardless of rank, could challenge the authority of the Almighty God. The fallen host, who once revered Lucifer, now condemned him, holding him responsible for their downfall. They refused to seek his counsel again, mocking the former son of the Morning and lamenting their foolishness in following someone arrogant enough to believe he could set his throne above the stars of God. As his six generals each went their separate ways, the once mighty stars of Heaven were fully disbanded, searching the chasms of darkness for what lay dormant within, a place they had been taught never to explore.

CHAPTER 16

The Creation

Genesis 2:8-9

"Now the Lord God had planted a garden in the east, in Eden; and there he put the man he had formed. The Lord God made all kinds of trees grow out of the ground—trees that were pleasing to the eye and good for food. In the middle of the garden were the tree of life and the tree of the knowledge of good and evil."

Genesis 1:26-30

Then God said, "Let us make mankind in our image, in our likeness, so that they may rule over the fish in the sea and the birds in the sky, over the livestock and all the wild animals, and over all the creatures that move along the ground."

So God created mankind in his own image, in the image of God he created them; male and female he created them.

God blessed them and said to them, "Be fruitful and increase in number; fill the earth and subdue it. Rule over the fish in the sea and the birds in the sky and over every living creature that moves on the ground."

Then God said, "I give you every seed-bearing plant on the face of the whole earth and every tree that has fruit with seed in it. They will be yours for food.

And to all the beasts of the earth and all the birds in the sky and all the creatures that move along the ground—everything that has the breath of life in it—I give every green plant for food." And it was so.

"**C**reation was underway," Rochelle continues, capturing my imagination. I can't help but be astounded by her knowledge of events that happened so long ago.

Where did she get so much information? Was it all given to her at judgment, as she mentioned before? I think to myself.

Surely not! Her story shows Lucifer vulnerable, even defeated. I can't imagine Lucifer, from what I have heard of him, would ever appear to any of his subjects as anything other than a god to be worshiped and feared. Where then was this incredible collection of memories coming from?

"Christopher? Are you listening?" Rochelle inquires, wanting to make sure I'm following.

"Yes," I respond, "I'm just in awe of your knowledge and the amount of detail you've shared."

"Naturally, how else could I convey it? Where was I?

As one third of Heaven's once majestic hosts lay within the empty abyss in the realm of darkness searching and mourning the terms of their damnation, Creation was in full swing. While Heaven had suffered great losses at the hands of Lucifer, the Eternal One could not waste time with His plans to move forward forming the realm of Earth and all that would inhabit it.

Lucifer was in turmoil over the loss of his seat, his position and above all his God. He cried and pleaded within the nothingness for redemption in hopes that his Creator would hear and have mercy. Even if he had been heard, mercy was not given, not to him nor any of the hosts. As time slipped away, life was engulfing the empty places of the Earth and revealing to all, the Creator's majesty through the work of his hands and the manifestation revealed through His spoken words.

Heaven and Earth were changing. Life, in all its intricacies, was being established in the realm of the living. The laws that govern time and space were being solidified for all to witness. Lucifer could only watch from a distance at the splendor of what the Creator was speaking into existence. It consumed him, plagued his mind with a hatred for the Almighty that made him seek deeper places within the darkness that none had ever imagined. The air was thick there, evidence of cataclysmic events from the Creator's works above that could still be felt even in these outer embankments of the darkness. Here, Lucifer could collect his thoughts and reconstruct a new purpose from the ashes of what remained of himself.

In his isolation, the darkness played tricks on his mind. He began to lose his grasp on reality until something finally broke out from within him. A spirit came forth and arose out of him, manifesting itself as if separate from Lucifer yet still one and the same. This spirit immediately began revealing secrets to Lucifer, revelations of who Lucifer truly was. The spirit exposed to Lucifer that light no longer defined him. In fact, it had been the light that held him back from entering into his true power all along, power that could only be attained through darkness.

Lucifer initially rejected the spirit still holding on to the shred of righteousness left within him that he wished to salvage. He was the Angel of Light, after all. The opposite of what this spirit was revealing himself to be! But the spirit was relentless in its effort to reveal the powers and principalities that lay waiting within him.

As the spirit worked, Lucifer's thoughts betrayed him; he had no control over his own mind. A new foundational belief was rooting within him that the darkness was safe, that it held the power to reclaim his position. He was captivated by these deceptive promises of reclaiming his title. The fallen hosts had rejected him and wanted nothing more to do with Lucier's self-proclaimed divinity. He would do anything to reclaim his rightful position and authority over them again.

In a moment of confused emotions, torn between the desire for everything he had known and the desperate need to reclaim his authority at any cost, he was driven to madness. The conflicting desires gnawed at his soul, leaving him fractured and desperate. In a frantic attempt to escape the feelings tearing him apart, he spread his wings and took flight from the depths of the chasm.

Transcending through one realm of darkness after another, he sought to escape the torment that lay within. Each realm presented new shadows and horrors, yet none were as relentless as the voice echoing in his mind. Fleeing from this unrelenting torment, he raced through the empty voids of the outer realms, his flight fueled by sheer desperation, as if his very life depended on it.

He soared like a fallen star, shooting through the firmament, his trail of light a fleeting beacon against the endless night. As he streaked across the sky, his light began to fade, dissolving into the darkness, symbolizing his relentless, yet ultimately futile, escape from the inner turmoil that pursued him.

After dragging his weary self through the endless wasteland, past the abyss of the seas and beyond the mountain range of fire that raged day and night, Lucifer finally came upon the first light he had seen since his fall. Sweet relief! The voice inside of him immediately hushed into silence upon Lucifer's arrival to the light because there, in the midst of darkness, he mistakenly stumbled upon the new creation.

The new world before him, glowing in a light recently birthed, was strangely familiar to him, as if he had been there before but could no longer recognize its majesty. He could feel the Spirit of the Creator's presence radiating throughout it and basked in the familiar warmth of the Almighty's presence. Fearful of being recognized in such a majestic place, Lucifer hid himself on the outskirts of this new wonder.

Dare he go any further? Dare he step any closer to the very presence that condemned him to the darkness from which he came?

He looked back at the vast chasms, awaiting the voice to console him in his unfamiliar hesitation. But, upon realizing the absence of the spirit, and believing himself to be safely concealed, he stepped forward towards the new world, curious at its perplexities.

Though he fell from the heavens, now walking in the midst of the Almighty's latest handiwork, he could not help but marvel at its beauty and creativity. A weight lifted off of him in the absence of darkness; the immersion of the Almighty's presence brought a peace back into Lucifer's *being that he had forgotten. A deep longing arose within Lucifer that still desired for when he basked in the Creator's presence and sang endless melodies in His courts.*

Lucifer felt welcomed back into the light from which he was first formed as he stepped into this new realm of creation—the realm that the Creator eagerly anticipated and birthed on the heels of Heaven's first war.

With outstretched arms, he reveled in the sensation of touch, the cool breeze caressing his skin and the rough texture of the earth beneath his fingertips. His senses awakened, allowing him to fully immerse himself in the physical realm. With each breath in his nostrils, he inhaled the earthy scent of the cedar forests, the tang of salt in the air, and the crisp freshness of the mountain breeze.

Enthralled by the Creator's boundless imagination, he marveled at the intricate beauty of the world around him. Every detail, from the delicate veins of a leaf to the towering peaks of the mountains, spoke of a divine craftsmanship beyond comprehension. With each step, he felt a profound connection to the natural world, humbled by its vastness and complexity.

As he walked among the giant cedar trees, he felt dwarfed by their presence, their branches reaching towards the sky like silent sentinels guarding the secrets of the forest. Shafts of sunlight pierced through the dense canopy above, casting a warm golden glow upon the forest floor.

Strolling along the endless crystal coastlines, he listened to the soothing rhythm of the waves, their gentle lapping against the shore a timeless lullaby. The sand beneath his feet was soft and warm, the salty breeze invigorating his senses as he gazed out at the boundless expanse of the sea. And in the distance, rising majestically against the azure sky, stood a grand mountain range with seven peaks.

Continuously captivated by the crystalline shores and the celestial embrace of sky meeting sea along the horizon, Lucifer embarked on his ascent of the seven peaks. Each summit shimmered in the luminous atmosphere, still reverberating with the Almighty's recent proclamation, their towering presence affirming their dominion over the lands below. Each peak, made different from each other in form and magnitude, postured itself in reverence to the seventh which sat in the center of a valley.

As he laid his eyes for the first time upon the seventh and most magnificent of mountains, he noticed a most peculiar thing. Though the other six were quite different, they were all bare at their summits and raised at their peaks. However, the seventh had no peak. Instead it appeared con-caved at its summit with a significant source of light that emanated from within it.

As he traversed the final summit, moving beyond the clouds and past the crystal waterfalls that fed the lakes below, he encountered a bounty of fragrant trees lining the edges of the peak. He stood in awe, gazing at the valley below, nestled within the mountain as if shielding itself from the outside world.

Created as a sanctuary for something dear to the Almighty upon His visitation, there before him lay a lush and magnificent garden, overflowing with succulent, flowering fruit trees and vineyards. The garden was a vivid tapestry of abundance, with an array of floral delights and bountiful harvests stretching as far as the eye could see. He paused in an orchard of trees whose branches were clothed in a display of exotic vines with flowers hanging over into a lake that sparkled under the pink hued sky like crystals gleaming in the sunlight.

Lucifer examined one of the fruits hanging off a branch before plucking it from its stem, noticing how the richness of the red skin and how the sweet fragrance caused the soul to yearn for a taste. Holding the fruit in his hand, Lucifer became very aware that this physical realm was awakening desires within that had never been awakened before. He was captivated by his surroundings and realized that this was not an unfamiliar creation as he had first thought.

Lucifer found himself once again in Eden, the garden of God, a place he remembered from long ago. But something was different. Now manifested within the physical realm, a new power resonated from within the garden, a power that had not existed before. As he drew nearer to the source of this energy, Lucifer scrutinized the garden with intense curiosity and caution, keenly aware of the unfamiliar force that now permeated this once-familiar place.

Following streams of turquoise water that contrasted beautifully against the black and white sands underneath his feet, Lucifer made his way down the valley to the heart of the garden. There, he was able to find the source of this unique power to which he was drawn. Two trees, unique to anything else he had seen, stood before him. They were magnificent, not because they rivaled the great Cedar for its height or the Oak for its strength. They were magnificent because of what was within them.

An energy emanated from each that could be felt within the earth beneath his feet. He could sense the connectivity they had with the rest of the garden as if each tree shared some symbiotic relationship with all of the other foliage. Upon closer examination of the two, Lucifer was very familiar with the first one.

Set ever so slightly higher than the other, her long outstretched branches, some kissing the earth, were adorned with radiant fruits stemming from wonderfully unique vines wrapping themselves across every branch. Her fragrance was more sweet and intoxicating than any before or any to come. Lucifer knew this tree never withered or grew old and that her branches and fruits never spoiled or tarnished. The pink and red flowers that adorned every branch were as vibrant today as they were the day Lucifer last gazed upon her.

The Tree of Life, he thought to himself.

When Lucifer tried to grab one of the small low-hanging fruits, he was met with opposition. A powerful presence radiated from the tree, reminding Lucifer of another familiar but distant being from a time long ago, one with whom Lucifer longed to gain an audience with again.

The Tree of Life turned her leaves and magnificence away from Lucifer almost as if ashamed by his presence. Realizing that she did not wish not to speak with Lucifer, he turned his gaze beyond her glory to the second tree.

Magnificent, *Lucifer thought to himself as he studied its unique design.*

Similar to a fir tree with long, thin, soft bristles at the ends of each branch, he too radiated an internal power as he majestically stood tall in Lucifer's presence. Unlike fir trees, though, large thorns, resembling teeth, were concealed beneath the soft bristles, covering the entirety of the tree. Even more peculiar were the bushels of fruit, reminiscent of those found on palms but vibrant in color and appearance, hanging ornately from its thorny branches.

"You're hiding something, aren't you?" *Lucifer questioned as he studied him, recognizing the conflict on the outside of his appearance that clearly radiated a similar conflict within. But, before he could turn from his presence, the tree welcomed Lucifer as one would welcome a friend.*

Dipping one of his branches low to the earth, the tree postured itself before Lucifer, allowing him to examine the fruit more closely. The fruit's vibrant colors seemed to radiate from within, casting a mesmerizing glow that captivated Lucifer's attention. The surface of the fruit shimmered with an intoxicating array of hues, each more alluring than the last. As he drew nearer, the smells that wafted from the fruit left Lucifer stupefied. The scents were a tantalizing blend of sweetness and earthiness, rich and layered, filling the air with an almost magical fragrance that overwhelmed his senses and drew him in irresistibly. Power radiated from within this tree as well but not the same sort of power as could be witnessed from the Tree of Life.

Gazing upon this unfamiliar tree before him, beckoning him to taste its fruit, Lucifer felt a strange recognition. Within the tree, he saw something that mirrored his own reflection upon the inky black seas of iniquity after his fall. The tree's aura, its dark allure and underlying menace, resonated with the same depths of despair and defiance he had seen in himself. It was as if the tree embodied a part of his own essence, twisted and corrupted, yet undeniably powerful and captivating.

"You were correct in surmising that a concealed power lay within the fruit," the familiar voice whispered to Lucifer once again. "The knowledge of good and evil pulses through its flesh. Anyone who eats of it shall be granted great power, equal even to the Almighty!" The voice's words echoed in Lucifer's mind, filling him with a sinister promise.

Intrigued by the obvious concealment of the power and guided by the voice within that somehow knew much of its origin, Lucifer delicately removed one of the fruits from its thorny branches. There was much to learn of this unfamiliar fruit, much insight that may be useful for a time to come.

Suddenly, he felt the air stir around him. The garden was awakening and singing praises to a familiar presence. The Almighty was descending within the cool mist of morning. Lucifer, ashamed to reveal himself, walked away from streams of living water and back to the edge of the garden as he heard the trees and grasses sing in excitement at the Almighty's majesty. There, in the midst of the garden, Lucifer witnessed the Eternal One present himself in physical form and walk towards the edge of the gleaming waters.

Stepping behind a tree, Lucifer peered through its branches to watch from a distance.

Then God said, "Let Us make mankind in Our image, in Our likeness, so that they may rule over the fish in the sea and the birds in the sky, over the livestock and all the wild animals, and over all the creatures that move along the ground."

He then bent down on one knee and began tracing His finger through the dirt, as though writing something upon it. A faint smile could be seen upon the Eternal's face as He leaned in closer, examining the work of His hands.

What is He doing? Lucifer wondered with glaring eyes as he looked down in disgust at the soil he stood upon. The material beneath his feet was foreign to him and stained anything it touched.

Why was the Eternal so fascinated by something so unclean? Lucifer pondered to himself as if reconfirming within himself his distaste *for what the Almighty had become. The Eternal One then reached deep into the earth and scooped up the dirt into His hands. Holding the formless dirt in front of Him, with particles falling through His fingers, He began to shape and knead the soil. Lucifer looked on, enraptured by the moment and how the Eternal took His time molding and shaping the earth within His hands.*

Of all the magnificent splendor that adorned this place, why has the dirt caught the Eternal's complete and absolute focus and attention? *Lucifer wondered.*

Just then, the windows of Heaven began to open from above for all of the heavenly hosts to witness. Lucifer found himself gravitating back into the shadows and out of the light that radiated from around the Eternal.

"What spectacle was so important that the Eternal One would want all of Heaven present to its creation, as if He had never done anything equal or greater than this?" *Lucifer scathed to himself, annoyed at the interference.*

Now sequestered in the shadows of the same fruit tree Lucifer found earlier, hoping he had gone unnoticed by the Eternal and His hosts, Lucifer began to look on at the Eternal's work. The Creator, carefully holding the dirt in one hand while the other fell to His side to collect water from the stream that flowed beside Him, sprinkled the dirt with the water. With divine precision, He began to pull and stretch the mixture, shaping it into forms that could easily be identified as arms and legs, a torso, and a head. As He worked, the essence of life and purpose seemed to infuse each movement. Finally, the Creator was finished with His creation, a small figure, frail in stature and weak in appearance.

Lucifer, observing this meticulous process, whispered aloud with anxious anticipation, "Surely all of this nonsense couldn't be about this frail collection of dust." *His words dripped with skepticism and curiosity, unable to comprehend the significance of such a fragile being.*

The Creator laid the tiny figure on the ground in front of Him. With a tenderness that transcended understanding, He leaned down and gently kissed the figure's forehead. Then, with a deliberate and profound breath, He slowly exhaled His majesty into the lifeless form.

In that moment, the atmosphere seemed to shift. The air was charged with an energy that was both ancient and new, as the essence of the Creator mingled with the earthly vessel. The lifeless figure began to stir, the spark of divine life igniting within it. What once was merely a collection of dust and water now held the breath of the Almighty, transforming it into something more—an embodiment of both the earthly and the divine, a testament to the Creator's boundless wisdom and love.

The form began to metamorphose in front of every witness. Color flowed across his surface; eyes formed out of the droplets of water sprinkled from the Creator's fingers; nostrils flared, inhaling the breath of the Almighty as life erupted from within it. It was hard for the heavenly hosts and Lucifer to understand what they had just witnessed. It was impossible to imagine that the same dirt beneath Lucifer's feet had been made into the living form that began to kneel on its knees before the Almighty. The Eternal One, overjoyed at His creation, declared over him, "Be fruitful and increase in number; fill the Earth and subdue it. Rule over the fish in the sea and the birds in the sky and over every living creature that moves on the ground."

Then God said, "I give you every seed-bearing plant on the face of the whole Earth and every tree that has fruit with seed in it. They will be yours for food. And to all the beasts of the earth and all the birds in the sky and all the creatures that move along the ground—everything that has the breath of life in it—I give every green plant for food."

Lucifer stepped back with a gasp of repugnant shock in reaction to the Creator's words.

The man kneeling before his Creator was oblivious to the world around him and the cosmic war waged in his honor. He respectfully acknowledged his Creator, laughter spilling from his mouth and joy radiating from his newly formed body. His heart, unburdened and pure, overflowed with gratitude and wonder at the life breathed into him.

The joy he saw from the man only reminded Lucifer of just how far he had fallen, and how this creature of the dirt, the stain upon the Earth, had taken the place of this once highly revered angelic being made from light on which no stain could be seen.

I give you dominion over all the Earth. *Lucifer replayed the words of the Eternal in his mind, trying to focus on any small detail that may give him an advantage.*

You are free to eat from any tree in the garden, *The Eternal had continued,* but you must not eat from the Tree of the Knowledge of Good and Evil, for when you eat from it, you will certainly die.

When you eat of it! *Lucifer pondered the very specific words used by the Eternal, knowing He did not use words flippantly.*

Very interesting choice of words oh Lord of Hosts! *Lucifer said with conviction.*

CHAPTER 17

The Consummation

Isaiah 14:9-17

The realm of the dead below is all astir
to meet you at your coming;
it rouses the spirits of the departed to greet you—
all those who were leaders in the world;
it makes them rise from their thrones—
all those who were kings over the nations.
They will all respond,
they will say to you,
"You also have become weak, as we are;
you have become like us."
All your pomp has been brought down to the grave,
along with the noise of your harps;
maggots are spread out beneath you
and worms cover you.

How you have fallen from heaven,
morning star, son of the dawn!
You have been cast down to the earth,
you who once laid low the nations!
You said in your heart,
"I will ascend to the heavens;
I will raise my throne
above the stars of God;
I will sit enthroned on the mount of assembly,
on the utmost heights of Mount Zaphon.
I will ascend above the tops of the clouds;
I will make myself like the Most High."

> But you are brought down to the realm of the dead,
> to the depths of the pit.

> Those who see you stare at you,
> they ponder your fate:
> "Is this the man who shook the earth
> and made kingdoms tremble,
> the man who made the world a wilderness,
> who overthrew its cities
> and would not let his captives go home?"

*W*alking back and forth along the murky shoreline of despair, Lucifer was lost in a haze of memories. The dark waters lapped at his feet, mirroring the turmoil within his soul. Each step he took seemed to stir the depths of his mind, bringing forth alternate realities and fears from what he had witnessed in the garden. Eden, with its vibrant colors and intoxicating scents, stood in stark contrast to the bleak and desolate landscape that now surrounded him.

He could almost feel the warm breeze that once caressed his face and hear the gentle rustling of leaves as he wandered among the trees that bore the fruits of life and knowledge. Yet, it was not the beauty of the garden that haunted him, but the last words from the Almighty that echoed endlessly in his mind. Those words alluded to something . . . something he needed to flush out.

As he paced the shoreline, his thoughts swirled in a tempest of regret and defiance. The memory of the Creator's voice was a constant presence, a reminder of the glory he had lost and the consequences of his rebellion. He replayed the moments of his transgression, the pride that had led him to challenge the Almighty, and the subsequent expulsion from the celestial realms.

The shoreline itself seemed to reflect his inner state—a place where light and darkness met, where hope was a distant memory, and despair reigned supreme. Each wave that crashed against the shore whispered tales of lost potential and unfulfilled destiny.

Lucifer's gaze was distant, his eyes reflecting the agony of his internal struggle. He was sheathed in remembrance, cloaked in the weight of his past deeds. The garden was a reminder of what he once was and what he could never reclaim.

When you eat of it . . . *Lucifer seethed in reflection of the Almighty's words.*

If the Almighty is truly omniscient, then He knows that His words carry the predetermined prophecy of the fall of this beloved child, *Lucifer mused to himself.* To emphasize "when" means it is not a matter of "if." *He pondered this with a sense of grim satisfaction, recognizing the inevitability woven into the Creator's proclamation.*

Unsure of his next steps, Lucifer decided to seek out one of the first ancient beings he had encountered after his fall: Folly. She was a spirit shrouded in darkness and mystery, cast out eons ago for her own transgressions. Her reputation preceded her, filled with tales of wisdom tainted by madness and insight wrapped in chaos. Lucifer knew what she was capable of and understood that her knowledge and cunning could be instrumental in his plans.

He ventured into the deepest shadows, where light dared not intrude, calling upon Folly. Her realm was a place of twisted paths and echoing whispers, a mirror of her own fractured mind. There, in the heart of darkness, he found her. Folly, with her enigmatic smile and eyes that gleamed with a dangerous brilliance, greeted him again as an old friend.

"There is much you can enlighten me with," Lucifer said, his voice a blend of respect and calculation. "Your guidance is crucial in bringing to fruition the Almighty's misspoken prophecy."

Folly regarded him with a knowing look, her presence both unsettling and alluring.

"Ah, Lucifer," she purred, "you seek to turn 'prophecy' into fate."

"Yes!" Lucifer replied with confidence.

Folly's expression turned serious, a hint of caution in her eyes. "Perhaps you underestimate things. There is much you still do not understand. *The time of my ascension is drawing near, but for now, you must await the Architect. Only he can give you what you seek."*

Confusion began to take root within Lucifer. "The Architect? Who is he? Why can't you help me now?"

Folly's demeanor remained unwavering. *"You must await the Architect. He holds the key to the knowledge and power you desire. My time has not yet come, and I cannot intervene further."*

Lucifer tried to press her, his frustration growing. "Tell me more! How do I find him? When will he come?"

But Folly remained resolute, her willingness to divulge any further details thwarted by the influence of the one to come.

"You will know when the time is right, Lucifer. Until then, you must wait."

With that, she cast him out, leaving Lucifer more perplexed and frustrated than before. Her enigmatic words echoed in his mind as he was forced back into the shadows, left to ponder the mysterious Architect and the uncertain path that lay ahead.

The words spoken by the Almighty still echoed in his mind, haunting Lucifer as Rochelle continued her tale. *His thoughts were consumed with a stratagem that would restore his place before the hosts of Heaven.*

Confusion and doubt manifested within his thoughts whenever he pondered the frail being within the garden. The man's fragility and apparent insignificance baffled Lucifer, making him question how such a feeble being could hold any importance in the grand scheme of things. Folly's words about the Architect only deepened his confusion: You must await the Architect. He holds the key to the knowledge and power you desire. *This statement haunted Lucifer, leaving him in turmoil as he tried to comprehend the true significance of the man and the mysterious Architect who was yet to come.*

"How could the Almighty completely overlook all the other elements that presented themselves before His Majesty for consideration?" Lucifer questioned. "In what ways did the Creator find dirt more worthy than so many others who were far greater than what was postured before the Almighty within the Garden?" He continued to dwell on these thoughts, his memories clouded by misguided perceptions. Lucifer could only see the man for what he was not, rather than for what he truly was.

Unwilling to see the good within the man, or why the Creator would choose this vessel to contain part of His spirit, Lucifer began examining other candidates that he felt more suitable for such an honor.

"Did He not witness the trees with their outstretched arms reaching high into the heavens and standing firm against the storms?" Lucifer remarked aloud. "How the blossoms and fragrances emitted from them carried life and created within themselves protection for all things upon such a fragile land, where the sun in the sky would consume them were it not for the breath from their leaves that shields the earth from its harmful gaze?

"Would He not consider the wind? As powerful as she is graceful, she carries herself across the land and sea like the spirit of a wild mare, galloping to and fro with effortless elegance. She moves with fluidity, her form ever-changing yet always breathtaking in her beauty.

Lucifer reminisced about the times he watched as the wind danced through the valleys, caressed the waves, and swept over the mountains, her presence felt in every corner of the earth. Her quiet whispers were heard through the trees as the rustling leaves shared her tales. Her gentle touch nurtured life, as they released their seeds to be carried by her to their chosen resting places. As delicate as she can be, when roused, she can unleash her full might, bending trees, stirring oceans, and shaping the very landscape. She embodies both serenity and strength, a force of nature that is both essential and awe-inspiring.

"Or what of the two brothers of the air, Thunder and Lightning, who guard the portals of the underworld? Mute is the first brother whose charge lights the sky as he parries his way across the particles of the air, striking the tongues of the beasts below from breaching the realm of the living. Sonorous, the other, possesses a voice that shakes the earth each time his younger brother strikes down intruders, warning all within hearing distance to remain still or endure their wrath.

"Better yet, consider the waters. What element of creation could better represent His glory and His diversity than water?" Lucifer mused. "In its many forms, water presents itself to His Majesty with unmatched versatility and power. It can be a gentle stream that nurtures life, a mighty ocean that commands respect, or a fierce storm that can take life away. Water can be still and reflective, capturing the heavens above, or it can rage and roar, carving valleys and shaping mountains. It has the ability to cleanse, to refresh, to sustain, and to destroy. There is so much opportunity to tell His story through the waters, with their infinite shapes and boundless capabilities. If He had imparted His spirit into the waters, they would have been the perfect testament to His glory and omnipotence," Lucifer stated, his voice tinged with both admiration and bewilderment.

"Would He not consider the Sun, the Moon, or the Stars?" Lucifer carried on with his blasphemous rant. "Surely the dirt would be no competition against the flame, the element that is all-consuming. How magnificent would His creation have been had He drawn it from the fires of Heaven, the birthplace of life, and simply imparted His spirit within the flame? The celestial bodies, with their brilliance and eternal presence, reflect His glory far more than mere dust.

"Had He drawn man from these celestial fires and imbued him with their eternal light, how remarkable mankind would have been under His guidance and wisdom," Lucifer fantasized, envisioning a creation far superior to the one formed from mere dust.

"If there is a likeness of the Creator upon this being that He pulled from the lowest of these, it is only revealing the weaknesses and frailty in *the Almighty for not considering greater candidates for His creation,"* Lucifer concluded.

"What Lucifer missed, though, was that man was, by design, unlike the rest of creation," Rochelle says pointedly. "To tell the story of love, the Creator had to choose that which was the least of all.

"So why isn't dirt considered great?" Rochelle asks rhetorically. After all, as the expression goes, 'you're as worthless as dirt.'" She chuckles, emphasizing the irony.

"Lucifer's powerful lie, his own curse against what he considered a worthless being, was the very foundation of man's significance. In choosing the humblest element, the Creator demonstrated that true greatness comes from within, transcending the material and the mundane.

"But," Rochelle begins to speak softly:

Lucifer overlooked something quite significant about the creation of man: he was not spoken into existence, as all of creation had been until now; he was breathed into existence. No other being nor living thing in all the universe had the fingerprints of the Creator all over them as man had. He was pulled from the earth, as were all the animals; however, unlike them, man was molded by the very hands of the Creator and given life by the Creator's own breath, leaving a part of the divine within him.

Lucifer, in his ignorance and arrogance, could not fathom that this frail creature formed from dust could ever possess power or authority that might rival his own. Confident in his superiority, he dismissed the true potential of humanity but could not deny the power they wielded within their tongues. He saw how the man's words carried authority over the plants and animals within the garden. And so, Lucifer devised a cunning strategy.

Lucifer's plan was deceptively simple yet profoundly insidious: to weaponize the very words spoken by God's children, turning the instrument of their divine inheritance into a curse of their own making. Each utterance would become a sharpened blade, slicing through the fabric of their destiny and relentlessly steering them toward their ultimate ruin.

But how can I approach the man to plant such seeds within him? *Lucifer pondered, debating within himself.*

"The least of these shall be the greatest in the Kingdom," Rochelle remarks as if emphasizing something important to me that I should recognize.

Jealousy oozed from Lucifer like a toxic chemical, his envy palpable. Rochelle continues on without explanation or clarification, leaving me in a constant state of confusion about what is to come. *Unsure of his place and finally acknowledging his lack of authority and power, Lucifer felt a deep and unsettling uncertainty.*

As Lucifer's countenance drifted further from the light, awaiting Folly's prophetic "Architect," the voice from the darkness within quietly came back to him, as though putting a gentle hand upon his shoulder.

"Your instincts were correct, Lucifer. In order to shift the celestial powers that center around the man, you must create within him the first seed of desire, sown by his own tongue. Are you ready, my son?" the voice said to Lucifer, who now stood unwavering before him as he welcomed it back into his presence.

"Teach me," Lucifer said in submission to the voice, as he sank back into the shadows.

"Teach me all I am to know so that I may gain the attention of the Almighty again and reclaim that which I deserve," he said, his voice quivering with growing hatred as he reflected on the Creator communing and walking in the garden with the man.

And so the darkness swallowed Lucifer up and took him back to its depths, where the inky black lakes of despair greeted him once again. The murky waters seemed to pulse with a life of their own, echoing the turmoil within his soul. As he communed with the spirit, Lucifer found the power of the darkness to be intoxicating. The more he surrendered to its embrace, the more he could feel its influence surging through his body, an electrical pulse that made him feel alive in a way he never had before. It was as if he were connected to an unending source of raw, untamed energy.

The spirit's power bewitched Lucifer, unveiling a side of himself he had never known. Under the spirit's direction, he became enthralled by the newfound abilities that it granted him. This dark voice, a whisper of malevolence and cunning, seemed capable of feats that had always eluded Lucifer. It could manipulate the elements around them, cloaking light behind shadow, and bending reality to its will.

Lucifer was instructed in the subtle arts of misdirection, learning to wield power with an elegance and finesse that was both beguiling and dangerous. This understanding led him to delve into mystic arts long forgotten and forbidden within the heavenly realms. Shapeshifting, light bending, and even teleportation became skills he mastered with increasing proficiency. Each new ability was a revelation, a step deeper into the abyss of his own potential.

As the power grew inside him, it became clear that his current form could not contain it. The light from which he had been created was now a burden, a relic of his former self that he needed to shed. Lucifer understood that to fully embrace this dark authority, he needed to be reborn. He needed to strip away the remnants of the light and be purified in the shadowy essence that now defined him.

This rebirth required a new vessel, one capable of wielding the immense power and authority granted by the Spirit of Darkness. The transformation would be total, a metamorphosis that would free him from the constraints of his past and allow him to emerge as a being of unparalleled power. In the depths of the darkness, Lucifer prepared for this ultimate transformation, ready to forsake his origins and embrace the full extent of his newfound abilities.

Revelation 13:1
"I saw a beast… rising out of the blackness of the sea
with ten horns and seven heads, with ten diadems on
its horns and blasphemous names on its heads."

The spirit led him to a realm he had not yet traveled, to lands cascaded by empty graves made in preparation for something to come. It held Lucifer upright as it carried him across the blackness of the sea, whispering to him of the prophecy of the child who would be born. The spirit spoke of the Great Red Dragon that lay dormant within the waters below, biding its time and awaiting the birth of the Son of Man to devour him. The sea's inky depths seemed to pulse with the dragon's latent power, a dark force lying in wait for the moment of destiny. Lucifer did not know at that time which child the spirit was prophesying, nor the significance of this child and how consumed he would become over him.

Rochelle stops talking for a moment. The way she spoke made it seem as if she was somehow unaware of the weight of what she had just said.

Why would she disclose something like this to me without truly knowing how much it could condemn her? I think to myself.

"Surely she knows whom the prophecy foretold," I whisper under my breath. "But then again, perhaps she doesn't." The thought hadn't even crossed my mind before, but time seemed to operate differently here, leading me to some radical thoughts.

"What if Jesus had not even died yet? What if He hadn't even been born yet? Could it be that all of death awaits the coming of the Son of Man, so that in His death, those that come after would not need another sacrifice of redemption because all had already been lost? Could His death transcend Time itself?"

I carry on, my mind racing with thoughts of possibilities and alternate realities, where perhaps quantum entanglements or even quantum superpositions could be real. I imagine universes where the laws of time and space were fluid, bending to the divine will, creating a cosmic tapestry where the past, present, and future were interconnected in ways beyond human comprehension.

As I ponder these profound ideas, my thoughts are abruptly interrupted. Rochelle, clearly annoyed, clears her throat, signaling her impatience with my rambling that had intruded upon her tale. She must have heard some of my mumblings, bringing me back to the present moment and the unfolding story before us.

"Shall I continue?" Rochelle snaps.

Ready to be rid of the light within himself that reminded him of the Creator, Lucifer agreed to a ritual baptism within the icy cold waters of the deep. He wanted to become a new creature, baptized in darkness and renewed by the Spirit of Darkness. He wanted the Spirit of Darkness to be of one mind with his own, no longer speaking at a distance but unified in the collective effort to obliterate the seed of man from the Earth.

They would use this union first against their adversaries dwelling in the lower realms, the other fallen, to gain their undying loyalty. Together, they would never be questioned about the mistakes of the past but instead be seen as a god who reigns over this realm, with plans of absolute dominion over the Earth and all who inhabit it.

Lucifer followed the spirit as far as he could as it disappeared within a hidden cove, where water cascaded off sheer cliffs above, forming an ominous curtain of liquid darkness. The cliffs, towering and foreboding, framed an opening in the sky that poured down light with perfect clarity and radiance. Lucifer looked in awe at the celestial beams that illuminated the cove, casting a stark contrast between the heavens above and the sinister waters below.

The light from the heavens was mesmerizing, a beacon of purity and hope, but as it filtered through the falling water, it seemed to struggle against the encroaching darkness. The waterfalls, a once remembered symbol of serenity, now appeared as torrents of shadow, their roaring presence filling the air with a sense of impending doom.

Below, the pool was an inky black void, its depths concealing unknown and hidden evils. The water's surface, reflecting the faint light from above, seemed almost alive, rippling with malevolent intent. The cove felt like a place where darkness reigned, a sanctuary of hidden dangers masked by the deceptive tranquility of the light from the heavens.

The spirit moved toward Lucifer with a chilling grace, its ethereal form gliding effortlessly through the oppressive mist. This cove, a realm where the beautiful and the sinister coexisted, mirrored the turmoil within himself. The light above was a distant reminder of purity, while the dark waters below held a foreboding promise of what lay hidden beneath.

As the spirit approached, a cascade of black mist enveloped them both, creating an ominous contrast against the ethereal light of the heavens. The mist swirled around them, thick and suffocating, while the radiant beam from above cut through it, casting an eerie glow on their meeting. Lucifer felt the cold tendrils of the mist wrapping around him, pulling him into the spirit's malevolent embrace.

The spirit's touch was frigid and intrusive, sending waves of trepidation rippling through Lucifer's core as it pulled him nearer. The dark power radiating from the spirit was palpable, filling the air with a sense of dread. Lucifer's heart pounded in his chest, a mixture of fear and reluctant curiosity taking hold of him. In the midst of the swirling darkness and piercing light, their forms intertwined, creating a moment of stark, terrifying contrast. The mist soon settled, an eerie stillness taking hold in anticipation of what was to come. The light from above draped over the scene, casting long, ominous shadows and highlighting the tension in the air. The celestial beam bathed Lucifer and the spirit in its ethereal glow, creating an unsettling contrast between the serene light and the malevolent darkness that surrounded them.

The water beneath was an inky void, a portal to the unknown, promising transformation but no return. As the spirit pulled Lucifer's head backward, his eyes were drawn upwards for one final glimpse of the heavens. The celestial expanse stretched out before him in all its splendor, *stars twinkling like distant memories of a time when he was an angel of light.*

The heavens seemed to pulsate with a gentle, sorrowful glow, as if they could foretell the coming events and were bidding farewell to their fallen kin. The majesty of this view, the vastness and serenity of the cosmos, stood in stark contrast to the dark waters below. Lucifer's heart ached with the knowledge that once submerged, the light of the heavens would be forever out of reach, a distant and unattainable relic of his past.

The spirit, sensing Lucifer's internal conflict, tightened its grip, its own form radiating an eerie, dark power. With a final, forceful push, it prepared to plunge Lucifer into the abyss, where the light above would be replaced by the consuming darkness of the unknown depths.

"You must have known," Lucifer whispered, his voice seething with fury, "that I would use the darkness You cast me into to build my throne until the day I sit upon Yours."

And with that, the spirit submerged Lucifer under the sea with abandonment, consumed from the inside out in total blackness, his very being painted in black, his thoughts invaded by the darkness.

When finally he arose, the inky blackness running off of his face, his presence grew twice in size, his wings draping behind him like cloaked armor as he emerged from the waters. His once soft and fair skin was replaced with scales of armor that shifted and moved like a flame kissed by the wind. The darkness within didn't fall from him as before. This time, it was a part of him; it armored him and cloaked him within shadow. He inhaled deeply his first breath of air as he rose to his feet from out of the water and exhaled a violent roar that could be heard throughout the realms as acknowledgment of his presence and new found glory.

The shadows from the abyss, who looked on at what was transpiring before them, bowed low to the ground in submission to Lucifer's ever-present authority. The air was thick with the palpable tension of ancient powers converging. Lucifer traversed the dark, churning waters without fear or concern, his presence commanding and unyielding. Beneath the surface, Leviathan stirred, sensing the approach of one who held dominion over the realm of darkness.

His form was immense, stretching across the seabed, coiled in on itself like a serpent of nightmares, the embodiment of chaos and untamed nature. His scales were impenetrable, each one a fortress of its own, shimmering with an eerie, otherworldly light that reflected the depths of the abyss. His eyes, glowing like molten gold, were said to pierce the soul of anyone who dared to meet his gaze. None could hide from him, nor escape his wrath.

As Lucifer moved closer, confidence permeating his presence, the waters began to churn more violently. Leviathan, with a mighty stir, uncoiled his massive body, causing the sea to froth and boil. With a thunderous breach, the great water dragon rose from the depths. Water cascaded off his enormous form, and waves crashed violently against the cliffs of the hidden cove. His breath, hot and sulfurous, ignited the air around him, creating a veil of steam that obscured the heavens above.

Leviathan's eyes locked onto Lucifer through the dense mist, acknowledging the dark power that had been bestowed upon him. Despite his size and ferocity, there was a keen intelligence in those golden orbs, an ancient wisdom that had seen the rise and fall of countless empires and worlds.

Lucifer stood unfazed, his own dark aura matching the intensity of Leviathan's presence. He raised a hand, a gesture of authority and recognition.

"Leviathan, ancient serpent of the deep, I come to forge an alliance."

Leviathan's massive head tilted slightly, the golden eyes narrowing as he considered the fallen angel before him.

"You bear the mark of power, one that commands respect even from the ancient depths. What brings you to my domain, Prince of Darkness?"

Lucifer's voice was clear and resolute, cutting through the roar of the churning sea.

"I seek your strength, oh master of the seas. Together, we can unleash chaos upon the Creator's favored realm. The power I wield is *but a fraction of what we can achieve united. With your might and my cunning, we shall bring forth a new era of darkness."*

The great dragon's nostrils flared, releasing another plume of steam. His body, covered in scales that glinted like polished obsidian, shifted as he considered Lucifer's words.

"The lord of this realm, Death, has granted you your authority, yet he remains unknown to you. To tread these waters is to embrace the unknown, to challenge the lord of this realm. Are you prepared for what lies ahead?"

Lucifer's smile was cold and determined. "I fear nothing, least of all the unknown. Together, we will bend the cosmos to our will and cast the light into eternal shadow."

In acceptance, Leviathan retreated into the depths, a promise of chaos and destruction lingering for a time to come when he would call upon the great serpent. Lucifer, with newfound determination, turned his gaze upward, ready to unleash the power of the abyss upon the unsuspecting world. However, in the midst of his newfound authority, something more powerful than either he or Leviathan began to manifest and materialize. An ever-growing darkness billowed around Lucifer, consuming the space with a palpable void, darker and emptier than the deepest chasms of the abyss.

As the darkness thickened, it began to take shape, forming the figure of a being whose presence exuded an overwhelming sense of dread and finality. This was Death, the ancient entity whose power and essence transcended even the darkest corners of creation. The shadows seemed to shiver and retreat in his presence, and the very air grew cold and still.

Death approached Lucifer, his form an intricate weave of shadows and voids, exuding an aura of inevitable finality. For the first time, Death unveiled his mask, revealing a face that was not one of horror, but of profound emptiness—a visage that reflected the ultimate fate of all things. His eyes, deep wells of despair, held an ancient knowledge and an indifferent understanding of the universe's ceaseless cycle of life and oblivion.

Lucifer stared boldly into the face of Death before bowing low in submission to him, sensing Death's higher authority under his cold stare. Death was pleased with Lucifer's submission, and so fashioned a crown from the grave to place upon his head as a gift to the new prince.

Lucifer accepted it, looking up at the faceless entity who was cloaked in a robe of obscurity.

"Rise," Death commanded. The voice emanated from the darkness, not a mere figment of Lucifer's imagination as he had once believed. This was an entirely separate being, masterfully concealed, so much so that Lucifer had never discerned his presence. Death had been with Lucifer from the moment of his fall, from the day of his banishment from the heavens into the abyss. He was cunning, cloaked in anonymity but always with Lucifer, speaking through his thoughts and conforming Lucifer's mind to his will. Death sought to reveal to Lucifer the authority that had been dormant within him, so that at the appointed time, when Death revealed himself to Lucifer, he would welcome Death to himself as one would welcome a brother.

Since before the hosts of Heaven, Death was there, always within the depths with none above aware of his presence nor understanding of his purpose. But, there he was nonetheless. When the thunders of war reached the lower levels, Death ascended, curious of the events that were unfolding above in the upper realms. He waited patiently as he observed the war within Heaven, anxious to bear witness to the prophecy that declared that the realms of Heaven would divide in war and the new prince of Death would emerge to fill his graves.

Unsure of its full meaning, Death could not discern whether this prince would be an ally or an enemy and so was on guard. The prophesied war was to set into motion events that would one day raise the trumpets and break the seals that Death had been waiting an eternity to occur. This was the day in which Death would ride straight out of the depths, his pale horse beneath him, and he would command the principalities of Hades and be given authority over a fourth of the Earth, to kill with sword and with famine and with pestilence and with wild beasts of the Earth.

And so, he waited. Decades went by . . . millennia gone. Here he mastered his skills and understanding of the lower realms in wait for the one to come that he could imprint upon as his vessel of ascension. Lucifer would become the vessel and Death the architect of the authority and power that would come against the world of men to fill the graves that Death had dug centuries earlier, awaiting this moment. The baptism was by design, and Death, the minister who performed the ceremony by which his power would start the transfiguration. But, it was far from over if Death was to use this vessel against the Almighty in the coming days.

Lucifer looked upon the face of Death in awe, for up until now, he had only ever heard of rumors of this lucid spirit's existence. The angels had once turned these rumors into a limerick long ago before the Eternal One forbade them of any mention of such a spirit in His heavenly realms. Lucifer had always held onto the fascination behind the mystery and existence of this spirit, and the other ancient kings and queens that came before the hosts. The hosts all knew of the one within shadow, who's kiss is eternal. He who wanders the outer realms of Heaven, lord of shadow and flame, powerful and ubiquitous by design, one of the harbingers from old retaining his omnipresence, unknown and unseen by any in the third realm aside from the Almighty. Lucifer examined the face of the spirit before him, gazing into the emptiness where in most there would be eyes, as the old limerick danced into his mind:

There's a shadow that lies in the deep,
Mawet is the name that he keeps.
A touch from his hand,
You'll fall where you stand,
To journey to lands beneath.

No one would journey to see,
If any truth lies in Thee.

For go as you may,
Eternally you'll stay,
Should he touch as you meet.

The concealment where he reigns,
There's neither pleasure nor gains.
A somber abyss,
Where no sunlight shall kiss,
And time flows in endless chains.

In the shadow realm, he resides,
Beware his deceitful guides.
With a frigid embrace,
He finds every face,
To share secrets that darkness hides.

The former angelic light bearer watched with intensity in his eyes as Death reached out his hand from out of his obscured cloak as an offering for Lucifer to embrace him. Heart racing, Lucifer slowly reached out to take ahold of Death's hand, the limerick echoing in his ear warning him not to. As Death forcibly grabbed hold of Lucifer, throwing him back beneath the water, a power the likes of which he had never felt surged through him while the waters filled his lungs and the light of the heavens above went dark.

Lucifer lay still under the water's surface as Death released him. With outstretched arms, Death looked upwards and spewed curses into the air, shaking the waters beneath, sending arrows from his mouth that collided with the portals of Heaven, forever closing them. A covenant was formed between them. Once his transferral of power into Lucifer was completed, Death sealed the realms from witnessing the birth of his son. He then called out in a booming voice:

"Lucifer ha-Satan. Arise Azrael my Angel of Death!"

As the lifeless corpse of Lucifer began to awaken, Death vowed to make his name be known more powerfully than his own so that when the name Satan would be spoken, Death's power would be backing it. Soon, every realm would know the name Ha-Satan, the accuser, in fear and trembling, for his name shall be known as the accuser who holds the power of Death. The spirit of Satan came forward and revealed himself to Lucifer, instantly recognizable as the same entity that had emerged from the mist earlier. This was the spirit that had baptized him within the dark waters, initiating the ritual that marked the beginning of his transformation. The connection between the two events was undeniable; the spirit that now stood before Lucifer was the very one that had enveloped him in the inky depths, performing the dark baptism that signified his rebirth into a new form of darkness and power.

As the spirit revealed itself fully, Lucifer understood that Satan was the vessel by which he would be granted greater authority and dominion for something yet unseen.

Lucifer! *The entity echoed deep into Lucifer's subconsciousness, speaking from within to the prince.* I am a god of this realm, Ha-Satan of the fallen, Prince of the Power of the Air, Ruler of Demons and Serpent of the Darkness through which I travel. In me you will ascend to the heavens and set your throne above God's stars. You will preside on the mountain of gods far away in the north. In the lower heavens, you will be like the Most High God and carry dominion over the Earth by which all authority shall be given. Yield your seal and be renewed by my hand. *The spirit commanded Lucifer.*

Without further deliberation, Lucifer accepted the terms of Satan's contract as instructed by Death's guidance, giving himself entirely over to the will of Death.

"I don't understand, Rochelle. Are Lucifer and Satan two separate beings or one and the same?" I ask, confusion taking hold of my mind as I try to grapple with the depth of her story thus far. I know I already asked this question earlier, but it still lingers, how two separate beings could operate as one.

"You must understand, Christopher," she replies, offering clarity, "some realms cannot be entered by certain vessels. Lucifer fell, cast out of the heavens never to return, yet Satan carried a knowledge and power that would allow him to ascend once again, should they be joined."

"Ok…I think I am more confused now than I was moments earlier," I admit sarcastically, knowing it might upset her but hoping she would give a little further clarification.

"My god," she rebukes, "you truly know nothing, do you? When you were alive, did you know your soul, your spirit, or just your body?" She questions.

"Um…"

"That's my point!" she exclaims. "You had vessels and yet you weren't even aware of them. Well, Lucifer was able to create the bond between himself and Satan just as the Almighty created the bond between your soul and spirit. By all accounts above, he would be known as Satan. He would look like Satan and carry Satan's authority, but deep inside, he was still Lucifer!"

Rochelle's eyes burn with intensity as she continues, "Lucifer and Satan are like two sides of the same coin. Lucifer, the fallen angel, and Satan, the master of deception and darkness. When Lucifer was cast out of Heaven, he lost his place but not his essence. Through a pact of unimaginable power, he merged with Satan, adopting his form and authority. So, while the world sees Satan, the essence of Lucifer lurks within, plotting and scheming with intimate knowledge of the heavenly courts and the Almighty God."

I listen, the pieces slowly falling into place. "So, Lucifer needed Satan's form to re-enter the realms he was banished from?"

"Exactly," she affirms. "Lucifer, in his pure form, could never return to the celestial heights. But as Satan, cloaked in shadows and wielding the power of Death, he could traverse the realms, sowing chaos and despair. It's a fusion of form and essence, power and knowledge."

Her explanation left me in awe, the depth of the cosmic struggle unfolding before me. It was clear now that the battle between the light and darkness was far more intricate than I had ever imagined.

"As I stated before," Rochelle continues on, "a covenant was formed between them that day. In order to fulfill Satan's prophecy, the stain, or rather the fingerprint of God, which Satan considers an abomination within man, needed to be exercised and purged in order for the realm of darkness to take the throne of the Most High. This is the purpose of judgment. Not to judge you because of the iniquities you have done upon the Earth, but to cleanse you from the stain that remains within you, left over by the Creator on the day you were made in His image. His imprint upon you, that has been with you since you were first formed in your mother's womb, is the image of the Almighty God.

"Death, in return, only wanted one thing!" Rochelle exclaims. "To have his graves filled, satisfying his insatiable appetite.

Once the covenant between them was made, Rochelle continues with her tale, my walls illuminating the story once more before me, *Death, kneeling down and pulling a dark substance from the ground below, spit upon it and rubbed it forcibly into Satan's eyes. Scales of protection were created over his eyes allowing him to see within the upper realms but preventing any light of the Eternal to bleed in. Darkness crashed in around Satan, crowding all around him and blackening his vision. A figure began to appear in the midst of Satan's mind. Unlike the powerful dark figure that emerged from the waters moments before, what was forming now would have been incomprehensible to Lucifer before the baptism with Death that brought about Satan.*

"This is the Devil, the dragon that shall be your vessel of power," Death hissed at Lucifer. *"Within the upper heavens, you'll move without fear. Not even the Eternal's presence shall harm you. When you invoke litigious destruction, by Heaven's own laws, all will obey. You shall be known as the Prince of the Power of the Air, Master of Lies, Tezcatlipoca or Σκοτεινός Αστέρας (Skoteinós Astéras) otherwise known as 'Dark Star.' None shall question your authority for you carry with you the authority of Death."*

The name *"Σκοτεινός Αστέρας (Skoteinós Astéras–Dark Star),"* resonated within Lucifer and Satan with a profound and sinister significance. It symbolized Lucifer's transformation into a celestial being of malevolence, an antithesis to the guiding stars of light and hope, that would become Satan. As the Morning Star, Lucifer would be a beacon of false hope to the unsuspecting victim, but to the principalities and powers that oppose him, Satan, through the vessel of the Devil, would be a powerful and ominous presence in the heavens. This dark luminary would cast shadows where there should be light, spreading fear and deceit across the cosmos.

The Devil's influence would corrupt the very fabric of the celestial realms, bending the laws of Heaven to his will. This star, unlike any other, would not shine to guide or protect, but to mislead and destroy. The unity of Lucifer and Satan in the vessel of the Devil would be a constant reminder to all who oppose him of his dominion, a harbinger of chaos and a testament to the depths of his cunning and deceit.

Like a dragon, Satan's body, within the concealment of the Devil, was long, serpent-like, and covered in scales, with eyes brimmed in flame and smoke pouring from his nostrils. Atop his head protruded ten horns, each skillfully adorned with princely jewelry, reflecting the grandeur of Lucifer who lay within. In his right hand, he held the sword of destruction; in his left, a scepter with seven chains dragging behind him, each chain ending in a collar to hold the heads of the seven fallen stars who would bear the names of blasphemy against Him after the fall, ensuring absolute loyalty moving forward.

Lucifer, the once brilliant Star of the Heavens, had now become the embodiment of the realm into which he was cast. Among the seven chains, one was even meant for him, a reminder of the price he would pay should he betray the covenant between them. Satan, now activated by the powers surging within him, revealed his ability to shift, morph, and change into different beings of varying size and stature, perfectly suited to steal, kill, and destroy all who would oppose him. And so it was, the Light Bearer of Heaven was no more.

Ascending into the newly formed earth above, Satan sought to declare his dominion over the world. He revealed his newfound authority to all, striking his scepter—a formidable artifact forged in the fires of Hades and quenched in the same black waters by which he was baptized—into the newly formed seas.

But the elements were not so easily subdued. The winds howled in defiance, whipping through the air with a ferocity that lashed at his face, cutting through the darkness like razors. The seas roared in unison, rising up to challenge him, their mighty swells threatening to engulf him. The very earth trembled under the strain of this cosmic conflict, refusing to bow to the dark authority that sought to claim it.

Satan, eyes glowing with a malevolent fire, stood his ground, his serpentine body coiled around the barrier island he had claimed. Yet, the combined force of the rebellious winds and waves proved relentless. They lashed out with unyielding fury, the winds howling in defiance and the waves crashing with unstoppable power.

Despite his formidable presence, the elements would not relent. They swallowed him, dragging him back into the abyss from whence he came. His eyes, radiating through the hollow shadows that encapsulated them, glared defiantly as he was pulled back down into the depths below. The darkness closed around him, but his fall was not one of defeat but of furious determination. The battle for dominion had only just begun, and the newly formed Earth trembled with the anticipation of the struggles yet to come.

CHAPTER 18

The Deception

John 8:44-47

You belong to your father, the devil, and you want to carry out your father's desires. He was a murderer from the beginning, not holding to the truth, for there is no truth in him. When he lies, he speaks his native language, for he is a liar and the father of lies.

Yet because I tell the truth, you do not believe me!

Can any of you prove me guilty of sin? If I am telling the truth, why don't you believe me? Whoever belongs to God hears what God says. The reason you do not hear is that you do not belong to God.

2 Thessalonians 2:9-10

The coming of the lawless one will be in accordance with how Satan works. He will use all sorts of displays of power through signs and wonders that serve the lie, and all the ways that wickedness deceives those who are perishing. They perish because they refused to love the truth and so be saved.

2 Corinthians 11:12-15

And I will keep on doing what I am doing in order to cut the ground from under those who want an opportunity to be considered equal with us in the things they boast about. For such people are false apostles, deceitful workers, masquerading as apostles of Christ. And no wonder, for Satan himself masquerades as an angel of light.

It is not surprising, then, if his servants also masquerade as servants of righteousness. Their end will be what their actions deserve.

*T*he endless black sea lay quiet, Rochelle continued to regale me with her tale, *its inhabitants gossiping and eagerly awaiting news of the prince's triumphant rise. Suddenly, the sky above ignited with electricity, a crack forming within the atmosphere. Sea water rained down from the celestial oceans above, accompanied by thunderous roars that echoed throughout the abyss, intensifying with each passing moment. The heavens above seemed to convulse with powerful energy that rippled through the sky, and the once-still black waters below began to churn in response. Flashes of lightning illuminated the dark expanse, casting eerie shadows across the undulating waves.*

The mystical creatures within, sensing the impending upheaval, retreated into the canyons and depths below, their whispers silenced by the overwhelming cacophony of the storm. It was as if the entire realm was holding its breath, bracing for the monumental event that was about to unfold. The newly formed fissure released its prisoner: the great dragon, plummeting from the physical realm above downward through the heavens and back into the endless black seas from which he had first ascended.

Earsplitting roars shook the realm as Satan fell back into the land of shadows, his authority unrecognized by any above. The impact from his breach sent a shockwave through the black waters, the energy emitted from his descent rupturing the molecular structure of the sea. The realm stood still, the water regaining its composure from his abrupt and forceful entry, unsure just how deep he was cast or when he would return.

Just then, Satan burst through the black waters, erupting in anger and sending a tidal wave of water in all directions, screaming in vociferation and protest to what had transpired. His fury was palpable, shaking the very foundations of the dark realm, and his malevolent presence reminded all that his struggle for authority was far from over.

"YOU SAID I HAD DOMINION!" *Satan screamed out to Death in rage. "You lied to me! You said my name would be known above all, and all would know my power."*

"SILENTIUM!" A voice screamed out at Satan from every direction.

"Your ascension was premature." Death lashed out at him in discontempt for his impatience.

"What did you expect? That you could just simply go to the upper realms as if you were a god?" Death laughed at Satan's naivety.

Irritated and inflamed by Death's callous response to yet another embarrassment, Satan conjured a newfound power within himself. With a guttural roar, he drew the darkness from the depths of the black waters below, channeling the raw, chaotic energy into his very being. The air around him crackled with malevolent electricity as he weaponized his spoken words, weaving the shadows into a ferocious torrent. The darkness surged forward, a living, writhing mass, enveloping Death with a terrifying intensity.

As the shadows swirled and consumed the space where Death stood, Satan poured every ounce of his rage and frustration into the attack. The water around them boiled and frothed, reacting violently to the clash of their immense powers. The sky above seemed to darken further, as if recoiling from the sheer force of the confrontation.

When the assault finally ceased, Satan raised his head, his eyes scanning the horizon as the vapor and darkness began to settle. To his bewilderment, there was no sign of Death. The space where he had stood was eerily empty, the shadows dissipating into nothingness.

"Surely he wasn't that weak?" Satan muttered, confusion and a hint of triumph coloring his voice. *"Then again, did not Death say that he would transfer his power over to me?"*

In the eerie stillness that followed, Satan gathered his thoughts and began to turn away, planning his journey to the marshes in the South. There, he intended to call upon Behemoth, as he did Leviathan, and seek an audience with the ancient beast. However, before he could venture far, the air grew thick with an oppressive presence. Something was beginning to stir.

Onlookers and demonic entities, both near and far, who had witnessed the event felt the shift. An electric charge crackled through the atmosphere, a foreboding energy that set their senses on edge. The oppressive aura was unmistakable, causing those within eyeshot to flee in terror once again, knowing all too well what was coming.

The ground beneath Satan's feet trembled, and the shadows around him seemed to writhe and retreat. The sky began to crackle with an electric energy, and a chilling wind swept through the abyss. The very essence of the realm responded to the impending arrival of its true master. The oppressive presence grew stronger, filling the air with a sense of inevitable doom.

Then, with a sudden and terrifying force, Death reappeared. His form materialized out of the swirling darkness, a towering figure of shadow and void. His eyes blazed with an unearthly light, and his voice, a thunderous proclamation that echoed through the abyss.

"You are a fool to believe you could defeat me!" Death roared, his presence overwhelming and absolute. The demonic entities that had not yet fled now scrambled in panic, their terror palpable as they sought to escape the wrath of the one who held ultimate dominion.

Satan, momentarily stunned by the sheer force of Death's return, felt the weight of his defiance crumble under the realization of his own limitations. The darkness that had been his weapon now felt like a shackle, a reminder of the insurmountable power that Death wielded over him.

Death advanced upon Satan, his aura radiating with an ancient, immutable power. The very fabric of reality seemed to bend and twist around him, acknowledging his supremacy. "You forget, Ha-Satan, by whose power you were created and who holds dominion over your fate.

"Do you truly think that I, the author and finisher of your transfiguration, would somehow be lower than you? There are few of us omnipresent principalities left in the realms from the days of old. You, who were created, can only use that which you are given, and even then, you are met with limitations. I do not share your limitations," Death mocked Satan, referencing his fall.

"There is much you must learn before you will truly understand the power you wield. There is order in all of the realms and we are all subject to the laws of the Almighty. Why else would I be down here in need of you, if I could simply breach the upper realms and contest the Lord of Hosts myself?"he asked Satan.

"While you possess my power," Death went on, "you now must separate the 'potter' from the 'clay.' Only then shall you release my power within the physical realm, thereby releasing your own as well!"

Satan had never considered this before and true as it was, Satan was unfamiliar with the laws that governed these realms and the powers given to him that he clearly could not control. So, Satan, submitting himself once again to Death's guidance, was enveloped by Death, who put him into a deep sleep sending him to another realm. He would awaken in a land far beyond the reaches of Sheol, where the fate of all hung in the balance of just two.

Light began flooding Satan's face, his eyes trying to focus from the piercing rays that were invading him, his tongue flickering out in utter distaste. Wondering where he was, he felt himself coil up in a tight posture around himself, his tongue flickering out again as it began tasting the air around him. It was then that he recognized his surroundings. He had returned to the Eternal's creation, in the midst of the garden, between two trees.

His tongue flickered back and forth from his mouth while he moved his body in a fluid motion towards the base of the tree before him. He was again drawn to the power that radiated from the Tree of Knowledge that he had studied on his last visit.

He slithered up and coiled himself around the branches, his tongue flicking out to taste the air. The fruit hanging from the tree was vibrant in color, each piece glistening as if beckoning to be plucked. Its sweetness was undeniable, but as he gazed at it, he saw with greater clarity than ever before the dark little secret it concealed. This fruit, so enticing and seemingly perfect, harbored a sinister truth, a deception that he now fully understood.

It started to become clear to Satan why Death had brought him back to this garden. Though he clearly recognized his serpentine form, he couldn't fully grasp why Death had chosen this disguise just yet. It was, however, undeniably clever to hide the wolf within sheep's clothing. As he slithered and coiled around the branches, he pondered Death's intentions, knowing there must be a deeper, more sinister reason behind this cunning disguise. But, at second glance at the fruit and the tree that bore it, Satan could sense that Death had a hand in the creation of this tree.

"An agreement had been made between Death and the Almighty prior to the creation of Man," Rochelle said pointedly, ensuring I grasped the significance of this contract.

In order for the Creator to tell the true story of love, mankind must have the freedom of choice, the freedom to choose life with the Almighty or experience an existence without Him. This agreement allowed Death to fashion a fruit, poisoned from its rotten core. When consumed by any creature, it would alter their eternal state, subjecting them to a deteriorated existence where they would experience the sting of death before ultimately being released to live out their new temporal state.

"The fruit!" Death's voice echoed from within Satan as he pondered the power radiating from within.

"The fruit is the seed by which the tree of iniquity shall enter into this world. To gain dominion over the earth, a betrayal must be committed by the firstborn of mankind," Death conveyed to Satan, as if telepathically, by a powerful means beyond his understanding.

"To turn the Almighty's most precious creation away from Him, shall invite a covenant between mankind and myself. You must present yourself as a counselor and friend. Gain his trust, then execute its finality!

"Imagine, Lucifer, the sting you could inflict upon Elohim, your begotten Father, if you were to persuade His beloved creation, through his own free will, to choose you over Him!" Death's enticement echoed in Satan's ears, a stratagem Lucifer found most intriguing as he lay dormant within Satan's subconscious mind.

Satan marveled at the thought of Man worshiping him and knew what he must do next. He began his search for the man he would seek to corrupt. Slithering back and forth amongst so many new creations in his attempt to locate him, he felt the familiar presence of the Almighty again. Hiding in the shadows, perched high within the tree tops, he peered through the branches to watch the Almighty interacting with the man. Thinking back at the last conversation the Eternal had with the man, Lucifer reminded Satan of the exact words spoken:

> "You are free to eat from any tree in the garden, but you must not eat from the Tree of the Knowledge of Good and Evil, for **when** you eat from it you will certainly die."

The remembrance confirmed to Satan what Death had already made known to him and reaffirmed within himself what he must do next. He waited, at the guidance of his teacher, for the Eternal One to leave before making formal introductions to the man. When the presence of the Almighty had left the realm, Satan started to slither down towards the man when Death intervened.

"Patience, Ha-Satan! In time you will learn that every enemy reveals their weaknesses to those who are willing to wait!"

Satan, heeding to the wisdom in Death's words, watched patiently in the background as time passed. Adam, as the man had been named, had great responsibilities. The Eternal had put him in charge of naming and caring for all of His creation. There was an interesting bond between the Eternal and Adam that Satan had not seen from Him before.

The Eternal was overjoyed to be in the presence of Adam. Their laughter could be heard by all of creation; their playful banter was intoxicating, even to the animals, as the creatures all began to join in the merriment, frolicing to and fro in the midst of their games. Satan had, for the first time, experienced with his own eyes, the gift of love on a level unseen before. He could see the way the Eternal looked upon Adam, as a father would look upon his own child. But Death, ever present within Satan's subconscious, reminded him to not be duped by the Eternal or his muse.

"Was it not this creature of dust that replaced you, oh Angel of Light?" Death reminded Lucifer, whose doubts were beginning to weigh upon the consciousness of Satan as his faint envies and longings were beginning to affect his judgment, potentially jeopardizing the mission.

"A whisper-thin veil of opportunity is all we have to accomplish what we must," Death reminded.

"Too soon and my plan will forever be void," Death whispered. "Too premature and my graves will forever be empty! Your time draws near, you must be steadfast in your resolve or lack shall be your name; want, your eternal prison!" Death exclaimed to Satan, aware that the presence of the Almighty was beginning to weigh on Lucifer's thoughts.

Determined not to let these doubts derail his mission, after Death's final remarks, he recoiled his body in a defensive posture, a physical manifestation to the internal conflict, and forced all of Lucifer's subjective desires from his mind. With the internal conflict settled, Satan realized the distraction had caused him to lose sight of the Creator and his muse. He made his way back to the outer edges, where God and Adam were just barely visible. There, he witnessed the Creator kneeling down to Adam and speaking over him:

"I am well pleased with your work, Adam. With every species I have created, which you have named, I have created both male and *female for companionship and procreation. It is time I now offer that companionship to you."*

Satan watched as the Eternal whispered something into Adam and observed as the man slowly lay in the Creator's arms, falling into a deep sleep. The Creator reached into Adam, His arm becoming formless, and passing through his skin not to disturb his slumber or harm his very delicate being. From out of the man, the Creator pulled a piece of bone. Satan watched on wondering why the Creator needed a portion of the man.

Why not simply take from the dirt to create a companion for Adam, as he had done before? *Satan thought to himself.* Or speak into existence this new creation, as He had done with every other living thing within the Garden?

"What they both did not understand at that time," Rochelle notes to me, "was that Adam and his companion were designed to be as one being. That's why Adam's rib was needed for her creation. She was separate and unique but still a part of him. Separated, they would be vulnerable, but together they would find a resilience within each other that was crucial for the days to come.

A beautiful creature emerged from the side of the man, fashioned from one of his ribs. She was a figure even more beautiful than the man himself, an exquisite work of divine artistry. The Creator spoke softly over her, whispering a beautiful melody, and creation harmonized within the garden around them. Every leaf, every flower, and every creature seemed to resonate with the melody, creating a symphony of life and beauty.

The Creator then gently stroked her head, carefully pulling each individual strand of hair, numbering them to ensure she was made to perfection. As she lay across the Creator's arm, He reached down into the river beside Him and scooped the life-giving water into His hand. With delicate precision, He let the water drip over her, each drop glistening like precious jewels on her skin.

Finally, the Creator leaned in and breathed His life into her, just as He had done with Adam. The breath of life infused her with a radiant glow, and she began to stir. Satan watched intently as the Creator laid His newly perfected work next to Adam. He stepped back, His eyes filled with satisfaction and love, as both beings began to awaken, their eyes opening to the wonder of the garden around them.

As they awakened, their gazes met for the first time, and an unspoken bond was forged between them. The garden seemed to hold its breath in anticipation, every element of creation bearing witness to this moment of profound significance. The Creator smiled, relishing the moments birthed by His hand and eagerly anticipating Adam's reaction, much like a father presenting his son with a cherished gift. Satan, from his hidden vantage point, observed with a mix of envy and intrigue, aware that this new creation would play a pivotal role in the unfolding story of mankind. Looking upon the beauty next to him, Adam spoke over her:

> "This is now bone of my bone,
> and flesh of my flesh.
> She shall be called 'woman,'
> for she was taken out of man.
> But she shall be known as Eve,
> the mother of all living things."

The Eternal left them to commune alone as Satan moved closer, keenly observing their every move and accounting for every spoken word. He noticed that their power and authority resonated through their tongues. Lucifer, having spent much time with the Creator, was acutely perceptive of their desires to be with their Father, a yearning he had also struggled to overcome after his banishment.

Satan, recognizing the potential behind Lucifer's keen perception, saw an opportunity. He collaborated with Lucifer to devise the only strategy by which they could execute their plan. Together, they plotted to exploit the very connection and longing that Adam and Eve had with the Creator, understanding that this deep desire could be twisted to serve their own plans.

"They must be separated," Satan conferred with Lucifer, reflecting on his observations and findings. "Together, they are too powerful. Separated, however, they are vulnerable. If I can get her alone, I could attack the—"

"Attack?" Lucifer interjected. "Remember, the fruit is the seed that will sprout the plans of Death to break through this realm. We must get them to eat the fruit from the forbidden tree."

"And how do you propose we do that?" Satan questioned Lucifer internally.

"Adam trusts Eve," Lucifer replied. "If we can convince her, she will convince him."

"I see," Satan mused. "So, we use their longing to be with their Creator as the means to exploit their bond and twist their desire?"

"Exactly," Lucifer acknowledged. "If the fruit is presented as carrying the power to ascend with the Creator and be like Him in spirit, they would see no reason not to eat of it."

"Let us see what the Creator's world is really made of when it becomes shadowed by opposition. Let us see what His creation becomes when faced with the paradox of choice," Lucifer finished his interjection into the consciousness of Satan.

A sinister smile spread across the serpentine face of Satan as he continued slithering closer and closer to the new couple.

"Yes, we will exploit their deepest desires, turning their longing for divine connection into a snare. Eve's trust in Adam and her curiosity will be our tools. She will become the unwitting catalyst for their downfall."

Lucifer agreed, his thoughts cold and calculating.

Satan's smile widened, the deviousness of their plan fully taking shape.

"Let us set the stage for the ultimate test. The Creator's precious garden will become the crucible of their choices, and we shall see if His creation can withstand the lure of forbidden knowledge."

With their sinister strategy in place, Satan and Lucifer prepared to execute their plan, eager to see the Creator's perfect world descend into chaos.

"As of now, the Creator's new world had only ever known of His light. What would creation do if darkness stepped into it?" Rochelle asks rhetorically. "How would it react if the Creator's light became challenged by another force? What if Man had the ability to feel the same convictions, hatred and betrayal that Lucifer felt so deeply within himself? Man only knew of God; what if Man was introduced to another? Man was created in light, in a garden of perfection, not yet knowing the realities of the darkness. But what if Man was introduced to the darkness? What if the darkness could find its way inside of Man and Man became the vessel through which darkness could walk the earth?" Rochelle again interjects into her story to bring insight to what was transpiring.

"With the new plan calculated and well thought out," Rochelle continues, "Satan waited for Eve to be alone before descending to make his formal introduction. He knew that in her solitude, his words would have the most profound impact, and his devious scheme could begin to unfold.

"You must understand," Rochelle pauses again to clarify, "a creature making an introduction to Adam or Eve was quite common. Before the dominion of Death breached the mortal realm, the animals regularly communed with Adam and Eve. "Even the trees and grasses had songs they sang and voices of their own," she concludes, her voice hinting at a deeper revelation she chooses not to share.

"How amazing that would have been to witness," I say to Rochelle, in awe of her knowledge and detailed descriptions on the subject.

"Indeed, Christopher. How amazing it truly must have been."

"But wait, I'm confused, you stated Death breached the mortal realm? Did I miss something? I thought Death couldn't break into the mortal realm yet, that is why he needed the union of Satan and Lucifer?"

"I am glad to see that you're somewhat paying attention," Rochelle replies. Her snarky comment not going unnoticed.

"Remember, the plan Death gave them was to introduce the fruit he fashioned for them and have them eat it. This would cause a reaction within the realms that I will get to shortly. But, to answer your question, Death had not yet entered into the realm. That was to come only if Satan and Lucifer could pull off their plan," she comments before continuing.

But that is why the plan was so masterfully laid out. Adam was the one who named most everything before Eve was brought into the Garden. She was not familiar enough with Creation to know that the serpent did not belong there, nor that he would have any intention to harm her. In fact, it would have been quite the opposite.

There was much that Adam was still teaching Eve and much that the Creator was still teaching Adam. Any knowledge given to Adam was passed onto Eve and vice versa. The knowledge the serpent would offer to Eve would be seen as precious and most valuable to her. So naturally, she would pass it on to Adam, knowing he too has a thirst for knowledge of all things pertaining to His creation.

The serpent slithered his way down the branches and over to where Eve sat collecting berries from the bushes in the garden.

"Greetingssss Eve," Satan hissed as she looked up in his direction in response.

"Oh, hi serpent," Eve responded. "What brings you to the gardens?"

"I have not seen you before. By what name are you known?" she asked.

"You are as observant as you are beautiful," Satan replied to her. "I am Belial, your humble servant," he spoke softly.

"When word spread of your beauty, I had to meet you for myself and make your acquaintance."

"I am very pleased to meet you then, Belial," Eve replied to the serpent.

"The pleasure is all mine, Eve," Satan flattered her.

"Can I ask you a question Eve? I see that you are collecting the fruits of some trees, but why do you not harvest from all of the trees within the garden?"

"Adam and I can eat from any tree aside from the tree in the middle of the garden. Even a simple touch of the fruit can kill us. You know this Belial! The same law applies to all of us," she replied.

"Die . . . ? You certainly will not die, Eve! Were you not told that tree is known by all as the Tree of the Knowledge of Good and Evil?" Satan boldly questioned her understanding of the law.

"Then surely you must know that He plans to let you eat of its fruit eventually, correct?" he asked Eve. "Do you not wish to have the wisdom of God and possess the power of the Almighty for yourself?" he proposed to her.

Unsure of a proper response to his questions and declarations, Eve reflected on her conversations with Adam about the matter. In pure innocence, an excitement was aroused within Eve of the possibilities that may be true within the serpent's bold claims. She pleaded with the serpent to tell her more, not suspicious of his intentions or motives within his assertions.

"Look upon the tree, Eve; how ripe is its fruit, how pleasing to the eye is its color? Surely you have misunderstood God's intention for you both. He never meant that you should not partake of the fruit ever, but only that you took of it when you were ready," Satan, now referring to himself as Belial remarked.

Knowing from his last visit to the garden that the fruit would not kill him upon touching it, Satan conjured a masterful deception to invoke the trust of Eve. He presented the fruit to her, clearly holding it within his coiled body and revealing her fallacies that it would kill her upon touching it. Seeing this, he intended for her to instantly trust what he said next.

"Do you not see what it is that I am holding, Eve?" Belial spoke aloud, revealing the forbidden fruit he was concealing within his tightly coiled body.

"Surely this would have killed me, correct?" he asked as she responded with shock and amazement that what he said was indeed true.

"Come now, I, as protector of the Tree of Knowledge, am giving you the authority to taste and see that it is good. Once you eat it, you will both be brought before the Most High in the heavens, as He intended. There, He will be greatly pleased that your knowledge and wisdom have given you power not only over this fruit but over all of Creation. Only then shall you become true heirs to this realm as was His intention for you both."

Not questioning the validity of Lucifer's claims nor consulting with Adam, Eve took the fruit from Belial and held it in her hand. However, before taking a bite of the fruit, she paused with it just inches from her mouth. She was hesitant to trust the counsel of this unfamiliar friend over the instruction of her love, Adam, and her Father, the Almighty God. Yet, there was no reason to distrust the serpent. At this point in time, no creature had ever defied the Almighty to bring the question into her mind of the validity of his claims to her.

"Why do you hesitate?" Satan rebukes, struggling to hold back his impatience.

"You're holding it in your hand now, are you not? Were you not told that you would die if you touched the fruit?"

"Yes, you're right," Eve replied to the serpent. "I am not dead, am I? Surely you must be right. Think of how pleased Adam will be to learn of my new discovery," she remarked as her lips pressed against the skin of the fruit, teeth sinking into its flesh, the juice from within slowly dripping from her mouth and falling off of her lips to the earth below. But, as the juice fell from Eve's lips onto a flower below her, the juice did not immediately kill the flower as Lucifer and Satan had expected.

Witnessing this, Satan knew there was another piece to this puzzle to solidify the plans and seal the contract that was only signed thus far by one half of the unity.

"Adam must also partake of the fruit! Only one half of the contract is signed," Satan remarked to Lucifer. "She must be the one who convinces Adam so as to not draw attention to us. Without Adam's portion, the power within cannot take its full effect since she was pulled from him."

"Yes," Lucifer agreed, understanding what Satan was implying.

"I don't feel anything, Belial," Eve stated to Satan, questioning the validity of his claims.

"I am sorry, my queen, pardon my ignorance, but you and Adam are of one spirit now, are you not?" Satan replied quickly.

"I do not know what you mean," she responded.

"Since you were pulled from him, created from his likeness, the two of you are now one. Therefore, he must partake of the fruit as well for the fruit's power to take its full effect and your unity and dominion over this realm be fulfilled," Satan explains.

"Once he partakes of the fruit, you will both possess the wisdom and power of the Almighty, and He shall be overjoyed by your new found power. He awaits you at the gates of Heaven with anticipation," Satan spoke joyfully to Eve, commemorating this event as one would celebrate a most joyous occasion.

"Why else would The Creator put this within the Garden and not remain herein?" he asked her. "Do you not wish to be with the Creator?"

"No, you're right, Belial. You have been forthcoming and honest with me. Of course I would wish for nothing more than to commune with the Almighty beyond just the morning visitations. If it is alright with you, I wish to take this to Adam and share the good news," she said to the serpent, completely unaware of the ramifications to her request.

"Why certainly, my queen. Go in haste, so as to not let the power in your hand spoil that which is your destiny," he replied with great satisfaction.

CHAPTER 19

The Covenant

Genesis 2:15-18

The Lord God took the man and put him in the Garden of Eden to work it and take care of it. And the Lord God commanded the man,

"You are free to eat from any tree in the garden; but you must not eat from the tree of the knowledge of good and evil, for when you eat from it you will certainly die."

Romans 5:12-20

Therefore, just as sin entered the world through one man, and death through sin, and in this way death came to all people, because all sinned—

To be sure, sin was in the world before the law was given, but sin is not charged against anyone's account where there is no law.

Nevertheless, death reigned from the time of Adam to the time of Moses, even over those who did not sin by breaking a command, as did Adam, who is a pattern of the one to come.

But the gift is not like the trespass. For if the many died by the trespass of the one man, how much more did God's grace and the first that came by the grace of the one man, Jesus Christ, overflow to the many! Nor can the gift of God be compared with the result of one man's sin: The judgment followed one sin and brought condemnation, but the gift followed many trespasses and brought justification. For if, by the trespass of the one man, death reigned through the one man, how much more will those who receive God's abundant provision of grace and of the gift of righteousness reign in life through the one man, Jesus Christ!

Consequently, just as one trespass resulted in condemnation for all people, so also one righteous act resulted in justification and life for all people. For just as through the disobedience of the one man the many were made sinners, so also through the obedience of the one man the many will be made righteous.

The law was brought in so that the trespass might increase. But where sin increased, grace increased all the more, so that, just as sin reigned in death, so also grace might reign through righteousness to bring eternal life through Jesus Christ our Lord.

1 Corinthians 20:20-28

But the fact is that the Messiah has been raised from the dead, the first-fruits of those who have died. For since death came through a man, also the resurrection of the dead has come through a man. For just as in connection with Adam all die, so in connection with the Messiah all will be made alive. But each in his own order: the Messiah is the first-fruits; then those who belong to the Messiah, at the time of his coming; then the culmination, when he hands over the Kingdom to God the Father, after having put an end to every rulership, yes, to every authority and power. For he has to rule until he puts all his enemies under his feet. The last enemy to be done away with will be death, for "He put everything in subjection under his feet." But when it says that "everything" has been subjected, obviously the word does not include God, who is himself the one subjecting everything to the Messiah. Now when everything has been subjected to the Son, then he will subject himself to God, who subjected everything to him; so that God may be everything in everyone.

"The last light of day painted the sky with hues of pink and gold as the sun slowly descended toward the horizon" Rochelle continues with her tale, *"while the wind danced gracefully, as she did every evening around this hour. The fields, carpeted with wheat grass, swayed and whispered praises to the Creator, anticipating His customary return in the coolness of the day. Adam, the first of his name, diligently tended to the garden's needs, following the Lord's instructions. It was in this tranquil moment that his* beloved wife, with joy in her eyes, sprinted towards him, eager to share the newfound knowledge she had gained.

"There you are, beautiful," Adam said joyfully upon seeing her. "Where did you get off to this afternoon?" he asked.

"Adam," Eve replied, "I had the most amazing encounter this afternoon. I cannot wait to share with you what I have learned," she remarked with great enthusiasm.

"Well, I cannot wait to hear about it," Adam replied with equal excitement. "Come, let us sit so that I may give you my full attention as you share with me what you have learned."

Adam led Eve to their favorite place, a serene spot where they sat and awaited the Lord upon His return each day as the cool breeze cascaded over the land. Perched at the garden's edge overlooking the valley below, they had a breathtaking view of the verdant paradise.

From their vantage point, they could see the life-giving river that split the garden's center into quadrants, each one a lush expanse teeming with life. The river sparkled under the soft light, its waters clear and inviting, winding gracefully through the landscape like a glistening ribbon of life.

To the north, a grove of towering fruit trees stood, their branches heavy with vibrant, succulent fruits of every kind. The air was filled with the sweet fragrance of blossoms and ripe produce, carried by the gentle breeze. Birds of every hue flitted between the branches, their songs blending into a harmonious symphony that celebrated the day.

To the east, a meadow stretched out, carpeted with wildflowers in a riot of colors, swaying gently in the breeze. The soft hum of bees and the fluttering of butterfly wings created a sense of peaceful industry, as every creature played its part in the tapestry of life.

To the south, a dense forest stood, its canopy providing a cool, shaded refuge for the animals that dwelled within. The rustling of leaves and the occasional call of distant creatures added a layer of mystery and depth to the scene.

To the west, rolling hills framed the horizon, their slopes covered in rows of perfectly manicured wheat fields that seemed to invite exploration and wonder. The gentle slopes led down to the riverbanks, where animals came to drink and play in the refreshing waters.

Here, at the edge of this tranquil sanctuary, Eve began to share with Adam her newly discovered wisdom. As they sat together, the cool breeze whispered through the trees, carrying with it the scents and sounds of the garden, a reminder of the perfection and beauty that surrounded them. The tranquility of the moment was profound, yet beneath the surface, a subtle tension hinted at the changes that were about to unfold.

"The most profound revelation was presented to me today," she began.

"I was tending to the currant shrubs, as I often do, when a wise creature from the canopy introduced himself to me. Do you know of Belial?" she asked Adam.

Thinking back on all of the creatures he had named, he could not recall one with such a name.

"I am sorry, my love, I do not believe that I have made his acquaintance yet," Adam replied.

"I was fairly certain you had not, for he made it known to me that I was the first with whom he had spoken. Nevertheless, he was wise and counseled me about a greater purpose for which we were made within the garden."

"A greater purpose?" Adam responded in an unfamiliar state of confusion.

"I had not really given much thought to such a thing," he remarked, clearly in deep contemplation over Eve's statement.

"I wish you were there, Husband. Fortunately, the serpent revealed to me a secret in the garden that will unlock a power within us, giving us wisdom and authority equal to the Almighty. We, too, can join Him in the heavenly realms each day with this new found power."

Intrigued by the possibilities of communing with God on a deeper level and even being capable of ascension as He does each day, Adam demanded to know more. Eve now presented the distinct fruit to Adam and began to explain to him what the serpent had shared with her.

"Eve!" Adam exclaimed, his voice laced with fear as he instinctively recoiled from what she held in her hands, "you are well aware we must not lay hands on that fruit. It is forbidden!" Adam admonished her.

"Our Father said that if we even touched it, we should surely die," he reiterated, his concern and obedience to God's command clear in his words.

"My husband, you are mistaken. Clearly I am touching it, am I not?" she begged the question.

"Am I dead as we had thought. No!" she pushed. "Did God actually say that we should not eat of every tree within the garden?" she asked Adam, following the same line of questioning the serpent had used against her.

"I have already eaten of the fruit. See here." Eve showed Adam the bite mark within the fruit.

Clearly observing that she was not dead as he was led to believe, doubt began to enter Adam's subconscious, leading him to trust his wife and drop his guard. Following Eve's instruction, he took the fruit from her hands. In an instant that would forever alter history, Adam bit into the forbidden fruit, unleashing a force upon the earth that forged a new covenant and law imposed upon all of creation. This act would reshape the entire world, binding its inhabitants to a fate of struggle and toil, holding them hostage to the dire consequences of their betrayal.

Lucifer watched as the fruit fell from Adam's hand to the earth. The earth reacted violently as the fruit, almost in slow motion, bounced across the soil, killing anything its flesh touched. Eve, still holding Adam's hand, looked upon Adam's face and fell backwards to the earth. Her eyes were indeed opened as the serpent had hoped, for she had not before noticed their nakedness and now felt shame coursing through her body. Adam, also feeling convicted for the first time and embarrassed by their nakedness, fashioned clothing for himself and Eve to conceal their newfound insecurities.

The garden fell silent and a mighty wind rushed in from the North. Satan watched on with anxious anticipation, fearful yet proud to have finally executed the masterful plan even in the midst of the Almighty. His beloved first born son and daughter to creation were now being altered and subjected to a different authority.

From the corner of the serpent's eye, an unnatural movement began to stir in the expansive wheat fields below. The forbidden fruit, glistening with an ominous sheen as the light refracted off of it in its final resting place, slowly sank deep into the earth, its descent opening a dark chasm within Eden. A blackness began to seep from the newly forming void, consuming every blade of wheat it touched. The stalks withered and disintegrated, vanishing into the encroaching darkness. This was not merely the absence of light; it was a tangible malevolence, a presence of sinister intent. It spread like a living shadow, an inky black substance that crept across the ground and encircled the newly formed portal, thick and suffocating like a puddle of tar. The air grew heavy, and an eerie stillness settled over the garden.

Shadows emerged in rapid accent and coalesced, spreading like dark tendrils across the vibrant landscape. The rays of the sun, which once bathed the garden in warmth and light, now struggled against the encroaching darkness. It was as if an unseen hand was dimming the brilliance, casting a sinister pall over Eden. The light fought valiantly but seemed to buckle under the strain of the dark force that sought to claim dominion.

As the shadows grew denser and more pervasive, they seemed to pulse with a malevolent energy, creeping across the ground like living entities. The animals, fearful and confused, began to retreat, their instincts driving them away from the heart of the disturbance. Satan, witnessing the chaos, recognized the significance of the moment. The garden was under attack, its sanctity being violated by the encroaching darkness.

The forbidden fruit, having triggered this sequence of events, had opened a breach—a gateway into another realm. The very essence of the garden, once a sanctuary of life and purity, was now tainted by the presence of an ancient evil. The stage was set for the true architect of man's fall to come forth.

The slow emergence of his head pierced through the dark void, casting a foreboding presence that struck terror into the hearts of all onlookers, even Satan. Pale and hollow, its eyes pierced through its black cloak like abyssal voids, devouring all light and instilling a primal terror in those who dared to gaze into them. Slowly, his body followed, his outstretched arms in a gesture of triumph as darkness fell from the tips of his long, spindly fingers. He too wore a garment of concealment, a shroud that granted him passage into the upper realms, much like Lucifer's vessel, Satan. His cloak, a haunting blend of silk and shadow, was inscribed with ancient and unknown symbols. Satan, transfixed and trembling, had never before seen his master in material form but recognized many of the symbols from the grand library of the heavenly courts. These symbols, wards of protection, must be part of its covering within the Creator's presence, amplifying the dread and awe that surrounded his arrival.

Death, the arbiter of finality, was now fully revealed for all to see. Wreathed in ash and fire, encircled by shadows that flickered like dark tendrils, he stood as the embodiment of despair. Light and Shadow bent to his will as he took a deep breath, inhaling the vibrant life around him. With each exhale, he spoke his curses upon the land and the animals. His voice, a chilling whisper, resonated with the authority of an eternal decree, sealing the fate of all creation under his dark dominion.

The once lush and vibrant garden began to wither under his words. Plants shriveled and trees groaned as if in pain, their leaves falling like tears. The animals, once peaceful and harmonious, began to exhibit fear and aggression, their eyes reflecting the newfound knowledge of mortality. The air grew thick with a palpable dread as the very fabric of the world seemed to respond to Death's dark influence.

Yet he paused as he stood before Adam and Eve, as if he did not have the authority to speak over them. They could feel the weight of their actions settling around them, a profound sense of shame and despair *enveloping them—unfamiliar emotions they had never before felt as the shadow of Death hung over them for the first time.*

The stratagem, conceived by Death but carried out by his new instrument, Satan, would forever shape the Earth and all who inhabited it. Time, an unending river, was introduced into the realm of the living, its current inextricably linked to decay and mortality. Death became its new master, and with its emergence, the era of innocence ended, replaced by a world where every living thing was bound by the inescapable reality of its end.

The garden, once a sanctuary of eternal life, now bore the scars of its first betrayal. The sun dimmed, casting a somber light over the fallen paradise. The ground beneath Adam and Eve's feet felt colder, harder, as if the very soul of the Earth mourned the loss of its purity.

Death stood triumphantly, his dark presence a stark contrast to the fading beauty of Eden. With his arrival, the world was forever altered, and the shadow of his dominion would loom over all creation, marking the beginning of an age defined by struggle, suffering, and the inexorable march toward the end.

"Well done, my good and faithful servants!" Death spoke arrogantly to Lucifer and Satan.

"He has been made aware of my presence. There is much the Almighty and I must discuss," Death spoke as he ascended into the higher realms to meet the King of Kings within the courtrooms of Heaven.

"Much was spoken that day," Rochelle pauses her story to remark. "Death introduced himself into the Earth in a way never before seen in all of creation. A contract was written upon the world called Law, and all who inhabited it would forever be under its dominion. A blood sacrifice would need to be made between Man and God for the repentance of sin. It would take thousands of years before any single offering would be pure enough to redeem mankind's curse and break Death's grip over the sons of Adam and the daughters of Eve.

"As for Satan," Rochelle continues her tale, "a curse was also laid upon him for his deeds in the garden. He was condemned to wander the Earth, unable to partake in its abundant blessings. The curse twisted everything he touched into the very dust from which humanity was fashioned—a substance he held in disdain.

"Similarly, Lucifer developed a hatred for Eve and her offspring because of the curse placed upon them in the wake of their further betrayal against the Almighty. So, they devised a plan to forever deceive men into believing women of the Earth the lesser sex: inferior to man and nothing more than merely a vessel through which a man could carry on his legacy.

"The garden too would forever be changed, removed from the Earth and hidden, locked away, and guarded by the most ferocious of the Cherubim until the day Man would deserve it again . . . if ever a day should come. Within obscurity these warring angels would forever conceal and protect the Garden from any who would dare pose a threat to its existence. With flaming swords capable of striking in any direction and throughout every realm, these Cherubim were not among the average of God's armies. They were elite warriors whose attacks would land before any could reach the entrance to the garden in the eastern ravine."

"As for Adam," Rochelle continues, "Satan would drive his first born, Cain, to kill his brother Abel, introducing into the world the first drops of blood shed out of anger.

"This is important, Christopher!" Rochelle exclaims to me so I understand the severity of her next words.

"The Earth opened its mouth to receive the body of Abel that day," Rochelle goes on once I acknowledge my undivided attention.

"His blood saturated the soil, the Earth feeling the weight of what had happened, and Abel's voice crying out from beyond death to the Almighty as the first mark upon Man was placed upon Cain. This mark would forever identify him to all those that would dare threaten him so that no one who found him would kill him."

"And you believe this *mark* is the same as the one I carry upon my forehead?" I question her in response to her tale.

"Yes, Christopher," Rochelle says pointedly.

"The same mark you carry on your forehead is both a blessing and a curse. It signifies a choice: to be redeemed through the ultimate sacrifice of the one betrayed or to be condemned by the treacherous act of the one who sealed his fate with a kiss of death," she tells me, now seemingly convinced of my identity or perhaps my allegiance.

" '*Condemned by the treacherous act of the one who sealed his fate with a kiss of death?*' What kiss are you talking about?" I ask, puzzled.

"When the Son of Man was betrayed, a kiss was the mark given to him," she replies. "I apologize if I assumed you knew what I was referring to. I've been here a long time, and sometimes I forget that others may not understand my references. Please bear with me.

"This mark," she continues, "invisible in the land of the living, is both a warning and a curse. A curse to those who bear it because of the target you will forever carry upon you. But a warning that any who should kill a marked man will suffer vengeance from the Almighty seven times over.

"This is why you are so important to the fallen kingdom, Christopher. You carry an authority over you still, even here, because of the relationship you have once had with the Almighty God. Though you have clearly fallen by your own choices, you cannot be separated from the Almighty's love. There is a timeline that you must be taken to our lord to be purged of the mark you bear, before Heaven intervenes and . . ." Rochelle stops, immediately realizing the consequences of her words had she continued to divulge any further information.

"Before Heaven what?" I immediately reply, as she catches herself.

"It is not good for you to know details about what cannot be changed," Rochelle replies.

"I stand before you already judged," she says, seemingly to distract me from answering my questions.

"I have been broken and shattered, like a clay vessel cast aside and forgotten. Anything found that was considered good in my heart has been conformed to darkness because it has been exposed to darkness. Any hope or prayer that was ever within me, has been lost to the darkness. Any part of myself that was still left in my heart has been consumed by my own actions and deeds. Since the day of my judgment, I was put on a path that only further consumed my once lively and loving self.

"The principalities of judgment convicted me, each of them spewing their curses over me, fighting for the right to claim me as they each read declarations and accounts from within their books that I could only gather were the recorded wrongdoings from my existence. The courtroom of Sheol undid me, Christopher," Rochelle says defeatedly to me.

"Though I was *saved* that day, the curse Lucifer imposed upon me corrupted all the good that remained within, even the memories of times before that I used to cling to for relief. Now, my heart is like a wild sea of storms casting me here and there leaving me broken and beaten. My bones have been crushed, resembling nothing more than dust. From dust I was once created and unto dust I am slowly returning. I am now counted no more than ash that has been left behind in a smoldering fire.

"This I can say though, in confidence," Rochelle says pointedly, interrupting her sorrowful self-loathing. "Due to Satan's interjection, Lucifer has temporarily pardoned the claim over my and my family's souls. For now, by the favor of my new master, I have not yet been handed over to the one who has a claim on me and my family. But, the price was still paid and accepted by Lucifer, securing my fate for a future time if I fail to uphold my end of the agreement. Though his judgment over me was harsh, the realms below are far worse. I am sure you have heard the screams of those below, have you not?" she asks, knowing I had.

Who could not hear the pleads and screams of those beneath that beseech others day and night to be freed? Their cries can be deafening until eerily all becomes quiet. Too quiet, as if something just silenced them, leading the mind to imagine sickening things that may have unfolded for them to be silenced as quickly and completely as they were. I ponder this in reflection to the days past and the terrible loneliness felt before Rochelle came along.

"I don't wish to be who I am, Christopher," Rochelle says to me apologetically. "Nor do I wish to do the things I must. But as I have mentioned before, it is because of mercy, however you may perceive it, that I have the freedom I have in this realm. If I am ever to see my beloved family again, I must do things that I wish not to do."

"But surely, Rochelle," I say in response, "you can't possibly believe Satan has your family. Do you truly believe . . ."

"Enough!" Rochelle screams, cutting off my assertion. "I haven't shared everything with you. But maybe you're right. Perhaps he doesn't have them, and I've been lied to all this time. But that's all I have. When everything else has been taken from you, as it has from me, you cling to beliefs that others might see as . . . ignorant.

"Quiet!" Rochelle says to me with urgency in her voice. "I will be right back."

"Wait, what? You'll be right back?" I mutter under my breath, trying to keep my voice low to avoid drawing any attention.

Where did she go? I wonder. *What did she hear or see that made her rush away so quickly?*

Seconds feel like hours as I listen more intently to my surroundings for any indications of what might have alarmed Rochelle, causing her sudden departure. Thinking back on everything she's told me, it's overwhelming to comprehend the vastness of this realm and the intricacies that I clearly know nothing about.

How will I ever manage to get out of judgment? Which principal demon will claim me? I wonder.

"Whatever I do," I say aloud, "I must do it quickly. Time is against me. If I am to gain any advantage, I must escape this fiery prison."

The sound of footsteps shuffling closer catches my ear, and I lean in when Rochelle's voice breaks the silence: "There's not a moment to lose, Christopher. My master will be here shortly."

"Where were you?" I ask, my voice tinged with urgency. "What alarmed you to hasten away so suddenly?"

"I don't have time to answer your questions, Christopher," she replies, her tone edged with a mixture of frustration and desperation. "I wish I did, but I have delayed things long enough. I must try and free you before it's too late."

With those final words, Rochelle begins to chant in a language foreign to my ears. Her incantations grow louder and more intense, the unfamiliar syllables hissing against the flames, causing the fire to shift and react violently in defiance.

The outline of her body becomes a stark silhouette against the raging inferno, standing resolutely as she battled to free me from my fiery prison. Each object she casts to the ground erupted in violent explosions, making the fiery walls tremble and recoil. It is clear she is invoking powerful spells, her voice growing louder and more commanding, reverberating through the inferno with an undeniable authority.

Her words cut through the roaring fire, each incantation causing the flames to shudder and crackle, their fierce light flickering as if struggling against her will. Fear begins to envelop me as I watch her wield an immense power, her chants becoming a relentless assault on the barrier that holds me captive.

The air thickens with tension and the acrid scent of burning sulfur. Explosions echo around me, each one a testament to her desperate effort. The flames seem almost alive, writhing and twisting in response to her spells, their resistance growing more aggressive yet showing signs of strain.

The ground beneath begins to shake more violently with each explosion, the heat intensifying as the fiery barrier slowly begins to crack. The realm itself appears to be fighting back, the flames lashing out in defiance. Yet Rochelle's resolve to free me doesn't waver, her silhouette a beacon of defiance against the overwhelming force of the fire.

As the flames rage with greater intensity, the heat begins bearing down upon me and becoming more and more intense.

"Rochelle!" I scream, my walls becoming more agitated and angered.

"Stop! Please stop!" I yell again in hopes she will cease her series of onslaughts against the flame as I lay helpless within it.

I don't think she can hear me, I think to myself, while the turbulence and tumultuous atmosphere she has created with her curses bear down upon me.

"We came from darkness, Christopher," Rochelle screams into the fire, her curses still having full effect, "and into darkness we shall return. Out of the ashes, we will rise, as foretold, and I will not miss it. Yield to me your flame and I will personally walk you to the gates of my Lord." Rochelle continues, her ferocity knowing no bounds.

After several inexhaustible attempts, Rochelle ceases her assault upon the flame, unable to breach its powers by use of force, unable to break through the impenetrable covering that continues to conceal my presence to the outside realm. In the moment of her silence, the flame yields its fury and stabilizes back to the original state. Defeated by her first attempt, Rochelle speaks directly to me, a longing evident in her voice as she begins to explain her actions.

"Christopher," she says, her voice softer now, "I know you may not understand everything that is happening. But believe me, every choice I've made, every action I've taken, has been to protect you. The forces we are up against are powerful, and their reach is far and wide. I've had to make difficult decisions, ones that I hope you never have to face.

"There is much I have not shared, and I recognize that I have not been willing to answer many of your questions or even allow you time to process what I have shared but time is of the essence. Time is so precious now that I thought I could release you from your capsule, and perhaps we could escape together," Rochelle says, leaving me speechless as to her reasons. Remembering back when we first met, she hinted that her son's name may have been Christopher.

Could it be that she considers me to be her son? I think to myself.

"Consider how much time I have spent with you and all I have shared with you that you may have knowledge to use within the council of elders, in the courtroom of shadows," Rochelle reminds me. "As I stated when we first met, knowledge is power, and power is position.

"Do not fear, Christopher, I am here with you," she consoles me as a mother would her child.

"Judgment will set you free, just like it did for me, and it will help you see things for what they really are. You don't have to be afraid anymore. You will see, Christopher. You don't have to be afraid of the darkness anymore. I am here with you and will be with you so that you may be charged into my care." She says to me before continuing another wave of incantations but this time much softer and more soothing, my eyes becoming heavy under the weight of her words spoken to me in reassurance that all will be ok.

Her words start to seep into my thoughts, a soothing caress that lulls me to kneel, then lay under an unfamiliar weight that overtakes my mind and body. My eyes flutter closed, my head shaking back and forth in a futile attempt to stay awake. Though she is not my mother, her voice carries the same comforting cadence, leaving me yearning for the embrace of my own mother. As I drift further into this trance, a thick cloud of darkness begins to encroach upon the walls of my fiery prison, transforming the bright flames into a curtain of inky blackness.

I look up, watching the once vibrant flames of my cylindrical prison slowly being swallowed by the encroaching shadow. My eyelids grow heavier, my vision narrowing as the light fades from the corners of my eyes. The darkness beckons, welcoming me back into its cold embrace. The weight of her words press me to the ground, anchoring me in place.

Just as I am about to surrender to the void, another voice cuts through the enchanting lull of her words. This new voice is sharp, insistent, radiating all around me and penetrating my mind. It urges me not to give in, to hold on. The whispers resonate within me, a beacon of resistance against the dark tide that threatens to engulf my consciousness.

"Don't let go," the whisper wraps itself around my crumpled being, reminding me that there is still something worth fighting for, though I don't know what it is or why it thinks I am worthy of receiving it. I lay my head down under the weight of her words when the silhouette of someone in the foreground of the fire catches my attention.

Did she break through the fire? I wonder. *Who is in here with me?*

"Rochelle?" I mutter, wondering how it was that she was able to breach through the fire. But the figure does not reply. Instead, it stands firm, arms outstretched against the flame, as though holding the fire back from engulfing us both.

As I try to focus, a sharp pain suddenly pierces my mind, and I can no longer witness the unfolding events as my surroundings begin to spin uncontrollably. Crying out in agony, the moment repeats itself over and over until the pain abruptly stops, leaving my collapsed body limp. Everything around me becomes still, sinking back into the blackness—everything, except a figure of a man walking in a radiant light, much brighter than my surroundings, a light that swallows the darkness, consuming it within itself.

A voice, like one crying in the wilderness of empty blackness, now quietly calls to me from inside my flaming prison. It is a voice in the stillness of the night, calling me by name.

"Christopher!"

CHAPTER 20

The Vision

Isaiah 40:6-8

A voice says, "Cry out."

And I said, "What shall I cry?"

"All life is like the grass. All of its grace and beauty fades like the
wild flowers in a field. The grass withers, the flowers fade as the
breath of the Eternal One blows away.

People are no different than the grass. The grass withers, the flowers
fade; nothing lasts except the Word of our God. It will stand
forever."

Psalm 90:5-6

"Yet you sweep people away in the sleep of death— they are like the
new grass of the morning: In the morning it springs up new, but by
evening it is dry and withered."

Luke 22:31-32

"Simon, Simon, Satan has asked to sift all of you as wheat. But I
have prayed for you, Simon, that your faith may not fail. And when
you have turned back, strengthen your brothers."

Jude 1: 12-13

They are waterless clouds, carried away by the wind; autumn's
lonely and barren trees, twice dead, uprooted; violent waves of the
sea breaking over the bow, foaming with shame; lost and wandering
stars destined to live forever in gloomy darkness.

Job 38:24

*Where is the field where the east wind is divided up and sent across
the face of the earth? Who cut the channels for the flooding rivers,
so that rain might fall on an uninhabited land, even on a wilderness
where no human sets foot so that the desolate desert and the
withering wasteland are satisfied, so that the grass is made to sprout
in that seemingly forsaken place?*

Deuteronomy 32:10

*He found him out in the wilderness,
in an empty, windswept wasteland.*

Jeremiah 50:44

*Like a lion that suddenly emerges from the dense undergrowth
beside the Jordan to attack a flock feeding in the lush pasture, so in
an instant I will arrive and chase Babylon from her land.*

Hosea 5:14-15

*For I will be like a lion to Ephraim,
like a great lion to Judah.
I will tear them to pieces and go away;
I will carry them off, with no one to rescue them.
Then I will return to my lair
until they have borne their guilt
and seek my face—
in their misery
they will earnestly seek me.*

An easterly wind rushes in. Blowing with a mighty force, it slings my long dirty blonde hair across my face; its heat is the rage of an open, blazing furnace, hot and smoldering on my skin. Shielding my eyes from its ferocity, I try to peer out over the land, hoping to see where I have traveled since collapsing within my fiery prison.

The earth is flat and barren. As far as my eyes can see, nothing but empty wasteland is before me. Waist-high stalks of wheat blew manically in the wind, hitting and whipping itself relentlessly against my legs. It is completely depleted of all color and life, as though the merciless spirit of the wind has sucked everything out of it, leaving its withered form to bow itself low and paint the land a shade of sickly gray.

A low and eerie howl sweeps through the fields, echoing from every direction, as though taunting and jeering voices are trapped in the wind, beckoning an orchestra of hushed whispers to rise as though the wheat was once alive.

Clearly disturbed by my presence, the voices rebuke my being there, as if I chose it or even knew where it was when I awoke. Notwithstanding my lack of clarity, I put my hands over my ears in an attempt to shut them out, but their taunts pierce further into my being.

The sense of barrenness in this region infiltrates the mind, leaving an emptiness inside that causes the soul to want to wither away and become just like the withering stalks of wheat: dead and devoid of life, angered and spiteful towards outsiders.

The state of decay of this region tells a story though, that life once existed here and was even flourishing. The corpses of broken trees that still stand as silhouettes in the backdrop of the fields showcase a story unknown to me of a time of plenty. Even old rotting fence posts randomly stick out of the ground as though this land was once cultivated and farmed. But now, all the life that once thrived here has either fled or withered away, just like the wheat stalks that once stood in ordered rows, showing they were intentionally grown and cultivated.

Looking to the horizon, dark clouds hang low in the sky. Moving slowly with the wind and gently kissing the hilltops as they pass, a rumbling groan resonates deep within them, as if they, themselves, are in a state of anguish from finding no trace of life to pour out the rains upon. Continuing their crawl across the sky, the clouds sift through the dying wheat as their low hanging bellies meet the earth, dragging themselves upon it, ever in search of what once was.

How is it that I escaped my fiery prison? I wonder to myself, still perplexed at the events that unfolded and led me here.

I cannot escape the reality that flame no longer confines me and yet, I won't allow myself to consider the thought that I have escaped, for I still feel the imprint of Hell's invading emptiness and pressing darkness swelling inside of me.

"Something isn't right here," I say aloud as an eerie feeling creeps within me, pressing on my chest and hinting that I should flee from here in haste.

Turning around to explore my surroundings in hopes it will trigger a memory of how I got to be here, something suddenly catches the corner of my eye. There, on top of a hill in the distance, stands a large shadowed figure peering down upon the wasteland below, where I remain frozen in fear. As the clouds continue to pass, the figure comes further into view, revealing a large beast standing on all fours!

With my heart pounding in fear that at any moment my location could be compromised, I muster the courage to peer up at him again. As I do, I begin to notice a fluid shadow whipping wildly around the beast's head from the fierce wind that catches and pulls at it in every direction. His silhouette stands darker than the clouds behind him, making him appear even more imposing. At the same time, a soft, mysterious light from an unknown source settles upon this creature, highlighting his form with a mystical beauty against the backdrop. I tremble in fear and in awe at the very sight of him, wondering what sort of beast is here with me.

The clouds billow darker. The wind's haunting howls bounce off the hillsides, like a voice from one lost in the wilderness, echoing throughout an empty land. It is then that I suddenly see the beast shifting his movement towards me, looking down from on top of his hill and lowering his head to meet my gaze. His wild eyes look straight into my own. I swallow a gulp of air in surprise, choking on it in my haste and quickly duck my head within the concealment in the long stalks.

My thoughts scream inwardly at me, *He knows that I am here!*

Every instinct inside me urges me: *Run!*

I do not stand a chance against such a preeminent creature as this!

In my attempt to save myself and flee, something catches my foot, pulling my entire body back to the earth and disrupting the blades of wheat who's decayed bodies crackle and break apart in a piercing racket that surely broadcasts my position. With the wind knocked out of me, I throw my arms over my head fully expecting the beast to be in full stride towards me to claim me as his next meal.

But a moment passes and the wind continues on its course, howling through the field of dead grasslands, causing every last blade to bend under its authority. I wait a moment longer in anticipation for what surely must be coming, but nothing happens.

In slow, methodical movements, I lower my arms and sit back up, the beast still standing there upon his hill, watching my every move without making any of his own. The shadows that once concealed him have lifted from his face, revealing the source of light that gleans from within him and possibly down upon him in the midst of the gloom that envelopes this place.

Peering above the stalks, I notice that the frenzied motion of the fluid-like shadows around his face is, in fact, a mane of hair. I look at his paws and notice that they are much larger than what I've seen any animal possess, with claws protruding and gripping deep within the earth. His tail agitatedly flings itself from side to side around his body, as though there is something urgent he awaits—as though he anticipates a great battle to come.

The feeling to flee subsides and is replaced by a desire to move towards him, to stand in his protective shadow. But I don't move. Fear and shame overtake me whenever the creature glances in my direction. Fear is understandable, but shame?

Why shame? I wonder to myself. *I don't even know who or what he is.*

Staring back in his direction, I examine his massive form. The unmistakable crimson sheen that drips from his jowls and streaks across his legs and paws paint a very clear picture of the battle he has just been in, and by all accounts, won.

As my eyes move up his body, meeting his own, I see that he still looks upon me with the same level of intensity as before. A familiarity within him that I can't quite put my finger on slowly plants a seed within me; a seemingly absent sense of hope and purpose begins to arise within me again upon gazing into his eyes. The fear and shame I felt before rips off me as if torn away by the wind that blows from beyond the hill on which he stands.

Without uttering a word, he exerts an unseen force that tugs at my spirit, a silent compulsion drawing me towards him, yet I remain unyielding. I feel paralyzed by who I have become—terrified that this is all another game or another sick joke or twisted perversion of a once begotten emotion in life that reminded me, on hard days, that the sun would rise again and things would be better. The feeling of hope had been absent in me for so long, ever since I awoke in Hell, that it now feels foreign; its warmth radiates within my body, though my mind struggles to accept it.

Looking over my shoulder and seeing the shadows from which I came, I hesitate at the thought of going back to the manifested horrors I had just escaped. Defeated and fearful of moving in any direction, I just lay there and watch on while the Lion upon the hill begins to turn and leave.

"Wait!" I yell out, a sudden and sharp sense of fear rises up at the thought of being left alone again. But he does not turn back. The Lion keeps walking from beyond the hill's edge until all the clouds and howling of the fierce wind swallow him up, hiding the evidence that he was ever here at all.

The mysterious Lion has left, and the wind left with him, for there is no longer any movement in the grasslands. Even the clouds dissipate into an atmosphere of hazy stillness. A stillness has settled over the ash-tinted hills bringing with it the hollow feeling of loneliness. Like stale air left to sit in a closed up coffin, the land here reeks with the stench of decay and death. The hope I felt from the Lion's gaze that started to plant itself within me has completely left with him.

"His eyes were calling out to you," I convict myself in rebuke. "Go to him! Go or you'll never leave this barren wasteland.

"GET UP AND GO!" I yell at myself, in hopes of swaying my fears and stepping out by faith. Before I fall victim to my fears yet again, my feet begin to move. With all my might, I begin to run towards the empty hill where the Lion once stood. My heart pounding, my thoughts racing, I fight through the thickening stalks of wheat, listening to it break and snap underneath my feet and turn into ash at my passing.

Now cresting the top of the lofty hill, out of breath and exerted, no trace of him can be found. In fact, I see no trace of him ever having been here at all. It is as if he has completely disappeared as mysteriously as he appeared.

The loneliness creeping inside of me manifests a panic and hysteria that is quite different from the fear I felt while within the fire. I don't want to be left behind in an eternity of loneliness, another kind of hell, especially in a place where the only sounds are the cries of the winds caressing the corpses of dead trees and dried up grasslands that once teamed with life.

How do I escape this wretched place? I continue to wonder.

"What is this lost and barren land and its valley of shadows that keeps everything locked in a perpetual state of decay?" I think aloud, still searching for any signs of the Lion.

"Why can't you remember anything?" I say to myself condescendingly.

"What was the purpose of the Lion appearing to me, only to vanish shortly afterwards?"

With my questions lingering, I continue forth, easing my way through the shadowed valleys with caution. With each passing step, the air transforms from a stale stench to the chilling presence of the frozen breaths of demise. The once stagnant atmosphere begins to bite at my skin, each breath I exhale turning into a visible, frosty mist that hangs in the air. The cold carries a sense of finality, as if every inhalation pulls me closer to an inevitable, icy end.

The light plays tricks on my mind here. There doesn't seem to be a single source of light, like the sun on Earth. Instead, the light emanating from beyond the hills shifts and changes direction unpredictably, casting eerie and ever-changing shadows. I know the shadows are from the dead trees above, but the shifting light makes them come alive on the ground before me, moving like phantoms in a stop-motion film.

After a few moments, I press forward, my urgency to find the Lion driving me onward. Navigating through the remaining cascade of dead trees, I emerge into a clearing. Before me lies an open area, flat and bare, dotted with abrupt and jagged black rock formations stretching beyond the horizon. As I walk among them, I notice they are engraved with letters and numbers. Each rock sits at the head of an empty pit.

Realization dawns on me—these are not rock formations. They are broken headstones, graves of varying shapes and sizes. Some are small, perhaps meant for an infant or child, while others are as large as a compact car, their purpose a mystery. The land is filled with thousands upon thousands of headstones as far as the eye can see.

Confusion grips me.

I don't understand, I think to myself. *The graves are all empty.*

Then it hits me. These graves are not for those already within the land of the dead; they are waiting for those still in the land of the living.

The oppressive emptiness drapes over me again, heavier and more suffocating than before. It clings to my shoulders like a malevolent cloak. The light, slowly fading upon the Eastern horizon, offers no solace as I step into the graveyard. To my horror, shadows stretch from the empty graves, reaching out with skeletal fingers, grabbing at my legs, attempting to drag me down into their abyss. No matter how I try to avoid them, their movements become erratic and desperate.

"The shadows aren't just lengthening from the tombstones in the fading light," I exclaim, my voice trembling as my eyes lock onto the surreal scene. "They're defying the natural order, moving in ways that shouldn't be possible."

Panic surges through me as a chilling realization strikes.

"They're emerging from within the graves!" I cry out, my heart pounding with terror. The shadows seem to react to my presence, their eagerness palpable, as if they have been waiting for this moment. Each tendril of darkness seems driven by a sinister purpose, casting a pall of dread over the already nightmarish landscape.

Though I don't understand their origin, nor trust my ability to discern whether they even exist at all, the feeling that something or someone is watching me, is obvious. A cold chill runs up my spine as I walk faster through this maze of graves. The air thickens the deeper I go, the shadows following my movements, unable to grab me as their long arms sweep through my legs.

As my pace hastens, so too does the desperation of the shadows to claim me. In panic, I begin running in the direction I think the Lion went, determined now, in a desperate sort of way, to find him no matter the cost. Faster and faster I run, jumping over the empty graves, bouncing erratically so as to avoid the dark shadows that cascade off the hillsides as I head further within the land of shadow.

"I have to find Him," I say aloud, my voice cracking in the fear that begins to overtake me. But, as soon as my fear elevates to panic, I hear the sound of a boy calling out to me by name.

"Christopher!" he says.

The sound echoes deep within the earth, as though he is in one of the tombs and trying to escape. I stop and listen intently, hoping to find a precise direction in which to search for the boy.

"Hello?" I ask.

"Is anyone there?" I voice, hoping to get a response.

No sooner than I stop to locate the child, lights shoot across the sky to the Western horizon and with it, the shadows flee in the opposite direction. Fixated on finding the young child, I turn my gaze to where I had just come. My eyes grow wide as I witness a deep, vast void of darkness breaching the horizon, like an enormous mouth opening to swallow the shadows within it. The scene is otherworldly, as if the very fabric of reality is unraveling before me. A cold wind from the West begins to blow, pushing me inexorably toward the ominous maw of shadows on the eastern horizon.

Panic surges through me as I feel the pull of the darkness, its gravity tugging at my soul. The light in the West grows dim, flickering like a dying ember. The ashen ground beneath me is soft and unstable, but I dig my toes into it, desperate to gain traction. I can't let myself be consumed by the encroaching void.

With every ounce of strength, I start to run toward the fading light, my legs moving sluggishly as if wading through water. The wind intensifies, howling in my ears, and the ground shifts beneath my feet, threatening to topple me. The darkness behind me feels sentient, its hunger palpable as it stretches ever closer.

The horizon ahead is a thin line of hope, the last remnants of light offering a fragile sanctuary. I push myself harder, my breath coming in ragged gasps, my heart pounding with fear and determination. The darkness is relentless, a creeping tide that promises oblivion.

As I run, the landscape around me blurs, the dead trees and jagged tombstones becoming indistinct shapes in the growing twilight. The world narrows to the path before me, a race against time and shadow. Each step is a struggle, each breath a battle for survival.

In the distance, the light flickers again, a beckoning beacon in the encroaching gloom. My muscles ache, and my strength wanes, but I refuse to surrender. The mouth of darkness is close behind, a cold, yawning chasm ready to devour me.

Suddenly, the urge to turn back and assist the child, though I can't pinpoint the source of the compelling voice, weighs heavily on my subconscious. As I glance back, a sense of foreboding washes over me. Everything that had existed in the place where I stood moments ago has vanished, devoured by the all-encompassing darkness, leaving behind nothing but a gaping void. The sight sets me on edge; the stark realization that I narrowly escaped a void of nothingness sends terror gripping at my heart.

"Whoever or whatever it was that cried for my help, is no more," I whisper aloud, knowing that I might have done more, but I unwillingly fled in fear and panic.

"Perhaps it was a trap," I say to myself as if to defend my cowardly actions.

Just like my last moments alive, when I was helpless to save myself, I feel paralyzed to assist any further in the search for the poor boy.

With the looming darkness closing in, my mind still reflecting on what more I could have done, it is abundantly clear to me that I am left with no other choice: Run or perish with the child!

Dodging the dotted landscape of graves and the stones that mark them, tears begin to streak down my cheeks. An overwhelmingly emotional pressure invades my chest while I play the child's voice over and over in my mind, as if he was still crying from beyond the void. The tears that fall from my cheeks are snatched up by the long fingers of the shadows that continue to rip at me from their graves, not allowing a single tear to land on the ground below.How did I get here? My thoughts tear at me again. How did I come to this place?

Is there no way out!?

Still running from the impending blackness that looms behind, a harmony of voices emerges across the land.

"Come lay down with us," the shadows whisper. *"Lay down your sorrows and sleep away your pain in the bed we have prepared for you."*

Sleep, I think to myself. Finding myself falling victim to their alluring gesture, my pace slows. Their words are tempting. The thought of resting instead of constantly fighting the barrage of emotions and foreign adversaries that try to claim me as their own is alluring.

"Come lie down with us," they whisper again. My eyes feel heavy; my legs slow down to the melody of their tune.

The shadows' whispers grow more insistent, wrapping around my mind like a soothing lullaby. Each step forward feels heavier than the last, my strength ebbing away with every word they utter. The ground beneath me feels softer, as if urging me to surrender to the dark embrace.

"Rest," they murmur, their voices harmonizing into a gentle symphony of temptation. *"End your struggles and join us in peace."* The promise of relief from the relentless fear and exhaustion is almost too much to resist.

My thoughts grow hazy, the need for respite pulling at my consciousness. The once sharp edges of my awareness blur, and I find myself teetering on the brink of giving in.

Leaning over the edge of an unmarked grave, I slowly begin to fall, allowing myself to be taken by the shadows. Their elongated hands grab mine and in a sudden and sharp motion they pull me downward; their soft and mesmerizing voices morph into demented screeching that fights over my flesh. I catch the edge of the grave with my hands and kick my feet into the opposing sidewall.

With the shadows now pulling at my torso, the image of the Lion standing on the hill enters my mind and gives me hope. Not wanting to give in to the shadows' false promises of rest, I fight. With every ounce of courage I have left, I pull myself out from their grasp and back upon the ashy earth. Laying next to the empty grave, I crawl further away as a peculiar thought emerges in my mind of how I came to be here: Rochelle had attacked the walls of my flame when I saw the figure of a man within the fire, appearing to shield me from the wrath of her words.

"I remember now!" I whisper to myself.

She was trying to break through my cell walls so she could deliver me to the beasts who would drag me to the courtroom of judgment!

But how did I get here? Did I hit my head? I wonder to myself, still trying to understand how it was that I came to be here.

Was this all in my mind or did I somehow forget a significant portion of events that unfolded that led me here? I wonder in fear and bewilderment.

No longer able to recall the events, fate finally catches up with me as the cascading black void engulfs me. The shadows retreat back into the graves, and the mouth of darkness takes hold of me. Like tidal waves in an angry sea, my body is consumed by the abyss, the darkness thrashing me back and forth like a log swept upon the rocks.

The force of the void is relentless, pulling me deeper into its maw. I feel myself being tossed and turned, my senses overwhelmed by the sheer power of the darkness. The world around me becomes a blur of chaotic motion, the void's currents battering me from all sides. My screams are lost in the deafening silence of the abyss, swallowed by the void.

Shielding my face with my arms, I suddenly hear a scream cut through the mouth of shadow; a scream so piercing that it invades my heart and becomes lost inside of me, my head ringing from its resonance and desperation. The scream parts the shadows around me like a hull parts the sea. I look up and see a tear forming within the roof of the dark chasm.

From the tear in the chasm's roof, fire begins to drip, each droplet sizzling as it touches the ground. The small tear widens, releasing torrents of fire that cascade down upon me. The shadows recoil, fleeing from the scorching light. The fire encircles me, creating a barrier of flames that then billows far into the sky, consuming the darkness that sought to devour me.

Suddenly, I am jolted out of the dream or whatever it was that had consumed my mind. The fire's brilliance, decimating the remaining darkness, pulls me sharply back into reality; back to my fiery prison. Just beyond the fire's edge, I hear desperate screams for help. The voice is all too familiar.

"Rochelle?" I call out, my heart pounding. "Are you okay?"

CHAPTER 21

The Dragon

Psalms 18:4-19

The cords of death entangled me; the torrents of destruction overwhelmed me. The cords of the grave coiled around me; the snares of death confronted me. In my distress I called to the LORD; I cried to my God for help. From his temple he heard my voice; my cry came before him, into his ears. The earth trembled and quaked, and the foundations of the mountains shook; they trembled because he was angry. Smoke rose from his nostrils; consuming fire came from his mouth, burning coals blazed out of it. He parted the heavens and came down; dark clouds were under his feet. He mounted the cherubim and flew; he soared on the wings of the wind. He made darkness his covering, his canopy around him— the dark rain clouds of the sky. Out of the brightness of his presence clouds advanced, with hailstones and bolts of lightning. The Lord thundered from heaven; the voice of the Most High resounded. He shot his arrows and scattered the enemy, with great bolts of lightning he routed them. The valleys of the sea were exposed and the foundations of the earth laid bare at your rebuke, LORD, at the blast of breath from your nostrils. He reached down from on high and took hold of me; he drew me out of deep waters. He rescued me from my powerful enemy, from my foes, who were too strong for me. They confronted me in the day of my disaster, but the LORD was my support. He brought me out into a spacious place; he rescued me because he delighted in me.

Micah 7:8-9

*Do not gloat over me, my enemy! Though I have fallen, I will rise.
Though I sit in darkness, the Lord will be my light. Because I have
sinned against him, I will bear the Lord's wrath, until he pleads my
case and upholds my cause. He will bring me out into the light; I
will see his righteousness.*

2 Maccabees 12:44-45

*For if he were not expecting
that those who had fallen would
rise again, it would have been superfluous
and foolish to pray for the dead. But if he
was looking to the splendid reward that is
laid up for those who fall asleep in
godliness, it was a holy and pious thought.
Therefore he made atonement for the
dead, that they might be delivered from
their sin.*

Isaiah 25:1

*Your dead shall live; their bodies shall rise.
You who dwell in the dust, awake and sing for joy!
For your dew is a dew of light,
and the earth will give birth to the dead.*

"Rochelle!" I yell out in desperation, hoping for her to respond.

With her screams growing faint as her body is dragged further and further away from me, I anxiously pace back and forth in my small confinement. I feel helplessness with each scream. Though I do not know what I would do to help her if I could get out, being forced to do nothing except stand by and listen to someone plead for their very soul is utterly tormenting on a profound level. Feeling half tempted to try and break through the fiery walls again, the flame surges above in fury, as if recognizing my motives and issuing a firm warning.

There's no way I can get through the fire without suffering irrevocable harm, I think to myself, still formulating a plan on how to help her.

The air feels thick. I begin choking on the sulfuric fumes that permeate the flames around me as I continue to call out her name. The sound of agony that hides itself within each blood chilling cry radiates an ache deep within my chest.

"You must do something, Chris," I say aloud, no longer wishing to hide and cower as I had done before. I ready myself to charge the flame, hoping to breach it by way of force.

Taking a deep breath, I brace myself and run at the flame. Not only do I bear an unrelenting pain and agony upon every inch of flesh that makes contact, but the flames also yield no ground from my blows.

I call out her name again, my words choking out of me as the flame emits a kind of gas similar to that of ammonia and so intense and suffocating that I can't even finish yelling.

"Roche—!"

It is of no use. I erupt into an unrelenting coughing fit. With each inhale, the fumes singe my vocal cords, forcing me to cough up a bitter taste into my mouth until I am spitting out blood all over the ground. The ammonia seeping from the ground around the flame in response to my attempted escape is unrelenting.

I must get lower to the ground, so I am no longer suffocating, I think.

Knowing the only way to survive this is to get underneath the gas, I fall to the ground, laying in the blood soaked soil in hopes of protecting my face from the fire's wrath, searching for any ounce of air to breathe.i my mind.

Rochelle was so vigilant and cunning. What did she get herself into that could have led to her capture? I think to myself, trying to remember back to the violent events that unfolded when my mind lost consciousness.

"Where is he, Little Rock?" the demon hisses, his countenance perturbed, voice angered at traveling such a distance from the upper realms at the request of his master, only to find nothing upon his arrival.

"I am not asking a second time, Rochelle!" the demon yells out in anger. His body shifts restlessly around her, bristling with provocation, as though seeking any excuse to attack.

"Forgive me, master," Rochelle says.

"Tell our lord that I have information that is of great significance to his campaign," Rochelle answers submissively without any sudden movements so as not to anger the demon further.

"What information do you have and where is this . . . *Seal Bearer* I keep hearing about that perturbs our Lord so?" the demon responds.

"I am sorry, master, I think it best to . . ."

"You think it best to what?" the demon angrily responds as it slings Rochelle to the ground, pinning her face into the dirt. "You're no more valuable than the dirt your face is pressed into. How dare you question me.

"Answer my question or my message back to our Lord will be quite different indeed," the demon demands, releasing her face with a forceful push as he shifts backwards and leaps upon the rock's face. He looks down upon her as she returns to her knees to respond.

"I am sorry, master. Forgive my insolence. I do not mean to upset your majesty or question your authority. I know not where the *Seal Bearer* resides but have vital information that must reach our Lord immediately," she responds, her face bowing low in submission, never making eye contact or lifting her head in equal height with his.

"Oh you do, do you?" the demon responds condescendingly.

"I was informed by way of the Watchers that the *Bearer of Christ* has been found and that you were beckoning an audience to beseech the Lord for contribution. Why then, is there such a change in information?" the demon questions her. "You know the Watchers see all within the realm. Shall we consult with them?" It hints of an aroma of deception emitting from her.

"Forgive me, master. Truthfully, I tell you I know not where he is but that the information I have is of great value. Valuable enough that contribution for us both may be recompense for your time."

Intrigued by her response, he allows her to continue speaking.

"Go on, Little Rock. What information do you have that is of such value?"

"The Lion of Judah has been seen, oh merciful one," she responds.

"Seen? Explain yourself. Did you lay eyes upon . . . *Him*?" the demon immediately responds.

"No," Rochelle answers. "I did not personally lay eyes upon Him. But, a powerful seer shared with me, unbeknownst to him as he was under my spell, that the Lion was seen in the land of shadow, just beyond the burial grounds."

"The shadow realm?" he asks. "What purpose would He have to visit the burial grounds?" the demon mused rhetorically.

"What else?" he demands of her.

"He wore Scarlet's cloak," Rochelle mentions hesitantly, knowing it would cause confusion and anger.

"**Scarlet's cloak?**" the demon lashes back at Rochelle, quickly making his way down from his stone perch and hovering over her in contempt.

"How could he possibly be wearing the cloak if he had not yet . . ." He pauses, as though something comes to his mind that disturbs his train of thought.

"Go back to the seer and find out any additional information you can," he says to Rochelle, his words hanging in the air as if echoing from all around her.

"I must consult with my master about what you have heard. Meet me here by the finality of the second gleaning," the demon commands Rochelle as he vanishes beyond the shadows from whence he came.

"Chri... op.er." I hear a voice saying, my eyes slowly opening to the sounds around me and my name being called.

"Christopher," the voice says again, this time more clearly as I regain consciousness.

"Christopher!" it repeats again. More insistently this time.

"I'm here," I respond, still trying to collect myself, confusion overshadowing my mind. *What's going on?* I internalize.

"Rochelle? Is that you?" I ask, confusion still clouding my thoughts as I regain consciousness. I struggle to comprehend how Rochelle stands before me, seemingly unscathed by the demon that had dragged her away just moments earlier.

Was it all just a dream? Perhaps a vision or a premonition of things to come? Or maybe it was my subconscious painting a picture of events unfolding around me, despite being under a spell. Could I have been unconsciously hearing the conversations, my mind playing them out while I lay there, unable to fully grasp what was happening? I wonder silently, grappling with the surreal nature of the events.

"Yes of course it is me. Who else would it be?" Rochelle remarks condescendingly. "There isn't much time," Rochelle pleads. "He is upon us. I have done all that I can to delay him, but he shall be back shortly and his wrath will be fierce.

Before any thoughts can materialize or comments escape my mouth, Rochelle hastily speaks: "Christopher, you spoke about the second coming; the Lion of Judah . . . something that I never shared with you. How was this revealed to you?" she questions.

"Did you have a vision?" she asks, clearly perceptive enough to distinguish from my ramblings that I had drifted off into another realm, which also means she must have seen these visions as well.

"Yes," I reply, not divulging any further information.

"Tell me what you saw," she quickly fires back.

Hesitant to respond, I share only what I recall from her attack.

"I remember the fire was enraged by your words. Though I don't fully understand why you were attacking me when I thought you were here to help. I . . ."

"Is that what you thought I was doing?"she interrupts. "Attacking you?

"Christopher, I was trying to free you so we could leave this place, together," she answers in a very sincere manner.

"Free me?" I reply, a clear confusion within the tone of my voice. "I thought you were charged to find and turn me over for judgment."

"I was," she answers honestly. "And it was my every intention to add you to my list of captives and continue my search for others, as I have done so many times before.

"But, upon speaking with you, something changed within me. You reminded me of feelings I'd almost forgotten or that I'd thought had been stolen from me. I told you about my family. You remind me of my own sweet boy. I so long to see his face again. I admit I used dark magic against the fire in hopes of breaching it, but I assure you I was not using it to harm you, Christopher. I would never harm you," she responds with a gentleness in her voice so different from our previous conversations.

"But now is not the time to discuss these things further. We must get you out of there. You have to trust me," she says with conviction.

"Do you know how you came to be within the fire? Better yet, do you know how to get out?" she asks, clear panic starting to set in.

"I wasn't lying earlier, Rochelle," I answer, "I don't know how I came to be here. I just awoke within the fire and cannot recall anything prior to Death carrying me into the blackness beneath."

"Does the flame respond to you?" she asks.

"What do you mean?"

"Does the fire cease when you are calm and become enraged when you are scared or fearful?" she questions, clearly on to something.

"Yes," I reply. "Now that you mention it, it does react to me and to my surroundings as though it is connected to me or seemingly alive."

"Interesting," she says under her breath but just loud enough for me to hear.

"What?" I ask. "What is interesting?"

"Nothing . . . I mean . . . something indeed but the likes of which are just limericks, tales of old. We call them sentinels or Pyr Titans. At the time of creation, the Pyr Titans were pulled from the flame by the Almighty. They were selected to shield God's chosen who remained and stood against the dark prince's attacks and curses before the redemption and fulfillment of the Son of Man. I've heard tales of these fiery sentinels enduring the wrath of the dark prince as he tried to breach the chasm and tear the spiritual Veil that separated the celestial bodies during the time when the great flood overtook the Earth and realigned the heavens.

"No one knows what became of them after the Son of Man ascended, following the tearing of the physical Veil in the temple. This event allowed the Almighty God to once again commune with His creation through His Spirit.

"Some say the pillars of fire that remain within Sheol are the remnants of the Pyr Titans and still remain loyal to Elohim, even to this day.

"They travel the barren wastelands, like pillars of fire and cloud, shifting and bending across the lands in search of the fallen Bearers of Christ. For those marked by the Seal of God, those who confessed with their mouths and believed in their hearts that He is Lord, a special protection is granted until a final choice is made. This is the eternal decision pronounced by the sound of trumps of the heavenly host. For it is written:

They who have slept in their graves shall come forth,
for their graves shall be opened;
and they also shall be caught up to meet Him
in the midst of the pillar of Heaven—
They are Christ's, the first fruits—those who
shall be the first to descend with Him.
Those upon the earth and in their graves shall be caught up to
meet Him, all at the sound of the trumpet of the angel of God."

"Are you saying that the fire encircling me is alive? The once chosen Pyr Titans seeking those who bear the Seal of God upon their foreheads?" I ask Rochelle.

"That is indeed what I am saying, Christopher.

"How else have you remained hidden?" she questions.

"How else have you been completely undetectable by the Reapers, the Watchers, the scouts and even the Prince of Darkness himself were it not for Elohim's continual protection over you?" she finishes, letting her words sink in.

"I've never witnessed such a display of power in this realm before, and I am certain it couldn't originate from within it. Unlike other powers I've seen here, which typically retaliate when provoked, this one solely shields and protects without any aggressive response."

Taking a moment to grasp what she says, I start to ask another question when Rochelle immediately interrupts me, something urgent catching her attention.

"Shhhh!" she says to me. "Not another word. Swear to me that no matter what you hear, Christopher, you will remain silent. Remember, they cannot see you or detect your presence though you are just feet from them, but they can hear you just as I can." She then falls to the ground, posturing herself prone in submission to something unseen or unheard by my ears.

As Rochelle submits to the unseen presence, I focus on the roaring fire, its crackles and pops forming a symphony of distraction. The flames weave a barrier that distorts the air, creating a shimmering veil that hides me from prying eyes as if it were alive and aware of my need for protection. Its glow casts an eerie light on Rochelle's prone form, making her appear almost ethereal against the dark backdrop. Time seems to slow, each second stretching into an eternity as I wait in the safety of the fire's embrace when a deep and ominous voice cuts through the air, freezing me in fear.

"Just who were you talking to, LITTLE ROCK?" the demon's voice echoes from the darkness, encircling Rochelle with an ominous presence.

"Master, be not angered by my ramblings. I only consult myself for guidance. You know well the frailties of our minds and the habits we create within them," she replies, her voice steady yet tinged with fear.

"Indeed," the demon replies, his tone dripping with contempt. "Your creation truly is weak and frail, unable to even control your own thoughts without influence or subjectivity. I care not for your ramblings. Have you done as I asked and met with your seer again?"

"I have, master. A foreshadowing event is upon us. Even as we speak, preparations are being made for an assault," Rochelle says, though my mind races with questions about her assessments.

What assault is she talking about? Is she referring to me being taken?

"At what point were you going to divulge this information had I not intervened?" he scolds, towering over her as she remains postured in submission.

"That is not why I am here though," he spews at her, kicking her aside upon the ground like one would kick at a piece of trash.

"Come forth, Draco," the demon calls into the darkness, summoning an unknown entity that must have been nearby. The rumbling footsteps of the dragon I heard when I first arrived are now at my doorstep again. It breathes down on Rochelle as the demon continues interrogating her, the fire bending at the force of its breath. I anxiously wait to hear what happens next, the tension palpable.

"I think you know more than you are leading me to believe," the demon suggests. "Yes . . . you reek of deception. DON'T DENY IT!" he screams at her.

"My lord, please—"

"MY LORD?!" the demon taunts, cutting her off. "Pitiful! Weak! What the lord of shadow saw in you I will never know, but my ears have heard troubling things of late, Little Rock. Do you know what I have heard?" he interrogates, offering no respite for her to reply. She maintains her silence, clearly accustomed to such harsh treatment.

"Little Rock . . . Little Rock . . ." he hisses, repeating the name as if playing a melody of contempt. "You know Draco, do you not?" he questions, this time demanding an answer.

"Yes, master. I know of your dragon and the powers it wields," she replies.

"Then why, OH WHY, do you persist in your lies? I know you have knowledge of the whereabouts of another *Seal Bearer*" he asserts, his tone demanding a response.

"As I stated earlier my Lord, I know not where the *Seal Bearer* resides, only that the prophecy is upon us.

"Indeed," the demon replies, "the Watchers have seen visions of the Lion prowling in the land of shadows!" His words hang stagnant in the air for an uncomfortably long time. Though I cannot see them, I hear a rustling from the ground and the sound of strangled breathing. I can only guess that the demon is lifting Rochelle by her throat. Her muffled squeals rise unnaturally high, painting a vivid image in my mind of her being held outstretched before him.

Her gasps become weaker, each desperate breath a testament to her suffering. From my hiding place behind the wall of fire, I strain to hear every detail. The fire crackles and flares, masking my presence but doing little to shield me from the horror unfolding just feet away. I imagine the demon's cruel grip tightening around Rochelle's neck, his claws digging into her flesh.

"You dare defy me with your lies?" the demon snarls, his voice filled with malevolent glee. "I know you conceal something. You forget, we created deception; birthed it out of our own transgressions. The smell is palpable upon your flesh.

"What is he to you that you would risk so much to protect him? Why would you risk going before the council of shadow again? Reveal his location to me, and I shall extend to you a very rare offering: forgetfulness. Tell me, Little Rock, and I will forget this insolence ever took place," the demon offers Rochelle.

With no response, my heart begins to pound in my chest.

Of course she is going to reveal my location, I think to myself. *She must. How could she not? As the demon said, what am I to her that she would offer herself as a sacrifice for me and risk everything . . . for me?*

"If this is how you wish to repay my mercy, then let me introduce you to my wrath.

"Duc eam!" the demon commands the dragon as his figure can be seen ascending onto the dragon's back.

"Ad iudicium revertaris!" the demon screams at Rochelle as she begs him not to take her back to the council of shadows, the throne room where she described her judgment. I can only assume what awaits her there as I reflect back on her earlier recount of events. She would likely be returned to the principal demon, who had received payment for her. As she hinted, she would either be redeemed by Satan, fulfilling her pledge, or condemned to the whip of her new master for failing.

In the dark, ominous scene playing out before me, the demon, assuming a commanding presence atop the dragon's formidable back, issues the order again, *"Duc eam!"*

Knowing what fate awaits, Rochelle leaps towards my flamed prison, crawling desperately towards me. For a fleeting, heart-stopping moment, the flames part just enough for me to see her silhouette.

Brief, momentary details about her that I have only imagined appear. Her hazel eyes meet mine, her battered face desperate but determined. Though we've known each other only a short time, I can see I mean something to her, and she to me. She reaches out towards me, her hand being consumed by the flame as my hand grips hers. The pain is unnoticeable in the moment as she mouths the words: "I'm sorry."

Gratitude and anguish flood through me in that fleeting instant. Then, with terrifying speed, the dragon's claws strike, seizing her with brutal force. Rochelle's face contorts in terror as she is violently thrust into the darkness. The sound of Rochelle's nails scraping the ground becomes a chilling prelude to her brutal fate. Her agonizing screams resonating through the surroundings as she is dragged out of sight, leaving me to grapple with the horror and the enormity of her sacrifice.

"ROCHELLE!" I scream out over and over.

Her voice fades away, and I remain helpless and unable to assist. Thrusting my fists hard into the ground beneath me, I peer up at the flame in her direction, pleading for something or someone to help.

"God!" I cry out, knowing the consequences of my action. "My God! Please, hear me," I implore with a tremble in my voice. "You knew this was going to happen. You saw her being dragged away in your vision. You saw her and did nothing when there was still time to intervene. You did nothing to warn her . . . nothing!!!"

My words falter, silenced by the realization that my primal plea reverberated in a space where God seemed absent. Looking in the direction Rochelle was just moments earlier, a single tear trails down my scarred cheek.

"Is there no one to help us?" I plead to the nothingness that returns to my cell.

"Is there no one to save us from this eternal Hell?"

What a fool I am for thinking anyone could be listening. How can anyone save someone who's been forgotten? I think to myself fully aware of the position I have put myself in by screaming the name of God within the land of the dead.

Time stands still as I await the inevitable. Given the circumstances, the demon, or perhaps something unknown, will likely be upon me shortly, just as before.

"This time though," I say with determination, "I will make it known where I am. Let them come!" I declare, standing slightly favoring one leg in a defensive posture for what is to come when I scream as loud as possible the name forewarned that should never be spoken within the realm.

"JESUS!"

The relentless heat of the flame presses against me in response. It billows around me angry at my outburst, crackling and releasing its gasses in a futile attempt to suffocate and silence my plea for help. But I no longer care; I continue to yell out as loud as possible. If there is nothing more that I can do for her, I can do this so that she may know that she is not alone. I have come to learn that there is no worse feeling than knowing that you are absolutely alone here.

The flame rumbles at me, spitting sparks of molten earth in my face as though to mock me in my helplessness. The flame acts alive in its persona of persistent warnings, trying to tell me to stop, to beckon me not to attract the attention that may be coming my way. But it is already too late.

"Whatever Rochelle's fate, it is inevitably mine as well," I declare aloud, resigning myself to the inescapable destiny that loomed ahead. "They will find me, too; it's only a matter of time."

Bowing low before the encircling flame, I acknowledge its unquestionable authority. I silence myself, surrendering once more to its control, my voice utterly stripped away by the searing heat and toxic fumes that envelope. Amid the silence, mournful wails from beyond my fiery barrier emerge. Though Rochelle's pleas are indistinguishable, the air grows heavy with the haunting cries of the damned, their lamentations enveloping the realm.

My plea seemed to infect the surroundings; countless voices joined in, begging for God's mercy. The air thickened with a blend of despair and hope, merging into a cacophony of desperate cries. Then, in a sudden, violent moment, a thunderous roar erupted, overpowering every sound. The roar reverberated through the air, spreading fear and silencing every voice within its vast dominion. The ground trembled, and the sky seemed to darken as if the very heavens recoiled from the force of the roar.

The roar's intensity was so overwhelming that I could feel it deep in my bones, enveloping me in a level of fear and anxiety I had never experienced before. The flames around me flickered wildly, casting erratic shadows that danced like specters on the ground. Its presence was unmistakable, its colossal silhouette emerging from the shadows with eyes gleaming with malevolence and scales shimmering with an otherworldly fire.

As the echoes of the roar faded, a heavy silence settled over the land. Every breath I took felt like a betrayal, and every movement a risk.

"He's almost here," I whispered to myself.

The dragon has returned!

CHAPTER 22

The Breach

Joel 2:1-11

Blow the trumpet in Zion;
sound the alarm on my holy hill.

Let all who live in the land tremble,
for the day of the Lord is coming.
It is close at hand—
a day of darkness and gloom,
a day of clouds and blackness.
Like dawn spreading across the mountains
a large and mighty army comes,
such as never was in ancient times
nor ever will be in ages to come.

Before them fire devours,
behind them a flame blazes.
Before them the land is like the garden of Eden,
behind them, a desert waste—
nothing escapes them.
They have the appearance of horses;
they gallop along like cavalry.
With a noise like that of chariots
they leap over the mountaintops,
like a crackling fire consuming stubble,
like a mighty army drawn up for battle.

At the sight of them, nations are in anguish;
every face turns pale.
They charge like warriors;
they scale walls like soldiers.

They all march in line,
not swerving from their course.
They do not jostle each other;
each marches straight ahead.
They plunge through defenses
without breaking ranks.
They rush upon the city;
they run along the wall.
They climb into the houses;
like thieves they enter through the windows.

Before them the earth shakes,
the heavens tremble,
the sun and moon are darkened,
and the stars no longer shine.
The Lord thunders
at the head of his army;
his forces are beyond number,
and mighty is the army that obeys his command.
The day of the Lord is great;
it is dreadful.
Who can endure it?

Ezekiel 1: 4-9, 13

I looked, and I saw a windstorm coming out of the north—an
immense cloud with flashing lightning and surrounded by brilliant
light. The center of the fire looked like glowing metal, and in the
fire was what looked like four living creatures. In appearance
their form was human, but each of them had four faces and four
wings. Their legs were straight; their feet were like those of a calf
and gleamed like burnished bronze. Under their wings on their
four sides they had human hands. All four of them had faces and
wings, and the wings of one touched the wings of another. Each
one went straight ahead; they did not turn as they moved.

The appearance of the living creatures was like burning coals
of fire or like torches. Fire moved back and forth among the
creatures; it was bright, and lightning flashed out of it. The
creatures sped back and forth like flashes of lightning.

2 Thessalonians 1:10-12

330

*On that day when the clouds draw back displaying His powerful
heavenly messengers in a fiery blaze, Jesus the Lord will appear
from heaven dealing out perfect justice to anyone who doesn't know
God and anyone who disobeys the good news of our Lord Jesus.
And what's to become of them? They'll pay for what they've done;
their punishment will be eternal destruction. And what's worse?
They'll be banished from the Lord's presence and glorious power.*

Daniel 12:1-4

*At that time Michael, the great prince who protects your
people, will arise. There will be a time of distress such as has
not happened from the beginning of nations until then. But
at that time your people—everyone whose name is found
written in the book—will be delivered. Multitudes who sleep
in the dust of the earth will awake: some to everlasting life,
others to shame and everlasting contempt. Those who are wise
will shine like the brightness of the heavens, and those who
lead many to righteousness, like the stars for ever and ever.*

Isaiah 45:7-8

*I am the Lord, and there is no other.
I form the light and create darkness,
I bring prosperity and create disaster;
I, the Lord, do all these things.*

*You heavens above, rain down my righteousness;
let the clouds shower it down.
Let the earth open wide,
let salvation spring up,
let righteousness flourish with it;
I, the Lord, have created it.*

The dragon's return heralded an inevitable confrontation, and the weight of that realization pressed down on me like a crushing burden. My heart began to race, and the flames that once felt protective now seemed fragile and tenuous against the looming threat.

Time felt suspended in this stillness, each second stretching beyond reasonable expectations. I could feel the dragon's gaze sweep across the landscape, searching, hunting. I knew it was only a matter of moments before it found me, and the final reckoning would begin. The dragon's return marked the end of all certainty, plunging my thoughts into the terrifying unknown, with Rochelle's stories vividly replaying in my mind of what may await.

Its powerful footsteps echoed heavily, and its purposeful movements brought it closer and closer. Clearly agitated at not having found me yet, the beast let out a resounding roar, a deafening cacophony that pierced my eardrums. In agony, I screamed out in pain. Realizing my mistake, I immediately fell silent, but it was too late. The dragon had heard me.

The beast lets out another roar that seems to convey an unmistakable expression of disdain, a visceral reaction to the discovery made by the dragon's heightened senses. Suddenly, the dragon takes flight, its massive wings beating with a force that stirs the air into a frenzy. It circles the area, honing in on my location. Its shreels are deafening, piercing the air with a fearsome intensity. Loud clicks resonate from its throat, a clear form of echolocation, guiding it as it searches for me. The unyielding flame between us flickers, struggling against the overwhelming force of the dragon's approach.

Landing in close proximity, the dragon advances toward me, the air thickening with tension and quivering in response to its commanding presence. Each step it takes sends tremors through the ground, amplifying the sense of impending doom until it settles just outside my fiery walls.

"Inveni illum intra!" a voice screeches from the shadow upon the dragon's back.

"Te inveneniemus!" the voice persists, very clearly making its intentions known that it shall not relent until it has claimed me as its own.

The imposing figure of the dragon comes into full view behind the illuminated walls, rising upward as if to rival the might of the flame and assert dominance. Prominent thorn-like scales are visible, protruding from the dragon's sides and top. The tail lashing back and forth in a manner reminiscent of a reptile confronting its adversaries.

Unyielding, the flame steadfastly withstands the onslaught of opposing forces, its defiant glow unwavering. The dragon, in protest, roars with a power that reverberates through the air, shaking the very ground beneath me. Another thunderous roar follows, and the beast emits a viscous, slimy substance that splatters against the wall of fire. For a brief, terrifying moment, the flame falters, a small section extinguishing and birthing a towering pillar of smoke, thick and suffocating. The smoke swirls around me, its acrid tendrils clawing at my lungs, as the dragon's menacing presence looms ever closer.

The dragon, not content with this small victory, slashes through my prison walls with its formidable tail, revealing my hidden presence. Roaring and hissing, the dragon acknowledges the revelation. Its enormous claw swipes at my flame, undeterred by the fire's effect on its scales. The menacing gesture narrowly misses me by mere inches. Swiftly, I duck and crawl as far to the opposing side as possible, the earth quivering beneath the dragon's forcible show of power.

Amidst the chaos, the flame, still consumed by the effects the viscous substance is having, momentarily fragments, seeking escape from the engulfing smoke. In that fleeting moment, I lock eyes with the dragon, a gaze filled with terror and horror. The piercing eyes of the dragon fixate on mine, an intense connection formed amidst the turmoil. With the demons eyes also affixed to my location, it commands:

"Effunde iram tuam!"

The dragon, rising in a triumphant display, tilts its massive head downward and unleashes a torrent of black fire that cascades across the ground. This eerie blaze absorbs light rather than emitting it, casting a haunting glow that twists and writhes like living shadows. The edges of the flame are tinged with a sinister purple, and as it spreads, it devours the very ground it touches. It leaves behind deep gashes in the earth, ashen scars that are unmistakable signs of the beast's unique ability. The air around it crackles with dark energy, creating an oppressive heat that suffocates rather than warms. This malevolent flame exudes an aura of dread, corrupting everything in its path and bending the protective barrier of my fire, weakening it further with its insidious power.

With a mighty sweep of its enormous wings, the dragon intensifies the assault, breathing more of its sinister flame upon the earth at the base of my fire, doubling down to ensure its full submission. The inky flames envelope my protective barrier, seemingly stunning or weakening it.

Now, with the flame seemingly pacified, an eerie chant begins to resonate from the demon rider. The sinister incantation reverberates through the air, creating an unsettling harmony that causes a gap to form in the flames, exposing me to the dragon's menacing gaze. Its eyes, gleaming with a terrifying intelligence, lock onto me once again. The scorching heat of its breath radiates outward, threatening to engulf me or, worse, snatch me from within my faltering protection.

The moment is fraught with terror as the beast, with an almost intelligent malice, exploits the weakness in my defenses. The dragon's gaze narrows, and I can feel its sinister intent bearing down on me. The chant from the demon rider grows louder, its cadence almost hypnotic, deepening the breach in my fiery shield. The flames waver and flicker, no longer the stalwart barrier they once were.

The dragon, sensing my vulnerability, prepares to strike. Its massive form coils, muscles tensing, ready to unleash its fiery wrath. I can see the predatory gleam in its eyes, the satisfaction of a hunter closing in on its prey. The demon rider's chant reaches a feverish pitch, and the flames around me diminish further, leaving me almost completely exposed.

In the face of impending doom, something in the background catches my attention. I watch as an inexplicable event unfolds in the sky above—a mysterious and deafening rupture, akin to glass shattering into countless fragments. The unexpected occurrence freezes the demonic beast in its tracks as a powerful energy begins to surge through a ruptured tear forming in the firmament. A desperate shriek emanates from the dragon, its shimmering black onyx body recoiling as the demonic rider tries to maintain control atop the cowering beast. The rider too looks over his shoulder to see the disruption in the sky.

For a moment, time seems to stand still as the terrifying figure upon the dragon, a creature I had only regarded as a myth, pauses. Instead of being consumed by their dominant presence, I witness the rider's panic. His previously commanding demeanor dissolves into fear as he desperately begins screaming, "Nos abire debemus!" His voice, usually filled with authority, now trembles with terror as he is petrified by the unfathomable force unleashed upon the sky.

The sky continues to crack and shatter, each rupture sending waves of energy that make the very air tremble. The once-unstoppable dragon, now a creature of fear, bucks and twists under the rider's grip. The rider's repeated cries of "We must leave!" echo in my ears as the dragon turns, completely forgetting I even exist, and flees. The desperate pleas that reverberated earlier in response to my prayer become celebratory cries at the flight of the enemy. *I wonder if they know what is happening,* I ponder, listening to the thousands of voices all celebrating the event.

"What is happening?" I question aloud, my heart still pounding within my chest at the recollection of the events. The moment that just transpired becomes all too real for me as I outwardly began thanking God, something that just slipped from my mouth unintentionally.

A rumble slowly ignites throughout the atmosphere, gaining in volume and movement. For the first time since finding myself here, a slight, cool breeze blows in, changing the movement of my flame as it begins to reawaken from the assault of the dragon. As the smoke gradually lifts and dissipates, a transformative spectacle unfolds. Emerging from the dissipating haze, an otherworldly power issues from the flame, its appearance undergoing a profound metamorphosis. The once-static flames now begin to exhibit a mesmerizing dance, resembling molten metal in a captivating flow that defies gravity. The radiant energy seems to pull the fiery essence in an opposing direction, creating a surreal visual display.

The flame that was fragmented and pacified from the attacks, now reveals itself as a dynamic force, commanding attention. As the smoke continues to clear, what stands before me is not merely a flame but a manifestation of elemental might, its essence reshaping the very nature of its own existence.

The charcoaled sky continues to fracture and break, groaning from long seasons of unrest. The rending sounds echo in every direction, bouncing off the ground and shaking the earth with a relentless intensity. The fissures in the sky widen, revealing veins of electric blue lightning that pulse with a formidable energy. Each crack spreads across the sky, casting an eerie glow over the landscape.

A tremor emanates from the depths of the ground beneath me, causing the earth to quiver and pulsate, dislodging loose bits of debris. Simultaneously, as the crackling symphony persists in the sky, the earth, now synchronized with this elemental dance, quakes in an irregular rhythm, reminiscent of a thousand drums beating in unison. It seems as though an army amasses to meet an opposing force that is seemingly breaching the firmament.

Pound… pound. Pound… pound. Pound… pound.

The strong force of the vibrations slowly reveal fragments of bone just buried beneath the ground, forcing them to the surface. Kneeling under the force of the impending opposing powers, I look on in shock upon seeing just how many pieces of bodily remnants were just inches under the soil beneath me. They cover the base of my prison floor, clattering together, as though they are trying to resurrect themselves one last time.

There's a noticeable response within the elements of Hell to the sudden shift and change in the sky. All I can do is observe from behind closed walls. The shattering sounds within the firmament cease, the cacophony of breaking glass giving way to an eerie silence. The shaking of the earth stops abruptly, leaving a stillness that feels almost unnatural. The veins of light in the sky stand frozen, their once-pulsing energy now suspended in time. The relentless beating of drums from below, which had been a constant rhythm in the background, falls silent, creating an oppressive quiet that hangs in the air. The entire realm seems to hold its breath, awaiting the next move in this unpredictable upheaval.

"My gosh, hell is being invaded," I say aloud, trying to comprehend the events unfolding before me. *What could be coming into this place that the dragon and its rider were in such haste to leave?* I contemplate. *More than that, unless my ears deceive me, what is arising from the depths to meet it?*

The gravity of the situation presses down on me as I ponder these questions. The silence is profound, as if the very fabric of Hell itself is waiting, poised on the edge of something monumental. The stillness is almost suffocating, a stark contrast to the chaos that reigned just moments before. My thoughts race, trying to make sense of the invasion from above and the response from below.

In the grip of anxious anticipation, I remain motionless. Every fiber of my being is attuned to the unfolding events. I hold my breath in the desperate hope of avoiding any direct involvement from what is to come.

As the fear within me swells, another subtle breeze weaves through the tumultuous realm, carrying with it an otherworldly fragrance that manages to momentarily temper the prevailing chaos. This unexpected respite stirs within me an elusive sense of peace and hope, feelings I had long forgotten.

Basking in the rare reprieve that falls upon me like cool water on a hot day, I notice the boundaries of my fiery prison extending outward. The once-confining walls reveal a mesmerizing dance as they split and expand. The central fiery core, akin to molten metal, undergoes a captivating transformation yet again, each undulating movement unfolding like a celestial ballet.

From the heart of this ethereal forge, four distinct beings emerge, untangling from one another with an otherworldly grace. These living entities assume forms reminiscent of human shapes, their colossal wings delicately interweaving a majestic display. Arrayed behind me, they now stand in harmonious formation, a collective force gently unraveling the fiery shackles that once bound me.

Gazing upon their majesty, their appearance transcended the ordinary, each figure adorned with celestial intricacies. Their heads were crowned with helmets fashioned from the dance of flames and iron, providing an ethereal shield. Human-like hands, untouched by their fiery sleeves, rested calmly by their sides. Feet, reminiscent of an ox's hooves, radiated with the polished glow of burnished brass. Their breastplates, forged from molten obsidian and inlaid with luminescent gemstones, were inscribed with ancient runes, pulsating with otherworldly power. These fiery sentinels stood tall, their armor shimmering with an ethereal glow that radiated divine energy. Forged from the very essence of fire and metal, these colossal beings exuded an aura of both power and serenity, standing as celestial guardians poised for the impending clash against the disturbance that had threatened to consume me mere moments ago.

As the wind subsides, revealing the true nature of the flame that had obscured it, a profound stillness in the air remains. The four ethereal beings, resembling soldiers, stand with towering stature behind me.

Though I should feel fear, I do not. I look upon them in awe, knowing that they have been protecting me this entire time, their backs outwardly facing their enemies as they took each stripe for me willingly. Now, however, their backs no longer turned, they stand firm, facing the indescribable army amassing from the depths below in response to the breach. These celestial guardians, their armor shimmering with divine light, embody both reassurance and power, ready to confront whatever horrors rise to challenge them. The air crackles with anticipation, but in their presence, I feel a profound sense of security, knowing that they will face the coming storm with unwavering strength and resolve.

What are they waiting for? I wonder, still awe struck by their transformation.

Without even realizing it, I escaped the confines of the fiery walls that had ensnared me since my arrival. I had been so mesmerized by the four beings' transformation that I completely overlooked the fact I am no longer imprisoned, no longer left to imagine what lay beyond the walls of my flame. I can now gaze out upon the scape of the land for the first time.

A sudden vulnerability and nakedness overwhelms me. The flame that had clothed me for so long now stands behind me as I rise to my feet and look upon the realm of Sheol in its entirety for the first time. In the midst of the fiery cell, I believed I had glimpsed the depths of my torment. Little did I know that the true darkness was on the outside of the flame, waiting to greet me with its ferocity.

No wonder Rochelle was so eager to find a way inside when first she came to me, I think in remorse.

As my gaze lingers upon the vast expanse where the land meets the sky, I witness the aftermath of the explosion—a rift materializing in the celestial canvas. What starts as a mere crack quickly expands, its jagged edges spreading across the heavens. Sections of the sky have already broken open, and beams of brilliant light begin to pierce through the darkness.

These rays of light, pure and radiant, slice through the shadowy expanse, casting an ethereal glow upon the landscape. The once dim and foreboding terrain is transformed, illuminated by the celestial beams. Shadows scatter in fear, and creatures of darkness scurry away, desperately seeking refuge from the illumination.

The light cascades in powerful streams, each beam cutting through the gloom with deliberate grace. It reveals the landscape in stark relief, highlighting the contrast between light and dark. Certain sections of the land are bathed in the radiant glow, while others remain shrouded in shadow. The creatures caught in the path of the light are exposed, their grotesque forms momentarily revealed before they can retreat into the safety of the darkness.

As the rift in the sky continues to grow, the beams of light intensify, pouring forth with relentless energy. The celestial light, unyielding and powerful, begins transforming everything it touches, bringing a sense of hope and purity to the once bleak and sinister landscape.

Taking a moment to savor the emotions and feelings thought eternally lost as the light passes over me, I gradually open my eyes, redirecting my gaze downward again to the lower realms below. An obscure panorama further unfolds—a landscape steeped in shadows with intricately placed snares, meticulously devised by the Reapers, revealing countless souls ensnared and entwined within.

What a horribly vivid portrayal of the destiny awaiting those who renounced Christ, I think to myself as my eyes continue to scan the lands before me.

In the ominous tapestry unfolding along the horizon, I see shadow-laden valleys fracturing the empty expanse. In the remote reaches, a menacing Basilica materializes. Sinister towers pierce the oppressive obsidian sky, looming ominously over the spectral landscape.

The temple defies logic, situated upon an ethereal island that hangs suspended above an abyss of unfathomable depth. A profound sense of foreboding shrouds this seemingly unsupported enclave. The effect gives an unsettling sense of defiance against the laws that were created to govern the realms.

My dread deepens as torrents of cascading fire can be seen surrounding the abyss, painting an ominous silhouette of the malevolent towers that preside over all within the realm. Molten magma, plunges into the depths, creating an eerie spectacle as it spills along the outer banks encircling the pit upon which the city precariously perches. The contrast between the stygian towers, the suspended island, and the fiery abyss is a hauntingly vivid image, an embodiment of an otherworldly darkness etched and silhouetted by powers foreign to me that I wish to never know.

"Surely, this is the palace where Rochelle was taken for judgment," I say aloud, convinced by the recollection of her description.

The wind begins to stir again but uniquely different than before. An ethereal force within it sweeps over me, frolicking within the wind as if alive, in search of something or someone. As it passes by me, I watch as it dances across the valleys, brushing across others as it did me. My eyes follow its path until they settle upon a scene that deeply unsettles me.

Wooden crosses by the thousands stand erect, bearing the weight of lifeless forms, suspended like grotesque ornaments across the hillside. The tortured souls, once human, now dangle in a macabre dance of agony—living beings, twitching and writhing in pain from their crucifixions. Their bodies, contorted and broken, hang limp, swaying with the wind, seemingly unable to even feel its peace.

The souls, once vivid in their humanity, now appear to be diminishing before my eyes. Their essence, a faint glow of what they once were, drips off of them, collected by grotesque creatures lurking below waiting to feast upon it, their insatiable hunger driving them to eagerly lap up every drop.

As I tread forward cautiously, my eyes keenly tracking the movements of the four fiery sentinels behind me, a foreboding apparition materializes upon the hill of crucifixion. Cloaked in a sinister shroud that stretches fourfold its ghastly form, as if woven from the substance of smoke or an obsidian tempest, the demonic entity hovers in an unholy dance. It defies earthy constraints, a malevolent specter presiding over the tormented landscape with an air of maleficent dominion. Each movement carries an ominous weight, casting an eerie shadow upon the desolation it commands.

I watch it staring directly into the firmament above, awaiting something when it immediately senses my eyes. In a sudden shift, it turns its gaze directly upon me, its eyes, deep and devoid of light, piercing the depths of my soul with an unwavering stare. Judgment and shame, fear and regret envelop me. There's a chilling familiarity that engulfs me as I sense this spectral being probing my essence, evoking an anxiety that traces the contours of my spine.

With deliberate motion, an outstretched finger points toward me, and in that instant, memories of childhood fears flood my consciousness. The realization dawns—this is the demon of my youth, casting scornful eyes upon me from a distance. Vulnerable to his admonition, I turn away, my anxiety mounting.

The reunion fades quickly as the sky once again splits with a resounding crack. The primal beats below echo in response, and an unseen force sends a shockwave through the realm from above, violently thrusting me off my feet. The impact knocks the wind out of me, not from hitting the ground, but from the shockwave's unknown origin reverberating through my entire being. Gasping for air, chest heaving in turmoil, I turn my head to the distant hill where the dark figure hovered, only to find it had vanished, leaving me lying there, grappling with the aftermath of an unseen force and the haunting gaze of a childhood demon now obscured.

A searing wave of agony erupts in my body, rendering me immobile and feeble, as if the very last vestiges of strength have been mercilessly drained from me. Prostrate on the ground, my arms clutch defensively around me and I struggle to contain the torment writhing within me.

In the breathless anticipation that hangs thick in the air, the flamed Titans stir. In perfect harmony, they slowly lift their hands, elbows bent, and position themselves to receive. Then, in an almost ritualistic fervency, they delve one hand at a time into their opposing sides, revealing a celestial arsenal of heavenly ordained weapons that they pull from within.

Each warrior now stands before me, presenting a spear unlike anything I have ever witnessed. The shafts seem woven from the very threads of starlight, glinting with an otherworldly brilliance. These spears, ethereal and powerful, reflect divine craftsmanship with every glimmer and shimmer.

In their opposing hands hang remarkably crafted shields, constructed from the scales of celestial dragons. These shields appear to be indestructible, radiating a subtle glow that matches their wearer's fiery helm. The scales, meticulously arranged, form a surface that not only deflects but absorbs the light, amplifying the protective aura around each giant.

The demon of fear, from the distant hill, unbeknownst to me, had not vanished in response to the impending invasion. Instead, it was relentlessly closing in on me, a shadow of dread creeping ever closer with each passing moment. With a rapid ascension to my location its gaze breaks the horizon line, and our eyes meet again. Fear immediately envelops me once more as my childhood nightmare unexpectedly re-emerges, surging forward with terrifying speed, its malevolent gaze fixed unerringly upon me. In swift response, the flamed guardians unfurl their wings, their presence a powerful threat to the encroaching terror.

Now hovering mere yards from me, the demon shows a slight trepidation at the sight of the Titans aligning behind me. Its head jerks rapidly from side to side, examining each opponent with quick, erratic movements.

Then, in a moment fraught with tension, the demon presents the flamed Titans with a choice, its gaze shifting between them and me, as if weighing the odds of confrontation versus retreat. The air grows thick with anticipation, the fate of this standoff hanging in a delicate balance.

"Release him to me or face the imminent wrath that looms in my infernal wake!"

The scene brims with intensity, neither force willing to budge. Unyielding and undeterred by the demonic authority, the flamed sentinels defiantly extend their spears toward the approaching menace, a silent yet potent response. Their resolve radiates intensity as they stand unwavering, each spear hovering above me. I look up, following the beaming rods to their points, then forward to the demon each spear is intently pointed at. The countenance on the demon's face lowers, its arrogance waning in the presence of such determined authority.

In the face of the Titans' immovable stance, the demon adjusts its focus directly upon me, still standing in the middle of the controversy. *He's not going to attack them,* I think to myself, *he's just coming after me.*

As if responding to my thoughts, the demon swiftly advances, its form shifting between the spear tips faster than I can react. In an instant, it wraps around me, one arm coiling tightly around my throat and the other raised above me, a protruding blade slowly extending from the palm of its hand toward my chest.

Time slows down as I watch the demon look up toward the fiery sentinels, a victorious look upon its gnarled face. It raises its hand higher, then swiftly brings it back down. The point of the blade is only inches from my chest when a sudden explosion erupts from within the depths of Hell, sending pulsating shockwaves that cast us both forcefully to the ground.

The air vibrates with the intensity of the blast, and the ground trembles beneath us. As I lay there, the demon's grip loosens, its confidence shattered by the unexpected eruption. The shockwaves continue to ripple through the realm, leaving a stunned silence in their wake. Looking back at the fiery sentinels, they remain steadfast, seemingly undeterred by the demon's advance or the eruption. It is as if they knew all along that the demon wouldn't harm me, clearly aware of what is breaching the firmament above and the authority that descends.

As the demon and I both turn to the origin of the explosion, clouds descend from the heavenly firmament in an inverted volcanic eruption, bathing the darkness below in the brilliance of white light. The demon, turning to face me, hisses in contempt, as it descends to the regions below, poised to join in the imminent war with a fervor matching the intensity of the impending conflict.

Turning my gaze back toward the sky after witnessing the demon's descent and the fiery sentinels lowering their guards, I see lightning erupt from the center of the tear. Streaking veins of energy spiderweb against the nebulous tapestry of clouds, casting an ethereal illumination with iridescent blue hues upon the crimson ground beneath, revealing the true magnitude of the celestial breach.

Each bolt of lightning, like a celestial brushstroke, highlights the vastness and depth of the rift in the firmament, exposing the raw, untamed power that now courses through the sky. The clouds exude an aura of sheer power and greatness. Brilliantly white and dense, they move with a precision that suggests an intellectual design, as if they are being instructed to breach but not descend too early, to yield and await further command. They resonate with an enigmatic force that deepens the mystery and evokes a sense of recognition, as though I've glimpsed this power in the eyes of a distant vision or dream in another time and place that eludes my memory. The interplay of light and shadow among these clouds creates a majestic spectacle, reinforcing the feeling that a grand, otherworldly intelligence is at work, orchestrating the unfolding events with meticulous care.

As the sky continues to pulsate with electric brilliance, the clouds suddenly descend violently upon the realms below. Their once meticulous and deliberate movements give way to a chaotic and forceful plunge, driven by an urgent, unseen command. The clouds, now a maelstrom of blinding white, crash downwards, bringing with them a storm of raw, celestial energy. The very air trembles with the power of their descent, and the ground beneath shudders as if bracing for the impact. The heavens, now fully unleashed, merge with the earth in a cataclysmic display of otherworldly might, marking the commencement of an epochal confrontation. In the presence of lingering hope that begins trickling into the realm, carried upon the winds that frolic to and fro upon the hillsides, small pools of moisture form in the corners of my eyes—a testament to an unexplainable sense of peace and hope, accompanied by a forgotten feeling of belonging. It's as if, against all odds, something remembers me—a reassurance that nothing in Heaven or beneath it can sever me from a love that endures. The very essence of this ethereal connection flows through me, offering solace and reminding me that, despite the darkness and chaos, a profound and enduring love holds me steadfastly in its embrace.

My legs quiver uncontrollably as I fall to my knees, surrendering to the release of my tears. Overwhelmed by the spectacle of demonic forces yielding to an overpowering celestial might, a sigh of relief escapes my lips. The breath of hope, now beginning to penetrate my being, inflicts a paradoxical pain, akin to the sting of rubbing alcohol on an open wound, yet simultaneously purging the infection of death that had settled within me. I wince as new vitality courses through my being, pushing out the stagnant decay that had taken residence.

Weakened by the conflicting forces within, my head heavy with thoughts and emotions I had intentionally suppressed, I lay my head upon the crimson earth. My words escape my mouth like desperate pleas of brokenness and confusion: "What next? I have nothing left." I declare aloud, the weight of striving, repressing memories, and the continual looming fears of being found weighing heavily upon me. Yet, lying here, an unexpected tranquility envelops me, washing over with a surge of indescribable peace that wipes away the fears, the brokenness, and the thoughts of being forgotten.

A celestial calm envelops me with the arrival of the cloud's presence, whispering the sacred words deep within my being *"Be Still,"* and I willingly succumb to its serene command. Yet, the grip of Death lingers, a constant reminder that, even amid this profound authority and display of majesty, I remain bound within, one of the afflicted.

Turning my head, I wince at the ongoing struggle between life and death vying for dominion over the remnants of my being. In that poignant moment, as I look upon the turmoil within the land, a divine spectacle unfolds—ethereal beacons of light descend from the heavens. Like shooting stars, streaks of radiant light descend from above, leaving luminous trails behind them. Their graceful descent is as ephemeral as their ascent, soaring back toward the fractured firmament from which they came, a celestial dance that repeats itself over and over.

Watching in awe, emotions long forgotten in the grip of Death resurface within me. I close my eyes, imagining the radiant lights to be angels, under the command of the Almighty God, here to retrieve His sons and daughters. For the first time in a long time, I feel a slight smile form upon my face at the thought. Then, an abrupt stillness envelops my body, the winds cease, and the lids of my eyes illuminate from an otherworldly source. Upon opening my eyes, feeling the peaceful warmth blanketing my once tattered skin, I find myself completely immersed and surrounded by the brilliance of one of the descending beams of light.

The light, radiant and pure, washes over me, and a darkness begins to drip off of my body like a blanket of onyx being pulled downward. As the blackness peels away, it reveals a different body beneath, one without scars or burns. My skin, once marred and tattered, now appears smooth and untouched, seemingly beautiful. The transformation is surreal, as if the light itself is healing and renewing me, restoring not just my appearance but a sense of wholeness I had long forgotten. Each drop of darkness that falls away takes with it a piece of the pain and suffering I had endured, leaving behind a renewed sense of self, radiant and unblemished.

Allowing the luminescence to envelop me like a warm blanket, I surrender myself within its ambiance, letting the gentle light caress me as I close my eyes and bask in its peace. Suddenly, the earth beneath my legs and shoulders begins to move, and I feel two objects slowly sliding under me. Opening my eyes to see the cause of the disturbance, I find a substantial pair of arms emerging from beneath me, lifting my battered body into the air. My head finds solace against its colossal forearms and in the security they offer.

Limp and yielding, my body rests against the opulence of a chest plate adorned with meticulous engravings that match those of my flame guardians. The celestial being holding my broken form exudes magnificence, a radiant assurance that I am shielded from any harm. Its presence is overwhelming, a beacon of hope and strength, instilling in me a profound sense of peace and safety. The warmth of the light and the firm embrace of the being together create an unshakable feeling of protection, as if nothing seen or unseen can now harm me.

Ascending into the unknown with this celestial being, I steal a final glimpse at the outer reaches of Sheol. A vast cloud infiltrates the depths of Hell, creating an imposing barrier that divides the realms of the deceased from the powers that govern them. Many of Hell's legions were already assembled before the ominous Temple of Fire, a prelude to the impending war.

Blinking away the tears in my eyes, relief floods my senses as I witness the lightning dancing across the sky, crafting intricate spider webs of brilliance as it begins striking the grounds below where the opposing army gathers. A profound transformation takes place as additional elements within the fiery depths pledge new allegiances that echo through the infernal abyss. The winds and flames, once chaotic and unruly, converge in a dance of unity, taking on tangible forms, reminiscent of a vision witnessed in a time before. Slowly, purposefully, they gather their strength, amassing into a formidable force that defies the tumultuous nature of the underworld. Additional fiery sentinels begin appearing by the thousands from the distance and marching to oppose the armies of Hell that were amassing.

Darkness begins to billow from the depths of the abyss in response. Large creatures stir, climbing out of the depths surrounding the Temple of Fire. Dragons and principalities breach the realm through portals that open within the ground below in response to the invasion with alarming haste. The creatures and demonic principalities stand in wait when an amassing darkness rises from a rift at the center of the battlefield.

A figure emerges from the portal, its size incomprehensible even from a great distance. Thunderous roars echo through the landscape, cheering its arrival. The ground shakes as the figure grows clearer, its immense form casting a long, ominous shadow over the assembled forces.

Speculating who or what this could be, I recall the tales Rochelle described to me. My attention is abruptly drawn to a tear in the firmament. A focused beam of light pierces the sky above, sending a powerful force to the ground below. The earth ruptures violently where the light touches, fissures spreading out in all directions as the ground erupts with a deafening roar. The clouds and elemental warriors stir upon the expected arrival of their champion, their movements synchronized and filled with purpose.

The scene is a clash of titanic forces. The light from the sky slices through the darkness, creating a stark contrast. The armies of darkness, now fully assembled, stand ready to confront the celestial intruders. The colossal figure, now unmistakably Satan, towers over his minions, his presence alone exuding an aura of dread and power. The dragon's roar, his scales glinting ominously in the dim light, while the principalities brandish their otherworldly weapons, preparing for the imminent conflict.

The tear in the firmament widens, the brilliance of the invading light growing ever more intense. The ground beneath pulses with the sheer energy of the celestial invasion, shaking in reaction to an encroaching might and superiority. The elemental warriors, their forms glowing with an ethereal light, turn, facing the heavens above, and kneel in acknowledgment to the One coming.

The earth and sky hold their breath as the two forces prepare His arrival. Satan's dark legions, filled with a ferocious determination, stand in stark opposition to the radiant army, setting the stage for a confrontation of unimaginable proportions.

In the final moments that I am able to witness, I watch as the ethereal armies, including the flamed sentinels behind me, rise to their feet, shouting praises to He who stands in conflict against the dark king of the realm. The vivid spectacle etches itself into my consciousness, a fleeting glimpse of a celestial drama ready for an unwritten war for the souls of those not forgotten—those He refuses to leave behind despite covenants made before kings giving false hope to false gods of authority never recognized by the true King of Kings.

Hoping to see the face of such a King as He enters, I imagine the look upon the demonic forces as He breaches the firmament with such power that fear turns upon themselves. My mind paints elaborate images of the unshakable creatures that were only moments earlier threatening to consume me. Now, I watch as they begin to flee, their retreat signaling a foreboding conclusion to their worthless show of power. These once formidable beings, whose presence exuded such malevolence and dominance, are now reduced to shadows of their former selves, their arrogance and might dissolving in the face of an overwhelming celestial force. The scene in my mind transforms into a vivid cinematic victory, as the forces of darkness scatter, leaving behind a landscape ready to be reclaimed by the light. But, as I look outward, in hopes to see what my mind fantasized, the canvas fades into an all-encompassing hue of white, leaving the aftermath of this otherworldly confrontation to the imagination.

Unable to see any further, as we cross the barrier above, a whisper, gentle yet profound, reaches the depths of my being, proclaiming,

"I found you, my beloved child."

Closing my eyes and resting my face against the brilliance and warmth of the angelic guardian, I drift into unconsciousness, transcending realms beyond the Milky Way and celestial galaxies, venturing into an unknown expanse unfathomed by my knowledge or intellect.

CHAPTER 23

The True Morning Star

Matthew 11:27-30

My Father has handed over everything to me. Indeed, no one fully knows the Son except the Father, and no one fully knows the Father except the Son and those to whom the Son wishes to reveal him.

Come to me, all of you who are struggling and burdened, and I will give you rest. Take my yoke upon you and learn from me, because I am gentle and humble in heart, and you will find rest for your souls. For my yoke is easy, and my burden is light.

1 Corinthians 20:20-28

But the fact is that the Messiah has been raised from the dead, the firstfruits of those who have died. For since death came through a man, also the resurrection of the dead has come through a man. For just as in connection with Adam all die, so in connection with the Messiah all will be made alive. But each in his own order: the Messiah is the firstfruits; then those who belong to the Messiah, at the time of his coming; then the culmination, when he hands over the Kingdom to God the Father, after having put an end to every rulership, yes, to every authority and power. For he has to rule until he puts all his enemies under his feet. The last enemy to be done away with will be death, for "He put everything in subjection under his feet." But when it says that "everything" has been subjected, obviously the word does not include God, who is himself the one subjecting everything to the Messiah. Now when everything has been subjected to

the Son, then he will subject himself to God, who subjected
everything to him; so that God may be everything in everyone.

Psalms 16:9-11

Therefore my heart is glad and my tongue rejoices;
my body also will rest secure,
because you will not abandon me to the realm of the dead,
nor will you let your faithful one see decay.
You make known to me the path of life;
you will fill me with joy in your presence,
with eternal pleasures at your right hand

Psalms 49:15

But God will reach into the grave and save
my life from its power.

Joel 2:30-32

I will show wonders in the heavens
and on the earth,
blood and fire and billows of smoke.
The sun will be turned to darkness
and the moon to blood
before the coming of the great and dreadful day of the Lord.
And everyone who calls
on the name of the Lord will be saved;
for on Mount Zion and in Jerusalem
there will be deliverance,
as the Lord has said,
even among the survivors
whom the Lord calls.

John 1:1-4, 9-14

In the beginning was the Word, and the Word was with
God, and the Word was God. He was with God in the
beginning. Through him all things were made; without him
nothing was made that has been made. In him was life,
and that life was the light of all mankind. The light shines
in the darkness, and the darkness has not overcome it.

There was a man sent from God whose name was John.
He came as a witness to testify concerning that light, so
that through him all might believe. He himself was not
the light; he came only as a witness to the light.

The true light that gives light to everyone was coming into the
world. He was in the world, and though the world was made
through him, the world did not recognize him. He came to that
which was his own, but his own did not receive him. Yet to all who
did receive him, to those who believed in his name, he gave the right
to become children of God— children born not of natural descent,
nor of human decision or a husband's will, but born of God.

Romans 8:36-39

As it is written:
"For your sake we face death all day long;
we are considered as sheep to be slaughtered."
No, in all these things we are more than conquerors through him
who loved us.
For I am convinced that neither death nor life,
neither angels nor demons,
neither the present nor the future, nor any powers,
neither height nor depth, nor anything else in all of creation,
will be able to separate us from the love of God
that is in Christ Jesus our Lord.

2 Peter 1:19

We also have the prophetic message as something
completely reliable, and you will do well to pay attention
to it, as to a light shining in a dark place, until the day
dawns and the Morning Star rises in your hearts.

Revelation 22:16

*I, Jesus, have sent my angel to give you this testimony
for the churches. I am the Root and the Offspring
of David, and the bright Morning Star.*

Awakening in a cocoon of warmth, I find myself immersed in a symphony of colors, vibrant with life. As I extend my hand, the image in my mind of the scars and burns I was accustomed to seeing fades with the revelation of the newly formed vessel before me, which I only briefly glimpsed as I was ascending. Hues of light dance around me, infusing me with their energy and majesty.

I stand with outstretched arms, my mouth wide open in a smile larger than I had ever presented before. A sensory reaction emerges within as something fine lands upon my tongue, its sweet taste juxtaposed against the bitterness of ash and sulfur that I was familiar with, transforming into an intoxicating essence that overwhelms my senses. The vibrant colors swirl around me, painting a vivid canvas of renewal and rebirth. The air is thick with the scent of blooming flowers and fresh rain, a stark contrast to the acrid stench of my past.

Every breath I take fills me with a sense of peace and vitality, each color offering a different taste and smell, my entire being resonating with the harmonious symphony of light and color. The pain and darkness that once defined me are washed away, replaced by an overwhelming sense of joy and wonder.

How is it that I can touch, smell and even taste the colors around me? I wonder, amazed by the physical responses that are manifesting, as the light plays on my skin.

With arms still outstretched in a posture of praise, allowing the colors to dance and wisp themselves around me, I embark on a sensory journey of discovery as the unexpected treasures, hidden within each shade, reveal themselves to me.

The regal purples reveal an essence of purity, rich and royal, as it moves from the bottoms of my feet to the top of my head, draping itself upon me. Its transformative properties cleanse the vile stains from my soul and wash over me with refreshing relief. Wisps and hues of yellow, bouncing off of the other shades, frolicsome and lighthearted, collide with me evoking the refreshing essence of joy that invites laughter to rise up within me again.

No sooner than my laughter ceases, serene and calming shades of blue twirl around me, akin to ballerinas—graceful and precise in their movements. They gently sweep across my being, providing a rejuvenating embrace that surrounds my soul. Immersed in their tranquil energy, I absorb the calming vibes and revel in the peace they bring.

Still soaking in the radiant tranquility of the rich blues, they begin to fade, and I find myself immersed in the emotional embrace of the color of red. Despite the poignant memories this hue triggers, there's a gentle elegance and pure warmth within it now. In this space, the red becomes a tender reassurance, radiating a soft glow that captivates my senses. As I gingerly reach for the scarlet shades, a gentle symphony of sensory delight unfolds, not only awakening my senses further but also delicately healing an unnoticed ache within my heart. Life, in all its richness, reveals itself through the soothing sweetness of this shade, drawing me into its tender embrace.

With every touch, the individual colors seemingly blend, giving rise to intricate spectrums that unfold like delicate threads on a spool, each one representing a unique palette and characteristic. As each color converges, the hues intertwining, they skillfully begin knitting themselves together and draping across my shoulders, adorning my nakedness with a myriad of colors that harmoniously come together in a vibrant tapestry of hues.

Basking in the warmth that now drapes across my skin, I feel weightless, suspended in the warm embrace of the light. I marvel at the harmony within, noticing how each individual shade works seamlessly with another to magnify the brilliance of God's creation. When I was alive, I never truly appreciated how wonderful light was, how it cooperated so perfectly to illuminate the world with such splendor. Like an artist painting upon every horizon, the luminescent marvel that awakens and sleeps each day was there to remind me of His grandeur.

I wonder if it was all created for us.

Each one of us, who God pulled from within the earth and breathed His life into, forming us within our mothers' wombs, are shown the majesty of His presence upon every sunrise and sunset.

Time is no longer connected to me, and I am no longer connected to Time. I am above the line of Time, floating into a vast space of unlimited possibilities. My eyes open to the wind as it welcomes me in a playful banter, slowly spinning me within as if rehearsing an exquisite choreography.

I watch it gracefully move across the quietness of a still pond, its movements stirring the waters and creating a melody that resonates from a frequency beyond my ability to hear. Words stream forth, carried on the very wind that embraced me moments earlier. They are as clear as crystal and pure as diamonds. They feel mysteriously familiar within my heart, but I have never heard them with my ears. These words have been hidden in secret places, perhaps so that they would never be tainted by the mouths of men, but now they sing out, as though being released for the first time.

Silent tears trace delicate paths down my cheeks, accompanying a melody that crescendos into a tapestry of harmonious tunes, each note delicately crafting a powerful word: love. This love is profound, extending deeper than the ocean's abyss and stretching wider than the East is from the West. Its purity weaves around the pain nestled within my heart, transforming my darkness into luminous light, and my ashes into a breathtaking beauty.

As the melody washes over me, a forgiving light wraps itself around my body, tenderly covering the deeper, generational wounds that once marred my soul. Even the deep lacerations of shame and guilt, concealed in the forgotten corners of my heart, find solace in this transformative embrace. My dry bones come back to life. As they awaken, the surrounding colors intermingle and reflect off one another in a mesmerizing dance. The winds, stirring up beads of water, create a perfect synchrony against the light's embrace, casting a radiant rainbow that emerges through the harmonious cooperation of each element.

Suddenly, the colors part like an intricately woven curtain, unveiling a window into another dimension. As I peer through it, the vastness of the universe unfolds before my eyes. Cautiously stepping into this surreal realm and onto a copious field of golden wheat, I look forward and see a small boy seated on the edge of the field, feet hanging over the edge and into the boundless expansion of the celestial heavens below. As he swings his feet in anticipation, I walk to the edge and gaze upon the vast galaxies. Joyfully, he welcomes me.

"Come," the Boy says to me, looking below with great anticipation. "Sit with me."

He reaches out his hand towards mine as he welcomes me to watch what is about to come.

"What are we looking at?" I inquire of the Boy beside me.

"Shhh," He whispers politely, placing a gentle finger to His lips. "My Father is about to speak. Watch as the heavens take shape through His words."

"Through his breath," He declares to me, "a mortal stage shall be constructed where the greatest love story ever written will unfold."

In the hushed stillness, we both sit there, our hands clasped tightly, as a resounding voice surges through the vast expanse of the heavens. Its origin defies explanation, coming from all directions, much like the echoing rush of a mighty river within a canyon. Our eyes remain locked onto the ethereal canvas before us, where the celestial realms begin their enchanting metamorphosis upon the sound of His voice, an awe-inspiring testament to the boundless power of the divine.

A breathtaking transformation unfolds before our eyes. The Earth, suspended in the cosmos, undergoes a remarkable metamorphosis. Time itself is warped and accelerates, as though it were a river racing to meet the ocean of eternity. The voice of God acts as the conductor of an awe-inspiring symphony of creation.

The void that was once the backdrop to a heavenly wheat field transforms into a kaleidoscope of color, celestial bodies emerge, and the expanse of the heavens takes shape. Light breaks through the darkness upon the Earth, and with it, the waters separate. Mountains rise, oceans ripple into existence, and the dance of flora and fauna unfolds harmoniously. Each element meticulously crafted as God's words breathe life into the canvas of creation, a masterpiece unfurling in the cosmic theater of existence.

Then, the scene shifts suddenly, and the sound of raging waters fills the air. My perspective abruptly changes. The entire universe becomes unveiled to me through the eyes of war. With drums beating and hearts pounding, the once calming sound of flowing waters is abruptly replaced by the cries of battle! Darkness creeps in like elongated, black fingers stretching across the earth, eager to inflict it with its violence and pestilence.

I observe in dismay as this darkness slowly envelops the world, intent on cutting off its source of life and suffocating whatever remains within. Sickness becomes rampant, afflicting all corners. Visions of kings succumbing to fleeting desires play within my subconscious, as if being shown to me in short glimpses through time, each scene unfolding upon the Earth like fragments of a grand, unfinished mosaic. Confusion rises like a dust storm, swallowing those unfortunate enough to be caught in its wake. War without opposition is a relentless plague, consuming everything in its path until nothing remains.

In the midst of this darkness, small lights flicker across the Earth.

"Behold, those are my beloved, in whom I am well pleased," the Boy declares to me, His gaze fixed upon each of them. As I continue to witness the growing shadow upon the Earth, I notice the once small Boy had aged with the transformations below, His growth unfolding subtly and gradually, almost without my realizing it. With His hand still holding mine, He rises to His feet and gently lifts me up. Our eyes lock as He says to me:

"It is time. The stage is set."

"Set for what?" I reply, our eyes meeting as a slight smile forms on His face before He descends below without another word.

Watching as He vanishes beyond the clouds, I am left in wonder as to where He was going and for what purpose. As I stare intently at the Earth from my vantage point, a sense of dread washes over me. Darkness violently covers the land, shadows moving swiftly to separate the Earth from the Sun's embrace. The ground shudders with violent earthquakes, tearing apart landscapes and igniting volcanic eruptions that send shockwaves globally. Massive landmasses collapse into the seas, transforming rivers and oceans into torrents of blood, reflecting crimson shades onto the celestial bodies. The Moon, now blood-red, looms ominously in Earth's orbit.

The atmosphere fills with ash and smoke, blotting out the remnants of daylight. With it, what little life remains begins to fade; the lush green landscapes that once thrived turn a sickly gray, the vibrant colors of nature withering away. Enormous storms gather strength, their fury breaking apart what remains of the fractured continents, shifting the landmasses with relentless force. The Sun then erupts, a third of it struck by celestial disturbances, casting eerie shadows over the Earth and triggering incredible solar events that burn and scorch anything in their path.

I continue to watch in disbelief as a cluster of meteors collide into the Moon, tearing it apart and sending fragments plummeting into the seas. Monstrous waves engulf the remaining untouched landmasses. The very fabric of reality seems to warp further as portals begin to open within the physical realm, releasing beasts of unspeakable horror upon the Earth.

Heavenly bodies converge against the imposing masses when suddenly the Earth explodes, sending fragments across the galaxies. The old world is destroyed, releasing a cataclysmic wave of energy that abruptly throws me off my feet. In that instant, Time itself seems to shatter.

Colors swirl and blend into a chaotic blur around me. It is as if the very fabric of Time has been torn apart, leaving nothing but a maelstrom of light and darkness. I struggle to comprehend the reality unfolding before my eyes, feeling the violent pull of temporal forces tearing at my very being.

For a moment, everything stands still. The fragments of the Earth, suspended in the void, glisten like jewels in the cosmic darkness. The silence is deafening, a void where sound and motion have ceased to exist. Time itself holds its breath.

Then, as if by some unseen hand, everything begins to rewind. The fragments of the Earth, now glistening shards, start to reassemble. The wave of energy that had spread outwards like a cataclysmic ripple starts to retract, pulling back into the core from which it came. The heavenly bodies, once scattered, converge back into their original orbits, the chaos gradually giving way to order.

The scenes of destruction play in reverse: cities un-crumble, oceans undrain, and mountains re-form. Fires extinguish, floods recede, and the sky clears. The Earth, once broken and lifeless, is restored to its former glory.

The rewind continues, faster now, as though the universe itself is eager to return to a pivotal moment. Time races back through the ages until it halts abruptly. The scene before me fades to white, and light stretches before my eyes as I am pulled off the ledge and into a world where time has focused, with pinpoint accuracy, on a specific moment, on a specific hilltop.

What just happened!—is my only thought. The event is so unbelievable that I can hardly fathom what I just witnessed. I look at my surroundings, noticing myself knelt down on my knees, postured in reverence. *Reverence to what*? I wonder.

Looking at the ground beneath me, the soil is rocky and devoid of life, an arid landscape under a stark sky. Yet, the weight of this moment stirs within me. The barrenness of the terrain is drowned out by what my heavenly eyes now see. Light paints the earth in the warmest of colors, each hue creating blankets of life unseen by my earthly eyes, as if showing me what could be or what once was. As I scan forward, my eyes settle upon the base of a wooden structure; a cross, with two others on either side. Thunder rolls around me, dark clouds hanging low with groans of pain lost inside them. The air is thick with an unsettling energy, as if the sky itself is mourning.

I look up, and droplets of blood drip onto my face. My gaze follows the trail of crimson to the feet above, soaked in scarlet hues, held fast by a nail submerged into the base of the cross.

The scene is raw, visceral. Each droplet of blood falls with a weight that echoes in the silence between the thunderclaps. The figure on the cross above me is agonizingly familiar, yet shrouded in an aura of profound suffering and sacrifice.

I feel a shiver run down my spine, the reality of the moment seeping into my bones. This isn't just a memory or a vision—this is a pivotal point in history, a moment of immense significance. I am here, witnessing the crucifixion, the ultimate act of sacrifice.

The sky darkens further, and the ground beneath me trembles. I am overwhelmed by the gravity of the scene, where the convergence of divine purpose starkly contrasts with the brutality of demonic influence. The weight of centuries, of countless souls and stories, presses down on me.

As the blood continues to drip, mixing with the rain that begins to fall, I realize that I am not just a spectator. I am part of this moment, intertwined with the threads of time and destiny. The cataclysm that rewound time has brought me here, to witness the culmination of sacrifice and redemption.

I gaze upward at Him, crucified and nearly unrecognizable were it not for those eyes. The eyes that just moments ago, stared into mine, offering reassurance that everything was going to be just fine, now look upward towards the heavens in anguish, crying to His Father:

"Eli, Eli, lema sabachthani?"—"My God, my God, why have you forsaken me?"

The silhouette of His figure is stark against the darkening sky, amplifying the solemnity of the moment. The sky transforms into hues of deepening shadows, His labored breathing resonating in the air, carrying an atmosphere of profound sacrifice. The blood flowing from His pierced hands and feet drips solemnly to the earth below. Each drop reverberates through the ground, the Earth itself responding to the weight of this sacrificial act. The world bears witness to the profound connection between suffering and redemption as the Messiah endures both physical and spiritual anguish.

Suspended between Heaven and Earth, Time shifts itself around Him, swirling the clouds into a dark chaos.

My Jesus, what have I done to you? I wonder, as I feel the weight of my every sin hanging in the balance upon the shoulders of this Man, where neither the Earth will accept Him nor the heavens take Him.

Darkness billows up from the Earth below and slithers its way up the cross like a snake. I hear a shout, "TESHLAM!"—"IT IS FINISHED!"

"No!" I scream in protest. The sound of my voice feels insignificant against the enormity of the moment. The ground trembles as if mourning the loss, and the heavens seem to wail in grief. The air thickens, pressing down on me, making it hard to breathe.

Suddenly, I am pulled away from the cross, the scene fading into a blur of colors and light. The wrenching sensation tears me from the crucifixion, pulling me into another moment, into another realm.

Colors blur, Time spins, and I awaken to find myself back in the golden wheat fields from moments ago. I look around in disbelief, my eyes drawn to a sparkling, crystal-clear stream winding gracefully through the center of the fields. I never noticed it before, but it now stands out to me, beckoning me to follow it. Walking alongside it, I see the waters trail off in the distance, cascading over the edge and into the heavens below. The crystal waters begin to evaporate, transforming into gaseous forms that shimmer like stars in the cosmic expanse. The hum of life buzzes through the blades of wheat, as though a choir, faintly singing with the birth of another cosmic heaven.

Staring at the beauty of the stars as they swirl below, movement catches the corner of my eye. There, at the boundary between worlds, stands a figure cloaked in robes of flowing white fabric, adorned with a sash of shimmering gold that catches the light of the heavens from the nearby crystalline waters.

With hair as white as freshly fallen snow and eyes ablaze like fiery orbs, the figure exudes a magnetism that draws me closer. Terrified, yet inexplicably calm and peaceful, I approach the man. As I take each step, the shroud of unfamiliarity begins to fall from my eyes, and glimmers of recognition take shape. His voice, gentle yet possessing the strength and resonance of a mighty river, speaks out: "Fear not, peace be with you."

With His outstretched arms, I notice the scars etched upon His bronzed skin, and the haunting echo of familiarity stirs within me.

Could this be the same man who was upon the cross? I wonder as I step closer to Him.

As I approach, the warmth and peace emanating from the Man is unmistakable. Our gazes lock. I am drawn into the depths of His eyes where an emerald glow now pierces through the flames within, seizing my full attention. In an instant, a wave of realization crashes over me, flooding my senses with the understanding of who this Man truly is, and I am overcome with a profound sense of weightlessness.

With tears of profound understanding streaming down my cheeks, I fall to my knees, embraced by the swaying wheat below, as the truth of his presence settles upon my heart.

"Jesus . . . my Jesus," I continue to repeat over and over. "I am so sorry. I am so very sorry."

My words cry out, my face now pressed against the ground below, at the recollection of the recent events.

I feel His hand gently lay upon my head, as He kneels down to speak.

"Why do you cry, child?" He asks, His voice so soft and loving even though my sins were just hung upon Him in the last moments of His death.

"I did not mean for this to happen," I sob. "I did not know that You would have to bear so much.

"I am not worthy to look upon you," I say to Him, my face still pressed against the crumbled blades of wheat, recollecting everything that had just unfolded. His sacrifice was the very reason that I knelt before Him now. Were it not for His boundless love for me, I would still be in the depths, facing unspeakable evils. But, before my mind can go any further, I hear His voice cut through my shame and guilt and fear.

"Rise, my child," He requests.

"Open your eyes and fear not," He says, His eyes locking onto mine through my tears.

Gazing into the vastness within his green eyes, a calming peace overwhelms me. My shame and guilt dissolve with every final tear that trails down my cheek, each droplet carrying away the burden of my regrets.

"I am the beginning and the end," He declares to me, my insecurity palpable. "The one who is alive. Though I died, behold, I am alive forevermore, and I hold the keys to Death and Hades." He reveals them to me with a joyful smile upon His face, hinting at an event unknown to all of what it took to acquire them.

"You have been through much," He says, again in a soft and loving way. "But, there is one more thing I must reveal to you.

"Take my hand," He says, extending His hand toward me, ready to receive mine.

He smiles an all knowing smile at me without saying another word. As I reach out towards His extended hand, the instant our fingers connect, a blinding white light surrounds us, immersing me in an otherworldly brilliance.

Life, a gift often undervalued, awaited me. Jesus brought me to one final, incredible place and revealed one more unbelievable moment that He wished to share with me.

In the final epilogue, I awake back in the bathroom where I died. Still grappling with the events that unfolded, and the shock and horror on the faces of those who presumed me dead, it has taken some time to fully process those last moments I was given with Him.

This is the final chapter of my journey and experience that led me Beyond Hell's Flames.

EPILOGUE

Revelation 22:1-3

Then the angel showed me the river of the water of life, as clear as crystal, flowing from the throne of God and of the Lamb down the middle of the great street of the city. On each side of the river stood the tree of life, bearing twelve crops of fruit, yielding its fruit every month. And the leaves of the tree are for the healing of the nations.

No longer will there be any curse. The throne of God and of the Lamb will be in the city, and his servants will serve him.

They will see his face, and his name will be on their foreheads.

There will be no more night. They will not need the light of a lamp or the light of the sun, for the Lord God will give them light. And they will reign for ever and ever.

John 3:16-21

For God so loved the world that he gave his one and only Son, that whoever believes in him shall not perish but have eternal life. For God did not send his Son into the world to condemn the world, but to save the world through him. Whoever believes in him is not condemned, but whoever does not believe stands condemned already because they have not believed in the name of God's one and only Son. This is the verdict: Light has come into the world, but people loved darkness instead of light because their deeds were evil. Everyone who does evil hates the light, and will not come into the light for fear that their deeds will be exposed. But whoever lives by the truth comes into the light, so that it may be seen plainly that what they have done has been done in the sight of God.

Matthew 7:13-14

*Enter through the narrow gate. For wide is the gate and
broad is the road that leads to destruction, and many
enter through it. But small is the gate and narrow the
road that leads to life, and only a few find it.*

Outside the confines of our world, Time loses its significance, yet within these earthly boundaries, we experience a complex duality. We are both constrained and freed by Time, limited by its boundaries and simultaneously blessed with the precious moments it affords us. Choice, therefore, has the greatest impact within our limited human experience because our decisions not only shape our individual journeys but often extend their influence to affect the trajectories of others. This interconnected narrative is purposefully authored by the Creator to convey a profoundly unique and individual story within each of us, setting us apart from all other creations and laying the foundation for the greatest love story ever told: ours.

Love, in its infinite diversity, is the essence of humanity. It is a part of our Creator, revealed when He shaped Adam from the earth and breathed life into him, igniting the first rhythm of our existence. Each of us were knitted together in our mother's womb, made in His image, in His likeness, so that we may rule over the fish in the sea and the birds in the sky, over the livestock and all the wild animals, and over all the creatures that move along the ground. Through love, we are given the power to choose, create, connect and even destroy if our hearts are misguided.

It is within the realm of choice that the complexity of human existence unfolds. In the profound narrative of history, every conflict, every war, and every moment of strife can be traced back to the love God had for us when He breathed life into our very beings. We fight for our beliefs, our ideals, and the ones we cherish because of the love that resides within our hearts. We yearn to protect what we hold dear, even when our interpretations of love lead us down divergent paths.

Yet, love is not solely responsible for the suffering we endure. Within this intricate narrative of conflict and war, it is also a beacon of hope for it drives us to seek peace, to heal wounds, and to reconcile differences. It is the love for our fellow beings that leads to acts of compassion, forgiveness, and understanding, transcending the darkest moments of our shared history. In the end, love is the catalyst that propels us forward, ultimately guiding us toward unity and reconciliation.

My journey through Hell left me with a complex mix of emotions—cursed by the torment I endured, yet strangely gifted with a newfound perspective. The specifics of my death remained shrouded in uncertainty as I was only able to collect bits and pieces from the distraught individuals, whom I just met, about how I was found and how long I had been there.

What I was able to gather was that they had stumbled upon my lifeless body when chaos then ensued as each consecutive person was made aware and further inspected me for signs of life. Arguments and differing opinions raged as they were torn between seeking help and the fear of legal consequences due to the drugs and negligence that led to my death.

When I finally returned, the shock on their faces subsided into joy and relief giving way to the revelation that more than an hour had passed since they had first discovered me. They revealed that when they heard commotion within the bathroom, terror struck them from the sounds resonating within as I regained consciousness. I remember in granular detail when I pulled my head out of the toilet, taking my first breath again and feeling life slowly and painfully reawaken within me. Never had I been so grateful to see the inside of a toilet but also extremely confused by what I was witnessing.

I don't know exactly how long I was in Hell, but you don't have to be in a place forever to feel like you've been there an eternity. Eternity was supposed to be my fate, and then God changed the dynamics of eternity for me. Out of grace, He gave me a new destiny—one where I had a second chance to live a life where each day brought a new unveiling of Himself, drawing me ever closer back to His warm embrace.

In the realm of death, time took on a peculiar quality—slowing down, almost freezing. While my body lay lifeless, by all accounts for an hour or so, my subjective experience within that span felt like an eternity. How this was possible, I am not sure, but if God can operate outside of time, it stands to reason that we might also experience time differently under His protection and guidance.

The first year after returning to life was the hardest. I was very absent. Much prayer and counseling was needed to keep my mind from slipping back into that place. Each night, as I laid my head down, I could hear Death's voice whisper to me that life was the dream, and I would soon re-awaken back in that place where I belonged. Rest was elusive. I would awaken, sweaty, palms hot as if I were still within the fire, the echoes of Rochelle's voice screaming out for me to save her.

I wonder whatever became of her. Was she among the countless I witnessed being saved that day? Perhaps returned to her own time?

How many more were redeemed to live again, given a second chance to start over and make the most of this precious gift of life?

How many testimonies were never written out of fear or confusion?

I was one of thousands, hundreds of thousands redeemed that day.

It's hard to hold onto the truth when it feels like there is so much evil trying to steal it away. Since returning, one Bible verse consistently plays over and over in my mind, reminding me not just who I am but whose I am:

Romans 8:38-39
For I am convinced, that neither death, nor life, nor angels, nor
principalities, nor things present, nor things to come, nor powers, nor
height, nor depth, nor anything in all of creation, shall be able to
separate us from the love of God, which is in Christ Jesus our Lord.

I came to realize that God's love for me was stronger than Death himself. We were created in His image, each of us carrying a piece of Him that He yearns to reunite with. He would go to any length, descend to any depth, to hold us once again in His loving embrace, much like a father would embrace his son or daughter. Just as the passage in Matthew 18:12-14 reminds us, He would leave the ninety-nine on the mountains to search for the one that strayed.

I came to understand that even in the depths of Hell, God never ceased to hold onto me. He never let go. His search for me never ceased because I was in Him, and He remained within me. This revelation echoes through the following verses:

Psalms 139:8
If I ascend to heaven, you are there!
If I make my bed in Sheol, you are there.

Jonah 2:2-6
"In my distress I called to the Lord,
and he answered me.
From deep in the realm of the dead I called for help,
and you listened to my cry.
You hurled me into the depths,
into the very heart of the seas,
and the currents swirled about me;
all your waves and breakers
swept over me.
I said, 'I have been banished

from your sight;
yet I will look again
toward your holy temple.'
The engulfing waters threatened me,
the deep surrounded me;
seaweed was wrapped around my head.
To the roots of the mountains I sank down;
the earth beneath barred me in forever.
But you, Lord my God,
brought my life up from the pit."

God grants us free will, and my choices led me down paths that ultimately led to Hell, yet God's choice was not to leave me there. As Ephesians 3:18-19 says,

"... how wide and long and high and deep is the love of Christ,
and to know this love that surpasses knowledge—that you
may be filled to the measure of all the fullness of God."

I will never understand the full cost of that love for me, but I now know the depths of His love for me. The depths of His love for each and every one of us. When I found myself enveloped in the white light that engulfed me after touching Jesus' hand, I was immediately ushered into the presence of the Lord. Transported to a place that defies adequate description, I arrived in a realm suspended at the heart of a luminous galaxy where darkness gave way to light. Celestial bodies glistened around us like jewels adorning the heavens, creating an ethereal panorama that transcended earthly understanding.

I've tried expressing the experience of being in the presence of the Lord numerous times, but the English language always falls short of truly capturing the moment. Whether it's my own limitations in conveying such a profound encounter or God's deliberate choice to remain a mystery, the answer remains elusive, leaving me in perpetual speculation.

What I can say, though, is that He was in everything, speaking to all of me all at the same time. He did not take on a mortal form, nor did He present Himself as a man or any physical being. Instead, He embodied the light, the sounds, and the smells, radiating an aura as if I knelt before the sun in our sky but wasn't consumed. It was as though every molecule of my being could hear Him, feel Him, and share His thoughts.

The light around me was not just bright; it was alive, pulsating with His presence. It enveloped me, bathing me in warmth and an indescribable peace. The sounds were not mere noise but a symphony of His voice, each note resonating deeply within me, filling me with understanding and comfort. The air was thick with a fragrance that carried memories of everything pure and beautiful, wrapping around me like a gentle embrace.

It was as if I had become a part of a greater whole, where individual boundaries faded away, and I could perceive His thoughts and emotions directly. The connection was intimate and total, far beyond any human experience of communication or closeness.

Kneeling there, I felt a unity with Him that defied explanation. It was a communion of spirit, where words were unnecessary because every aspect of my being was already in dialogue with His infinite consciousness.

As I knelt before Him, I remember asking Him five questions, yet upon my return to life, I could only recall receiving an answer to one of those five inquiries. For over 18 years I wondered if I would ever know the other four questions and corresponding answers. But then the second question and answer revealed itself to me in the form of a dream after a debilitating medical diagnosis.

Why five questions? I don't know. Why He allowed me to ask anything at all remains a mystery to me, but perhaps in time, I will have the answers to the other three. Each question and subsequent answer have become foundations within me. Cornerstones of my very being that define me and cannot be dismissed or questioned. I have carried these five questions inside of me waiting for the time to come when I can finally recall every part of that conversation I had with the Father.

Throughout my short, linear existence, every hardship has been met with the memory of His words from that day. Their impact is indelible, eliminating any need for proof of His existence or reassurances of His love. His word serves as a guiding lamp to my feet and a light on my path, testifying to His true nature.

It has taken my wife and I over 13 years to write this experience. The Devil has tried to claim my life and the lives of my family several times, each instance occurring within weeks of resuming this project. I truly hope that this book transcends expectations of fire, brimstone, and suffering. My hope is that the recounted experiences within these pages create a portrait of a love so great and so wide and deep that nothing in all of heaven or beneath the earth can sever it from each and every one of you.

From life's inception, its struggles, its constant ups and downs, a resounding message of hope reverberates—love is awaiting us all within His son, Christ Jesus. The love that He has for us resonates through the heavens that neither death, nor life, nor angels, nor principalities, nor things present, nor things to come, nor powers, nor height, nor depth, nor anything in all of creation, can separate us from Him.

In bidding my farewell, I present to you this concluding collage of scripture—a reflection encompassing my entire journey, narrated solely through the word of God. My earnest hope is that this compilation mirrors the intrinsic essence of each of our ongoing journeys—a tapestry woven with the thread of the greatest love story ever told, unfolding through the lives of each and every one of us:

Great is your faithfulness, Oh Lord.
So great is your unfailing love.[1]
For you created my inmost being;
you knit me together in my mother's womb.
I praise you because I am fearfully and wonderfully made;
your works are wonderful, I know that full well.[2]
Even the very hairs of my head are all numbered.[3]
The Spirit of God has made me; the breath
of the Almighty gives me life.[4]
You are my shepherd; I shall not want.
You make me to lie down in green pastures;
You lead me beside the still waters.
You restore my soul:
You lead me on paths of righteousness for your name's sake.
Though I walk through the valley of the
shadow of death, I will fear no evil;
for thou art with me; thy rod and thy staff they comforted me.[5]
But in my weaknesses, the thief came.
Like a roaring lion the devil rooted himself in
my heart and sought my destruction.[6]
My wickedness ensnared me.
For I did not listen to my father's instruction
nor heed my mother's teaching.[7]
Because I was lukewarm—neither hot nor cold—
You spewed me from thy mouth.[8]

---

1   Lamentations 3:23-24
2   Psalm 139:13-14
3   Matthew 10:30
4   Job 33:4
5   Psalm 23:1-4
6   1 Peter 5:8
7   Proverbs 1:8
8   Revelation 3:16

My wickedness led me to the realm of Death
because I forgot your goodness.[9]
I exchanged the truth about you for a lie,
and worshiped and served created things rather than You.[10]
But you are still the God of my salvation;
day and night I cry out to you.
May my prayer come before you; turn your ear to my cry.[11]
I am now counted among those who go down to the pit;
set apart with the dead, like the slain who lie in the grave,
whom you remember no more, who are cut off from your care.
You have put me in the lowest pit, in the darkest depths.[12]
I called to you; I spread out my hands to you.
Do you show your wonders to the dead?
Is your love declared in the grave, your faithfulness in Destruction?
Are your wonders known in the place of darkness,
or your righteous deeds in the land of oblivion?[13]
I cried to you for help, oh Lord;
when everything had been taken from me,
darkness became my closest friend.[14]
But vengeance is yours.[15]
Like a lion that suddenly emerged from
the dense undergrowth, you found me.
The eastern wind came—a dry desert wind sent by You.[16]
Though Death came to everyone because of one man,
the resurrection of the dead comes also through one man.[17]

---

9   Proverbs 5:23
10 Romans 1:25
11 Psalm 88:1-2
12 Psalm 88:4-6
13 Psalm 88:9-12
14 Psalm 88:18
15 Romans 12:19
16 Hosea 13:7
17 1 Corinthians 15:21

If it were not for you, I would still have
dwelt in the silence of death.[18]
Praised be your name that you descended first into the lower
parts of the earth before ascending up far above all the heavens.[19]
For you go with me; you will never leave me nor forsake me.
You are always with me, even to the end of the age.[20]
Praises be your name that your mercies are renewed each morning.
Yahweh, you alone are my inheritance.
You are my prize, my pleasure, and my portion.
You hold my destiny and its timing in your hands.[21]
You made a way for me when there was none.
I shall not fear, for you have redeemed me;
You have summoned me by name;
I am yours.[22]
When I walked through the fire, I was not burned;
the flames did not set me ablaze.
For you are the Lord my God, the Holy One of Israel, my Savior.[23]
Your word is the lamp for my feet and a light on my path.[24]
Whirlwind and storm are your ways and
clouds are the dust beneath your feet.
You disperse the clouds of your lightning.
Vengeance is yours O Lord.[25]
When I looked up, I beheld a white
cloud billowing from the heavens.
For you have come down from heaven, with a loud command
and with the voice of the archangel and with the trumpet call

---

18 Psalm 94:17
19 Ephesians 4:9-10
20 Deuteronomy 31:6, Matthew 28:20
21 Lamentations 3:23-24, Psalm 16:5
22 Isaiah 43:1
23 Isaiah 43:2-3
24 Psalm 119:105
25 Nahum 1:3, Psalm 97:2

of God, and the dead in you rose first. Then, we who remained
were caught up together in the clouds to meet you.[26]
You commanded your angels to guard me
and lift me up within their hands.
You covered me with your feathers, and
under your wings I found refuge;
You delivered me from the power of the grave;
You redeemed me from death.[27]
I was once darkness, but now I am the light of the Lord.
Where, O death, is your victory?
Where, O Sheol, is your sting?[28]
Your faithfulness is my shield and rampart.
You are my refuge and my fortress, in whom I trust.
I no longer fear the terror by night, nor the arrow by day,
nor the pestilence that stalks in the darkness,
nor the plague that destroys at midday.
Thousands fell at your side,
Ten thousand at your right hand,
but it did not come near me.[29]
Where can I flee from your presence?
If I go up to the heavens, you are there;
if I make my bed in the depths, you are there.[30]
Because of my belief in you, my heart no longer aches.
You prepared a place for me in your Father's house.
The moment you first left, to prepare a table for me,
your words stayed faithful and true:

---

26 1 Thessalonians 4:16-17
27 Psalm 91:11-12, Psalm 91:4, Hosea 13:14
28 Ephesians 5:8, 1 Corinthians 15:55
29 Psalm 91:4-7
30 Psalm 139:7-8

You prepared a place for me, and when you came back, you
took me to be with you in the secret place where we first met.[31]
You wiped every tear from my eyes for there is no more death or
mourning or crying or pain, for the old order of things has passed away.
You are making everything new.[32]
You are the Alpha and the Omega, the beginning and the End.
I was thirsty and you gave me water
from the spring of the water of life.[33]
In the beginning you were there. You were
with God because you are God.
In you all things were made.
In you I found life, and that life was the light for us all.
You are the light of the world, the true
light that shines in the darkness.
You are the way and the truth and the life.
No one goes to the Father except you and
those whom you choose to reveal to Him.[34]
Great is your faithfulness, O Lord.
I stumbled because of my wickedness but I
was brought back to your Eternal presence.
In your kindness, You forgave my sins and received me graciously.
You brought me back so that I may offer you the fruit of my lips.[35]
Your love reaches to the heavens, your faithfulness to the skies.
Your righteousness is like the highest mountains,
your justice like the deepest seas.
How priceless is your unfailing love, O God![36]
You healed my apostate heart and loved me freely.

---

31 John 14:1-3
32 Revelation 21:4-5
33 Revelation 21:6
34 John 1:1-5, John 14:6
35 Hosea 14:4
36 Psalm 36:5-7

You turned your anger away from me.
Because of your goodness, you are like the dew and
have remade me to blossom like the lily. Like a cedar of
Lebanon, I will send down roots whose splendor will be like
an olive tree, my fragrance like a cedar of Lebanon.
People will dwell again under the shade I provide and
will flourish like the grain, they will blossom like the vine.
Because your fruitfulness pours from
me, I will flourish like the juniper.[37]
You are that you say that you are.
For all of your promises are Yes, and Amen.[38]
Your steadfast love never ceases; your mercies never come to
an end; they are new every morning; great is your faithfulness.[39]
For I am convinced, that neither death, nor life, nor
angels, nor principalities, nor things present, nor things to
come, nor powers, nor height, nor depth, nor anything in all of
creation, shall be able to separate me from the love of God,
which is in Christ Jesus my Lord.[40]

---

37 Hosea 14:5-8
38 2 Corinthians 1:20
39 Lamentations 3:22-23
40 Romans 8:38-39

To discover more about Christopher and Jamie, book a speaking engagement, find upcoming appearances, purchase merchandise, or get your copy of the audiobook, visit www.beyondhellsflames.com.

ABOUT THE AUTHORS

Christopher and Jamie Harper are philanthropists, venture capitalists, and entrepreneurs with a passion for helping others and exploring the world. As the authors of *Beyond Hell's Flames*, they have brought their faith-driven message to a wide audience.

Christopher is an outspoken, unapologetic believer in Jesus Christ, with national awards and certifications spanning numerous industries. Jamie is the creative writer, dedicated mother, and visionary whose prayerful obedience to the Lord serves as the sails to his ship.

Together, they boldly follow wherever the Lord leads them, trusting in His guidance and provision, with their work deeply rooted in faith. The Harpers are dedicated to seeing the Kingdom of God come, using their resources and skills to assist those in need. Their commitment to philanthropy and adventure is a cornerstone of their family life.